COMMAND OF HONOR

GENERAL LUCIAN TRUSCOTT'S PATH
TO VICTORY IN WORLD WAR II

H. PAUL JEFFERS

NAL
CALIBER

NAL Caliber
Published by New American Library, a division of
Penguin Group (USA) Inc., 375 Hudson Street,
New York, New York 10014, USA
Penguin Group (Canada), 90 Eglinton Avenue East, Suite 700, Toronto,
Ontario M4P 2Y3, Canada (a division of Pearson Penguin Canada Inc.)
Penguin Books Ltd., 80 Strand, London WC2R 0RL, England
Penguin Ireland, 25 St. Stephen's Green, Dublin 2,
Ireland (a division of Penguin Books Ltd.)
Penguin Group (Australia), 250 Camberwell Road, Camberwell, Victoria 3124,
Australia (a division of Pearson Australia Group Pty. Ltd.)
Penguin Books India Pvt. Ltd., 11 Community Centre, Panchsheel Park,
New Delhi - 110 017, India
Penguin Group (NZ), 67 Apollo Drive, Rosedale, North Shore 0632,
Auckland, New Zealand (a division of Pearson New Zealand Ltd.)
Penguin Books (South Africa) (Pty.) Ltd., 24 Sturdee Avenue,
Rosebank, Johannesburg 2196, South Africa

Penguin Books Ltd., Registered Offices:
80 Strand, London WC2R 0RL, England

First published by NAL Caliber, an imprint of New American Library,
a division of Penguin Group (USA) Inc.

First Printing, June 2008
10 9 8 7 6 5 4 3 2 1

LIBRARY OF CONGRESS CATALOGING-IN-PUBLICATION DATA:

Jeffers, H. Paul (Harry Paul), 1934–
Command of honor: the heroic story of a World War II general/H. Paul Jeffers.
p. cm.
ISBN: 978-0-451-22402-6
1. Truscott, Lucian King, 1895–1965—Military leadership.   2. World War,
1939–1945—United States—Biography.   3. World War, 1939–1945—Campaigns—Europe.
4. World War, 1939–1945—Campaigns—Africa, North.   5. United States. Army—Biography.
6. Generals—United States—Biography.   I. Title.

D769.J42 2008
940.54'1273092—dc22   2007026779
[B]

Set in Adobe Garamond
Designed by Ginger Legato

Printed in the United States of America

PUBLISHER'S NOTE
While the author has made every effort to provide accurate telephone numbers and Internet addresses at the time of publication, neither the publisher nor the author assumes any responsibility for errors, or for changes that occur after publication. Further, publisher does not have any control over and does not assume any responsibility for author or third-party Web sites or their content.

For Arlene and in loving memory
of our sisters, Jean and Doris

CONTENTS

CONTENTS

"Wars aren't won by gentlemen. They're won by men who can be first-class sons of bitches when they have to be. It's as simple as that. No son of a bitch, no commander."

—General Lucian K. Truscott, Jr.

★ INTRODUCTION ★

Taps

Of a time in 1931 when he was a young officer in charge of honor guards at the National Cemetery in Arlington, Virginia, General Lucian King Truscott, Jr., wrote, "A military funeral is a beautiful and impressive ceremony. One learns that there is beauty in death and in the respect accorded the dead by the nation and those who live on after them. There can be no more fitting honor to a departed comrade or to the end of a funeral ceremony than a bugle sounding taps."

When the traditional burial rituals of a black riderless horse with cavalry boots backward in the stirrups, flag-draped coffin on an artillery caisson, muffled drums, farewell volleys, and taps were rendered for Truscott at Arlington on Wednesday, September 15, 1965, the iconoclastic World War II cartoonist Bill Mauldin remembered a speech by General Truscott on Memorial Day 1945. At the American cemetery in Anzio, Italy, Truscott had turned away from the crowd to speak to the graves of men he had commanded there. "It was the most moving gesture I ever saw," said Mauldin, "because it came from a hard-boiled old man who was incapable of planned dramatics."

Less interested in garnering fame than in earning the respect of his soldiers and his peers in the officer corps, Truscott refused to court the attention that correspondents showered upon Generals George Patton, Mark Clark, and others with a hunger for headlines. In a lengthy profile for *Life* magazine on October 2, 1944, with Truscott on the cover, the war correspondent Will Lang depicted a gray-haired man of forty-nine, with stocky build, jutting jaw, squinting gray eyes, and perpetual scowl who didn't trail his clouds of glory before the public. A year earlier, a *Time* magazine article had called him a hell-raising cavalryman. Wearing an old pair of tan riding breeches, knee-high cavalry boots, waist-length brown leather combat jacket, a khaki shirt with a white silk scarf tucked under the collar, and three gleaming stars studding a "luminous" enameled helmet, Truscott had earned a reputation for toughness and victories by turning the Third Division into one of the greatest combat divisions of the war.

Reporting Truscott's death at the age of seventy, *Time* recorded that he had been a "brilliant tactician and master of amphibious landings." The *New York Times* remembered "a World War II hero" whose distinguished combat record began in early 1942 with an assignment to form an American-style Commando unit that he named Rangers. In a raid on the French port of Dieppe, he became the first American general to see action in Europe. For the 1942 invasion of North Africa, he led troops under Patton in the taking of a key port in Morocco. After serving as field deputy to General Dwight D. Eisenhower in Tunisia, he led divisions in the invasions of Sicily and Italy, and after months of bloody stalemate forged the breakout from the Anzio beachhead for a drive north to capture Rome. Leading an invasion of southern France a month after the D-day landings in Normandy, he took command of an army corps in a sweep into the Rhone Valley in France. Returning to Italy to take over the Fifth Army, he conducted a campaign that crushed a desperate German last stand in what was known as the Forgotten Front.

"In these campaigns," notes the military historian Roger J. Spiller, "he led his troops from the front as they fought their way over some of the worst terrain and against some of the most determined enemy the European theater had to offer."

When Supreme Allied Commander General Dwight D. Eisenhower evaluated the seven army commanders under him in February 1945, he listed only George Patton ahead of Truscott, and cited Truscott as an experienced, energetic fighter who inspired confidence and possessed a keen analytical mind and the ability to learn the right lessons from combat.

A later generation of Americans who had no personal memories of the Second World War as they flocked to theaters in 1970 to see the movie *Patton* were provided a glimpse of Truscott through the burly, gruff character actor John Doucette in a scene that was misleading in its portrayal. When he expressed concerns about the cost in American lives by rushing to carry out Patton's order to execute an amphibious assault in a drive to beat the British general Montgomery in taking the port of Messina, Patton, played by George C. Scott, tells him, "If your conscience won't permit you to conduct this operation, I'll find somebody who can."

According to Truscott in his World War II memoir, *Command Missions*, an impatient Patton actually said, "Goddammit, Lucian, what's the matter with you? Are you afraid to fight?"

Bristling at this aspersion on his character by an old friend under whom he'd served with valor in North Africa and shared a passion for polo, skills in the use of profanity, and a flair for flamboyantly distinctive uniforms, Truscott retorted, "General, you know that is ridiculous and insulting. If you don't think I can carry out orders, you can give the division to anyone you please. But I will tell you one thing, you will not find anyone who can carry out orders which they do not approve as well as I can."

Patton's mood changed instantly. He threw an arm about Truscott's shoulder and said, "Dammit, Lucian, I know that. Come on, let's have a drink of your liquor."

In the film, Truscott declined to imbibe. In reality, they did and Patton left in good spirits. When he swaggered into Messina ahead of the British force a few days later, Truscott was already there. When Truscott was given command of the Third Army in vanquished Germany in 1945 after Eisenhower fired Patton for his controversial comparison of Nazis to the Republican and Democratic parties, Patton told the troops assembled for the official handover ceremony, "A man of General Truscott's achievements needs no introduction. His deeds speak for themselves."

Yet, when taps sounded at the old warrior's funeral more than two decades later, Lucian King Truscott, Jr., had faded in the memories of all but the soldiers he had commanded and the most serious students of the war. Having heard of him during the war from newspapers, on the radio, and in the newsreels when I was in elementary school, I knew that he had significant roles in invasions and fighting in North Africa, Sicily, Italy, and France, but when I needed to learn more of him in 2006 in order to depict him in a biography of the founder and leader of the U.S. Army Rangers, Colonel William Orlando Darby, I was amazed to find that, except for *Command Missions*, published in 1954, there was no book devoted to recording the exploits of the only American officer to command a regiment, division, corps, and army in World War II.

That he had been a unique general was evident in his foreword to *Command Missions*. He wrote, "I have no great controversies to pursue, no individuals to castigate." He structured the writing of his wartime experiences not as a self-serving autobiography, but as a record of the "accomplishments of the American soldier who has no superior and few equals when adequately equipped, properly trained and afforded good leadership in the various echelons." The result was a volume containing almost nothing about his personal life before and during the war and after his retirement. Although his years in the army before World War II were the subject of a second book, *The Twilight of the U.S. Cavalry: Life in the Old Army, 1917–1942* (edited by his elder son and published posthumously in 1989), he again revealed virtually nothing about himself.

Truscott's fingerprints can be found on plans for the decisive battles in winning the European war. His footprints can be followed across the desert sands of North Africa, over invasion beaches in Sicily, Italy, and southern France, and into the bitter final battles along the way to victory. Tributes to him and his military career are found in the form of condolences to his widow that fill several boxes in the Truscott archive at the General George C. Marshall Library and Museum at Virginia Military Institute in Lexington, Virginia. These files enshrine his steady ascent from a "shave-tail" second lieutenant in the horse cavalry in 1917 to a three-star general in World War II.

For their assistance and courtesy during my exploration of General Truscott's records, I gratefully salute Senior Director and Editor of the Marshall Papers Project, Dr. Larry I. Bland; Paul B. Barron, Director of the Library and Archives; Peggy Dillard, Assistant, Library and Archives; and all of the museum's volunteer staff.

My gratitude is also extended to James J. Truscott for reviewing the manuscript and for providing a son's perspective.

Thanks are due Sid Goldstein for providing tactical support in the form of air transport to and from Virginia, and to Al Leibholz, Cathe Giffune, and Janet Zinner for their enthusiastic encouragement throughout the writing of this book; and to my literary agent, Jake Elwell, and my editor, Brent Howard. For superb work in locating photographs I extend thanks to Janet Holsinger and the staff of History Associates.

In searching the historical record for insights into the character of a general who kept his mouth shut about himself, I confirmed Bill Mauldin's assessment of Truscott as a hard-boiled officer who was incapable of planned dramatics, and, as Lucian K. Truscott III wrote of his father, that Truscott belonged "to that generation of remarkable military leaders who emerged from the small peacetime army to play vital roles in the defeat of the Axis powers."

My intent and my hope is that in presenting the first biography of General Lucian King Truscott, Jr., I will have restored him to his proper place in the history of the Mediterranean and the European theaters of World War II.

★ ONE ★

Boots and Saddles

With his crisp new army uniform soiled by coal dust blowing through the open window of the only passenger coach at the end of a long string of empty gondola cars rattling behind the laboring locomotive of the El Paso & Southwestern Railroad, twenty-one-year-old Second Lieutenant Lucian King Truscott, Jr., could smell the rotten eggs odor of sulfur long before he could see yellowish smoke columns. Rising from smelters of the Copper Queen Mining Company and Calumet and Arizona Company, they blemished the clear sky of the Arizona-Mexico border as he stepped from the train at the town of Douglas in August 1917.

Four decades later, General Truscott would look back nostalgically and tell a reporter for *Life* magazine that joining the United States Army had "rescued" him from a life of obscurity.

He was born on January 9, 1895, in Chatfield, Texas, on his mother's birthday, and was there for six years before his father and namesake moved the family to Oklahoma. Although he recalled very little about Texas, General Truscott would tell correspondents who interviewed him during the Second World War that the fact that he was born in the Lone Star State allowed him to claim, as did Dwight D. Eisenhower, who was born in Denison, Texas, but grew up in Kansas, that he was always a Texan at heart. While Ike's ancestors were German, Truscott had English-Irish roots. His maternal grandfather, John Calvan Tully, was born aboard a ship en route from Ireland to the United States. He grew up to be the pastor of the First Christian Church in St. Louis, Missouri, and later in Paducah, Kentucky. Truscott's great-grandfather, Thomas Truscott, emigrated from Cornwall to Illinois in 1815. His son, James Joseph, called J.J., was born in England and was sixteen when they arrived. He became an American pioneer in the Mexican territory of Texas. After it won independence and became a state, he was one of the founders of Texas A&M College. To honor him, the town of China Lake changed its name to Truscott. When Knox County was formed in 1886 and the town got a post office, J.J.'s son, also named Thomas, set it up in his house. He was also the teacher of the Truscott School. Established in 1888, it had one room and served the town until it and much of the community burned down in 1907. It was then rebuilt about a mile away to be closer to the newly constructed Kansas City, Mexico and Orient Railway.

When J.J.'s second son, Lucian King Truscott, gave up work as a cowboy to become a physician, he left Truscott for the town of Chatfield and married Maria Temple Tully. The only doctor in a community of about five hundred, he was also the pharmacist, and the room that served as his office had shelves of tins with colorful labels and bottles filled with pills, lotions, syrups, and mysterious liquids that proved much too fascinating for his inquisitive toddler son to resist. While Truscott was examining a patient, Lucian, Jr., wandered unnoticed into the office. The flask of sparkling liquid that he chose to taste contained carbolic acid. A quick reaction by Truscott to the boy's screams saved his life, but the burning poison scarred the lining of Lucian's throat, leaving him with a raspy, gruff-sounding voice, described by Will Lang in *Life* in 1944 as "a rock-crusher" that gave his orders to officers and troops "an awesome ferocity."

For reasons that remain obscure, but possibly because Dr. Truscott dabbled disastrously in racehorses and venturesome investments in farmland, the family pulled up stakes in Texas in 1901 and moved to the village of Maud in Pottawattamie County in the Oklahoma Territory. It was a period in which the U.S. government decreed that the Indian Territory of Oklahoma above the Red River, which formed the northern boundary of the State of Texas, and west of the Arkansas River was wide open for the taking. The result was that land that had a population of less than 400,000 in 1901 mushroomed to nearly 1.5 million by the time President Theodore Roosevelt welcomed Oklahoma into the Union as the forty-sixth state in 1907. Some impatient pioneers who scrambled across the borders ahead of a pistol firing at the official time on the date chosen for the land rush added the term "jump the gun" to subsequent dictionaries, earning for them and all Oklahomans the nickname "Sooners." As more than 100,000 of them dashed across the Kansas border to grab 6 million acres, the famous New York newspaperman Richard Harding Davis witnessed "tent towns" with thousands of inhabitants springing up in a single day. A traveler from Iowa in the year the Truscotts arrived reported, "On every quarter section of land there is a house. Some are only one-room shanties. But as a general thing they consist of one or two rooms. There is also the sod house and dugout. A sod house is built by making the walls entirely of sod. The roof is made of boards like corn cribs, there being no shingles on the roof. In the interior of them, the walls are plastered. They seldom have a board floor. The floor is of dirt. In the one I examined, the floor was covered with straw and a carpet over the straw. Other houses were dug out of the ground and resembled caves in the side of a hill. Uncle Sam keeps soldiers all the time for fear of an uprising of the Indians."

For a six-year-old boy in the Oklahoma Territory in 1901, there were exciting stories to be heard from U.S. Cavalry "old-timers" about pitched battles between the Cherokees and the horse soldiers stationed at Fort Sill, Fort Cobb, Reno, Gibson, Towson on the Kiamichi, and Fort Wichita, including a bloodcurdling yarn about a massacre. After General George Armstrong Custer led the Seventh Cavalry in an attack on the winter camp of Black Kettle's Cheyennes on the Washita in 1868 and the bugler sounded "recall" at ten o'clock on that morning, Chiefs Black Kettle and Little Rock, along with more than a hundred Indian men, women, and children, lay dead in the snow. There were riveting stories about men in cavalry-blue shirts answering the bugle's calls and riding in double column out across the rolling plains with flags flying and their horses raising clouds of dust. The troopers sang "Garryowen," "The Girl I Left Behind Me," "Yellow Rose of Texas," "(If you want to have a good time, jine the cavalry!) Jine the Cavalry!" and one that exhorted:

> *Up! for the bugles are calling*
> *Saddle and boot, and away!*
> *Sabers are clanking and lances are glancing*
> *The colonel is fuming and horses are prancing*
> *So up with the sabers and lances*
> *Up and away! Up and away!*

Because General Lucian K. Truscott, Jr., chose not to describe his Oklahoma childhood in his memoirs, there is no record of what he thought and how he felt as he listened to these army tales and songs, or if they stirred in him a desire to become a soldier. The most Will Lang was able to learn from Truscott about his youth was that his mother's father was "belligerently Irish and there is a stubborn Cornish-English on his paternal side."

Among personal documents in Truscott's papers at the George C.

Marshall Library are copies of notes written by Truscott's wife, Sarah, that provided Lang background on Truscott's early years in Oklahoma. They show that the Truscotts moved many times. They left Maud for Konawa, returned to Maud, shifted to Remus, and settled in Stella, Cleveland County. With a father described by Lang as "a sickly country doctor with three daughters and a son to support," Lucian chose to help out by going into teaching.

"In 1911," Sarah Truscott wrote, "schoolteachers still earned their certificates by attending Normal Schools, so that summer Lucian and his mother attended Summer Normal School at Norman, and Lucian was granted a certificate. Only sixteen at the time, he stretched his age to eighteen, applied for and got [assigned to] a country school, six miles from his home at Stella, and during the eight-month term walked to and from school daily."

In the fall of 1912, the family moved to Creek County to a settlement known then as Edna. After the school terms were out, Lucian and his mother followed the family to Edna and attended Summer Normal School at Sepulpa. That winter, the doctor decided to move to a town in the Kiamichi Mountains, but when he reached Eufala, which was knee-deep in mud, he stopped. Lucian and Mrs. Truscott followed, but when Dr. Truscott moved to Onapa, Lucian stayed behind and taught at nearby Mellette.

Sarah Truscott stated proudly in her biographical notes,

During this period, he was instrumental in construction of the First Christian Church, Eufala, and introduced the idea of leaving the church doors open to the public throughout the week, because the church belonged to the people, and he believed religion should be an all-week practice rather than a Sunday gesture. He was just a normal healthy specimen of American youth, only different in that he did not drink, smoke, nor swear. He hadn't much time for play, though he took part in annual track meets, minstrel shows, and everything the teachers' organizations and schools participated in. Perhaps the only thing remarkable about his career was that as a boy his one ambition was to become an army officer.

Without stating that he'd found this period of his life boring and frustrating, Truscott described it as "drab little one- and two-room schoolhouses in Oklahoma's hinterlands." His selection of adjectives goes a long way in explaining what he meant when he stated that he was rescued by World War I. A signal that the United States might be drawn into the conflict that had been raging in Europe between the English, French, and Russians on one side and Germany and its allies in the Balkans since 1914 took the form of the National Defense Act of 1916.

Signed by President Woodrow Wilson on June 3, it provided for expansion of the U.S. Army to 175,000 men at once and to 223,000 over five years. It also authorized a National Guard of 450,000 and created the Reserve Officers Training Corps (ROTC) at universities and colleges and in military camps. The act was not only a reaction to events in Europe, but what Truscott in *The Twilight of the U.S. Cavalry* termed "troubles along the border" fomented by a rebel leader Americans called "the Mexican bandit Francisco 'Pancho' Villa" and who Mexicans admired as a revolutionary hero. During a raid on the border town of Columbus, New Mexico, on March 9, 1916, 485 men known as Villistas left ten U.S. Army officers and soldiers killed and seven wounded, with eight civilians killed and two wounded. Villa's losses numbered approximately one hundred killed, with seven wounded and captured. For the next eleven months, a "Punitive Expedition" of more than 14,000 troops under the command of Brigadier General John J. "Black Jack" Pershing operated in northern Mexico in pursuit of Villa with the objective of capturing him and putting a stop to his forays. Although Villa escaped, 140,000 Regular Army and National Guard troops continued to patrol the border to discourage raids.

The United States finally declared war against Germany on April 6, 1917. The National Defense Act called for raising the number of cavalry regiments from fifteen to twenty-five and offering provisional commissions in the Army Reserves to men who could complete an officer training school at a military camp. After two satisfactory years, the lieutenants would become Regular Army officers.

Truscott took notice. Easily passing the written and physical examinations, he found himself ordered to a basic training program at Fort Logan H. Roots in Arkansas. Established in the 1890s at Big Mountain in North Little Rock and named for a Civil War veteran, congressman, and notable Arkansas businessman, the military facility was on the site of a former resort with Romanesque Revival and Greek Revival architecture. Another prospective officer recorded,

> Everything is business, and there is no time to fool around. It is go from 5:30 in the morning to 10:30 at night, with very little sleep. However, I am getting used to it and am eager for the work. It comes hard to me, of course, but am gradually acquiring a little knowledge of something about company drill in close and extended order. We have a program of the entire work for infantry, and I see that it gets harder as it goes; but suppose as it comes I will be able to absorb enough to understand something about it. There are three study periods each day, one in morning, evening and at night, and really more study than actual drill. As one of the officers expressed it, they are trying to cram into us in three months what they put into West Point men in four years.

The term coined by the professionals for these newly minted lieutenants was "ninety-day wonders." Truscott wrote, "Even after our training, our military background was sparse. Most of us were completely ignorant of things military and had never seen an organized unit of the army or a Regular Army officer until admission to the training camp."

With the shiny brass bars of a second lieutenant in the U.S. Army Reserves pinned to his khaki shirt collar, and eagerly anticipating joining a unit of the Regular Army, where he would learn soldiering from professionals, he boarded a train with other graduates of the First Officers Training Camp in August 1917 bound for Douglas, Arizona. He had been assigned to the Seventeenth Cavalry at Camp Harry J. Jones. Established on the U.S.-Mexico border just east of Douglas and named after the town in 1910, it was renamed Camp Jones in February 1916 to honor a corporal who had been killed on November 2, 1915, as he stood guard at the U.S. Customs House in Douglas during a raid by Villa's large army. In the unsuccessful attempt by Villa to capture the adjoining Mexican town of Agua Prieta, Jones had been the only American killed.

When Truscott arrived at the camp to join the ranks of the Seventeenth Cavalry, he found "a sea of canvas" sprawling more than two miles from the edge of Douglas and encompassed by a high barbed-wire fence, the south side of which designated the Mexican border. A flat mesa between the camp and fence was a drill area for the First Cavalry, and a similar area to the north of the camp was for the Seventeenth. The site also housed the Tenth and Eleventh Field Artillery regiments, a hospital, several mule-drawn ambulance companies and wagon trains, signal companies, pack trains, and other mounted units. Tents for enlisted men flanked each of the camp's fifteen streets. Officers had several small adobe houses. Running the length of the regimental area were open stables for about a hundred horses in two-horse box stalls. Adjacent to the stables were the tack rooms and other buildings for storing equipment, horseshoers, saddlers, and feed.

Truscott learned that, like himself, most of the fledgling officers had come from towns, farms, and ranches of the Southwest and had been riding all their lives, but knew nothing about the requirements of military horsemanship that the army manual called "equitation." It was a kind of riding learned only by intensive drilling in the complexities of mounted and dismounted formations and issuing commands by voice, whistle, and hand signals.

There were other things for the new officers to grasp. First sergeants and clerks in every troop introduced them to the mysteries of preparing morning reports, sick reports, duty rosters, and details of troop administration. Mess sergeants explained how they fed soldiers for thirty and forty cents each per day. Burly sergeants taught secrets of supplying men and horses. In an era before radio, there were lessons in telegraph, semaphores, and "wig-wag" signal flags. Officers were veterans of the hunt for Pancho Villa and an insurrection in the Philippines under the command of General Arthur MacArthur. Some claimed to have raced up the San Juan Heights in the Spanish-American War behind Colonel Teddy Roosevelt. These instructors stressed the obligations of officers to respect the dignity of the enlisted man. A ninety-day wonder who began to explain a movement to his troops by saying, "Now, boys," was certain to evoke a stern rebuke from a supervising officer, along the lines of a dressing-down given to Truscott by the commander of the Seventeenth. Barked Lieutenant Colonel James J. Hornbrook, "They're men, damn it! They're men! Every one of them! They're men! Men! *Men!*"

"In those days of 1917," Truscott recalled, "military life in Camp Harry J. Jones was a succession of hectic changes, as it usually is when a nation gathers its military, economic, and political strength for war. General Pershing was in Europe beginning the buildup of the American Expeditionary Force. The two artillery regiments departed the camp, as did signal, ordnance and quartermaster units, all destined for overseas duty. Most of the Regular Army officers in the regiments received temporary promotions and departed for other assignments. Nearly all of the senior noncommissioned officers were commissioned and, along with more experienced enlisted men, were transferred from the regiments for assignment to the divisions in the national army then being formed."

As the United States mobilized for a war that no one in 1917 imagined would come to be known as the *first* World War, young officers of whom Lieutenant Truscott, Jr., had never heard but would get to know very well in the second were either already in France or scattered in posts across the country and hoping to receive orders to prepare to go "over there."

Colonel George S. Patton, Jr., having served as Pershing's aide-de-camp in the Punitive Expedition, was assigned as Black Jack's adjutant and headquarters commandant at Chaumont.

The future commander of all American forces in World War II as chief of staff, George C. Marshall, had just been made temporary major. A graduate of Virginia Military Institute in 1901, he was commissioned as a second lieutenant in February 1902, then served with the Thirtieth Infantry in the Philippines and at Fort Reno (1903–1906). Promoted to first lieutenant in March 1907 at Fort Leavenworth, he graduated from the Infantry and Cavalry School (1907) and was a student (1908) and instructor (1908–1910) at the Army Staff College, inspector-instructor of the Massachusetts National Guard (1911–1912), and served with the Fourth Infantry at Forts Logan H. Roots and Crocket and the Thirteenth Infantry in the Philippines (1913–1916). Promoted to captain in July 1917, to temporary major in August, to lieutenant colonel in January 1918, and to colonel seven months later, he would serve in France as the operations officer of the First Division and First Army, chief of staff of the Eighth Corps, and participate in the Cantigny, Aisne-Marne, St. Mihiel, and Meuse-Argonne operations.

Two years and two months out of West Point, the future Supreme Commander of the Allied Forces in Europe in World War II, Dwight D. Eisenhower, was a lieutenant and expectant first-time father who had been stationed at several posts in the south and west.

The commander of Land Forces on D-day, June 6, 1944, Omar N. Bradley had graduated first in the West Point Class of 1915 and been stationed with the Fourteenth Infantry at Yuma, Arizona. When the United States formally entered the war, he was made a captain. Rather than moving to Europe, his regiment received orders to return to the

Pacific Northwest to guard the Montana copper mines. Throughout the next year, he tried in vain to be assigned to a unit bound for the fighting in France. Promoted to major in August 1918, he received orders to command the Fourteenth's Second Battalion as the Fourteenth became part of the new Nineteenth Infantry Division, which was organizing at Camp Dodge, Iowa. But the great influenza epidemic of 1918, coupled with the armistice in November, ensured that the division would never go overseas.

Mark Wayne Clark, from whom Truscott would take over the Fifth Army in Italy in 1945, had just graduated from West Point.

Terry de la Mesa Allen, the commander of the First Division in North Africa, Sicily, and Italy, had dropped out of West Point in his final year and finished his education at Catholic University. Rejoining the army, he attended the Army Command and General Staff School at Fort Leavenworth at the same time as Eisenhower, finishing 221st in a class in which Eisenhower ranked first.

Allen's future deputy, Theodore (Ted) Roosevelt, Jr., and three of his brothers had made their illustrious father proud by enlisting. All would eventually be wounded. The youngest would garner glory for the family name by dying in action as an aviator. Their distant cousin Franklin Delano Roosevelt was beginning a political sojourn in Teddy Roosevelt's footsteps that led from assistant secretary of the navy to governor of New York and ultimately to the White House.

While Truscott was learning to become an officer in Arizona in the fall of 1917, in New York City a famous writer of popular songs was becoming an American citizen. Born in Russia in 1888, Israel Baline had come to the New World with his family in 1893. When he launched a musical career, he changed his name to Irving Berlin. After taking the oath of allegiance on February 6, 1918, he discovered that U.S. citizenship made him eligible to be drafted into the army. Called up almost immediately, he was assigned for basic training to Camp Upton in the town of Yaphank, Long Island.

"I found out quickly I wasn't much of a soldier," he recalled. "There were a lot of things about army life I didn't like, and the thing I didn't like most of all was reveille. I hated it so much that I used to lie awake nights thinking about how much I hated it."

The result of his distress was a song about a private's desire to "murder the bugler." Titled "Oh! How I Hate to Get Up in the Morning," it was introduced to the public by one of the country's most popular entertainers, Eddie Cantor. When the song was published by Berlin's sheet-music publishing firm, it quickly became a hit not only with the public but in army camps across the country, where, as Truscott notes in *The Twilight of the U.S. Cavalry*, the soldiers were ordered to take part in songfests. "Singing was a military formation," he wrote. "Troops were marched to it by regiment, columns of fours winding along the dusty roads and into the great recreation hall, a huge barnlike structure sheathed in galvanized iron, with a floor space where ten or fifteen thousand men could stand."

Led by a "chorus master" who toured all the camps, the men bellowed "K-K-Katy," "There's a Long, Long Trail A-Winding," "Pack up Your Troubles in Your Old Kit Bag," and "Tipperary," which were churned out by songsmiths of New York's Tin Pin Alley, such as Berlin and George M. Cohan, whose "Over There" became an unofficial second national anthem. The songfests became not only a welcome break from training routines but rousing morale boosters and marching cadences.

Yet, none of this music would mean as much to Truscott in memory as the sound of the bugle. "At Camp Jones the bugler of the guard regulated all of our day's activities," he wrote. "He ruled our lives with the clear notes which penetrated to every corner of the camp. During those war days, reveille sounded at half past five in the winter months, so our days began well before dawn. Troops' officers took turns standing reveille with their troops and, after roll call, reported to the officer of the day midway down the regimental street. Such reports were made again at retreat in the evening and again at taps at eleven o'clock at night after a bed check by the noncommissioned officer in charge of quarters. The bugle blew on numerous other occasions during the day at prescribed intervals: Mess, Police, Sick, and Drill calls early in the day; and later, Recall, Stable, Officers', and First Sergeants' calls. No bells, PA systems, telephone calls, or radio messages. Just the bugle. And we followed its orders."

It was an army rooted in the warfare techniques of the nineteenth century. Mobilizing for the kind of fighting they soon would face in France required the conversion of millions of young men who had been wrenched from civilian lives on farms and in towns and cities by the draft into soldiers. Their immediate commanders were predominately recently commissioned ninety-day wonders. Truscott recalled that to learn what was expected of them as leaders, most of the new officers studied a relatively new, small cloth-bound red book entitled *Officers' Manual.* A compilation of the "Customs of the Service," it presented matters of "a practical, worth-knowing nature, and things of value and assistance to the inexperienced, most of which cannot be found in print, but must be learned by experience, often by doing that which we should not do or failing to do what we should do."

Half a century later, General Truscott would write that effective military leadership was attained only by recognizing that to a very high degree the measure of success in battle depended upon the ability to profit from the lessons of the past. While training could approximate physical conditions of battle, including the extreme of fatigue, discomfort, and noises of warfare, it was not possible to create in peacetime all of the psychological conditions and tensions that result from the fear, uncertainty, loneliness, and horrors of the actual battlefield.

"Nor can we foresee in peacetime," he wrote, "the conditions under which future battles will be fought. No greater mistake can be made in military leadership than that of clinging to outmoded concepts, outmoded methods, and outmoded equipment."

Noting that these were the realities of the U.S. Army in the autumn of 1917, he depicted the cavalry clinging to romantic associations with the western frontier, the Indian Wars, and the Spanish-American War. Until the rampages of Pancho Villa in 1916, there had been no great threat to national security and no feeling of urgency in the government and among the majority of the American people to become involved in a war in Europe. Reluctant to "get in it," eager to end it as fast as possible once they were, and thrilled when it ended on November 11, 1918, the nation celebrated and looked ahead to what the 1920 Republican presidential candidate Warren G. Harding vowed would be a return to "normalcy."

Armistice Day was a joyous occasion throughout the country. Truscott noted that peace "deflated the hopes for service in France for many adventurous souls." Including himself. Without using the personal pronoun, he wrote, "Among the professional soldiers were the group of provisional officers who hoped for a permanent career."

Fretting over the possibility of having to return to civilian life, he was relieved to receive a copy of Special Orders Number 74. Issued by Headquarters, Southern Department, U.S. Army, on March 20, 1919, it directed the Seventeenth Regiment of Cavalry to proceed from Douglas, Arizona, to San Francisco "in time to debark on Army Transport sailing from that port on or about April 5, 1919," for station in the Hawaiian Islands.

One week after receiving the order, First Lieutenant Lucian King Truscott, Jr., took a step that would alter his life as profoundly and lastingly as his decision to abandon teaching to make a career of soldiering.

★　　　　TWO　　　　★

An Army at Ease

Beyond the gates of Camp Jones, Douglas was a thriving town with a population of about fifteen thousand that was no longer supported economically entirely by copper companies. The border troubles and the war in Europe brought a sudden influx of free-spending soldiers whose pockets had been swelled by a burst of congressional largesse in the form of an increase in the pay of privates from thirteen to thirty dollars a month and proportional boosts for higher ranks. Although Arizona had instituted a prohibition law seven years before the rest of the nation would go dry in 1919, fifty miles away, just across the New Mexico border, stood the town of Rodeo, offering saloons and gambling houses. For thirsty men unable to make the trek, a brisk bootlegging trade developed along the Douglas–Rodeo road. In Pirtlesville and other nearby places, soldiers with a different yearning could find relief in the company of what Truscott termed "the usual array of camp followers."

Officers were welcomed at Douglas's small country club with tennis courts and a nine-hole golf course with oiled sand for greens instead of grass. The town also provided upscale restaurants and cafes, billiard and pool parlors, and the first-class Hotel Gadsden.

Opened in 1907 when Arizona had yet to become a state, the hotel was named for the businessman James Gadsden, who had been named by President Franklin Pierce to negotiate the purchase by the United States from Mexico of territory that had been in dispute since the end of the Mexican-American War. The treaty, signed in 1854, was celebrated as the Gadsden Purchase and acquired land intended as the southern route for a transcontinental railroad. The hotel became a plush home away from home for cattlemen, ranchers, miners, and businessmen, a centerpiece for Douglas high society, and a lavish resort for eastern visitors. Among the guests in the winter of 1919 was a vivacious and beautiful twenty-three-year-old fourth-generation granddaughter of President Thomas Jefferson.

Sarah Nicholas Randolph was born a week before Christmas in 1896 on the site of the third president's childhood home, Edge Hill in Albemarle County, to Dr. and Mrs. William M. Randolph of Charlottesville, Virginia. She grew up with all the benefits of lofty social standing, privilege, and comfort that were the legacy of one of the most prestigious families of Virginia. Declaring that no family in the colony of Virginia was more prominent or more powerful than the Randolphs, a French visitor in the 1780s, the marquis de Chastellux, wrote, "You must be prepared to hear the name Randolph frequently." Seven decades later, the novelist Herman Melville cited the Virginia Randolphs as the quintessential "old established family in the land."

The family dynasty, founded by William Randolph in 1680 at a home below the falls of the James River, developed eleven major plantations. Merchants, ship owners, and the landlords of thousands of acres worked by hundreds of slaves, Randolphs dominated the economic affairs of the Virginia colony. As lawyers, they influenced the administration of its government and played a significant role in the Revolution and creation of the United States. Sarah's namesake, the first Sarah Nicholas Randolph, was Jefferson's great-granddaughter. A successful author, she published a best-selling intimate biography, *The Domestic Life of Thomas Jefferson*, in 1871 and in 1876 provided a lively account of the life of another distinguished and dynamic relative, the Confederate Civil War hero Stonewall Jackson.

In the preface to Truscott's memoir of life in the U.S. Cavalry between the World Wars, Lucian Truscott III said of his mother that she was a true Southern woman, even more so than Scarlett O'Hara and other belles in the pages of *Gone With the Wind*. "In an earlier generation," he stated, "my mother could have *been* a Scarlett." Although neither she nor General Truscott provided an account of the moment they'd met, it is evident in their son's portrait of the couple that the rough-around-the-edges former schoolteacher from the Oklahoma hinterlands being smitten by the Virginia belle was proof of the old adage that opposites attract. Recording that Sarah had the fire, will, and ambition to convince Truscott that he could succeed in anything he attempted, Lucian III recalled, "She knew all of the social amenities, and she taught them to him over the years: the silverware, the linen, the beautiful furniture, perfect manners, neatness, orderliness, only the best in clothes and food and wine. She helped him become the gentleman who in later years would feel perfectly at ease with both infantry privates in foxholes and royalty in palaces."

Her family nickname, Truscott learned, was "Chick." Neither recorded details of their courtship. Motivated by the order transferring Truscott to San Francisco no later than the fifth of April 1919, they were married on March 27 in Cochise County, Arizona. Sarah was twenty-three. At age twenty-four, Truscott had held the permanent rank of first lieutenant for three months. While he traveled with the Seventeenth Regiment by train to San Francisco, arriving early on the morning of April 5, she and other officers' wives went ahead of them by a few days. Aboard the U.S. Army transport ship *Sherman* for the trip to Hawaii, they learned that because of a lack of cabin space, the wives of junior officers would have to sleep on sofas and settees with older women and their daughters. "A few hours later," Truscott wrote, "the good ship *Sherman* passed out through the Golden Gate and headed into the swells of the Pacific, loaded to the gunnels with dreams."

The newlyweds settled into sparse quarters that the army provided to married officers at Castner Barracks. An area that soon would be renamed Schofield Barracks and become the home of the army's Hawaiian Division, it was occupied entirely by the Seventeenth Cavalry. For journeys to and from Honolulu (twenty miles away), married officers formed partnerships to purchase cars and shared their use on alternate weeks. The center of the social activities was the Officers' Club. Sarah observed that during conversations at the dinner table, her husband was inclined to be silent, but on subjects involving a principle or ideal about which he felt strongly he became a tireless talker. She also noted that he was never happier than when he was chatting with younger officers. "I would like to put iron into their souls," he explained.

It was at the Officers' Club that Truscott observed the work of a staff of Chinese mess stewards. He was so impressed that wherever General Truscott set up command posts throughout World War II, Chinese cooks and waiters prepared and served his meals.

In their modest home he demonstrated what impressed Sarah as "an unusual interest in things domestic." She recalled, "He began by helping to hang the first curtains that we put up. He also made little picture frames for Hawaiian scenes that he loved, and later he made tables and smoking stands, a couch, a desk, lamps, and many odds and ends."

It was a period that Truscott called his "Hawaiian interlude." He took up polo, a sport that became a lifetime passion, and it would forge an unbreakable bond between him and Patton. Lucian III recalled that in polo his father was absolutely fearless and determined to win, and that this gave him an advantage over many opponents, who would eventually back off a little when he pushed them too far. In a father-son talk following a match that Truscott's team almost lost because Truscott had deliberately fouled an opponent to keep him from scoring a goal, Truscott explained, "You play games to *win*, not lose. And you fight wars to win! And every good player in a game and every good commander in a war, every damn one of them has to have a son of a bitch in him. If he doesn't, he isn't a good player or commander. And he never *will* be a good commander. Polo games and wars aren't won by gentlemen. They're won by men who can be first-class sons of bitches when they have to be."

As Truscott's Seventeenth Cavalry settled into a life that moved at what he viewed as a leisurely pace in the delightful climate of an island paradise, the Congress decided in the form of the National Defense Act of 1920 that the strength of the U.S. Army, which had gone from 200,000 men before the war to nearly 5 million men at its end, 1,390,000 of whom had seen active combat service, should be drastically reduced. The act provided that a peacetime Regular Army would consist of 14,000 officers and 365,000 enlisted men. But when the moment came to appropriate funds, Congress provided money for only 150,000. That the United States would have no need for a large standing military force was enunciated by President Harding on March 4, 1921. In his inaugural address he said, "We seek no part in directing destinies of the world."

Describing the army's situation immediately after the war in the foreword to Truscott's cavalry memoirs, the historian Edward M. Coffman noted that with a strength of under 150,000 the U.S. Army ranked eighteenth in size among the world's armies, lower than that of Belgium. "To be sure, at the tiny garrisons, one day seemed much like the one before and the one before that," he wrote, "as officers and men went about their daily rounds in units that were usually at half strength or less. Indeed, a cavalry veteran of the Indian Wars of the late nineteenth century would have soon felt at home in one of the Texas or Arizona posts in the 1920s and 1930s."

A result of these limitations was a reorganization of the army that reduced the size of the cavalry from seventeen to fourteen regiments. When this was achieved by the inactivation of the Fifteenth, Sixteenth, and Seventeenth, the Truscotts found themselves packing for a return to the United States. In a little more than a year in Hawaii they'd had two children. Mary Randolph was born on May 3, 1920, and Lucian III on September 17, 1921. Their father had also earned a promotion to captain (July 1, 1920). Fifteen years would pass before his next boost in rank.

Transferred to the Presidio of Monterey, California, and assigned to the Eleventh Cavalry, Truscott was at the post overlooking the quaint fishing town and tourist attraction less than three months, but it was long enough to take advantage of the plush Del Monte Hotel's polo field and the golf courses of nearby Pebble Beach, where the putting greens were carefully manicured grass. When orders to his next post arrived, he was directed to return to Douglas, Arizona. In command of 460 enlisted men and assigned to the First Cavalry Brigade "for duty and permanent station," he joined the nation's oldest cavalry regiment. Organized in 1832 to fight in the Black Hawk War, the outfit was expanded into the Regiment of Dragoons the next year, and in 1861 it was designated the First Cavalry Regiment for service in the Civil War. Its second in command as Truscott reported for duty, Lieutenant Colonel Julian E. Gaujot, was a certified American hero who had been awarded the Medal of Honor for an exploit in the Border Wars. During the raid on the Mexican town of Agua Prieta in which Corporal Jones was killed, gunfire by Pancho Villa's men endangered the people of Douglas. Gaujot rode alone into Villa's camp to tell Villa that if the Villistas fired another shot into Douglas, American troops would respond. Truscott saw Gaujot as the perfect picture of a cavalryman.

With the Mexican border long since pacified, and Prohibition in full swing in the United States, officers and soldiers from Camp Jones who ventured across the line into Agua Prieta in 1922 did so in pursuit of liquor. While its plentiful cantinas thrived, the town of Douglas found itself enduring hard times that resulted from the drastic reduction in the population of the camp. This dire situation became a crisis when the War Department decided to abandon the camp and shift the cavalry regiment to Camp Marfa, Texas. The stated purposes were to save money and to merge the Fort Jones cavalry with the Fourth Cavalry Division at Fort Clark to create the First Cavalry Brigade. Although political influence exerted by Douglas merchants delayed the move until after Christmas 1922, the regiment departed the next day. After a grueling journey that took almost a month, the troops arrived at the little town of Marfa in the Big Bend cattle country of Presidio County, Texas, on January 23, 1923.

In the short span of Truscott's second posting at Douglas, he continued his indulgence in his favorite sport and in June 1922 participated in a Junior Polo Tournament under the auspices of the First Cavalry Division at Fort Bliss, Texas. Because there were no funds available for transporting the horses by rail, at a cost of about two hundred dollars, and no trucks to take them by road, the polo ponies had to be walked to the site. Despite this arduous trek, the team beat the Fort Bliss favorites and went on to triumph at a Senior Tournament.

The joy that he felt in helping his team win the matches in the state where he learned to ride horses was tempered that year when he learned of the death of his father at his home in Haywood, Oklahoma. Maria Truscott would live another sixteen years, residing for much of that time with her son. Lucian III recalled that when she died in 1938 while Truscott was serving at Fort Leavenworth, Kansas, it was the only time as a child that he saw his father cry.

For Sarah Truscott, now with two small children to care for, the shift from Douglas to Marfa was the fourth change of address in three years. This time, however, she arrived at her new house in the middle of January in the midst of a severe cold snap in which the temperature fell well below zero and stayed there. Truscott remembered, "Kitchens in some of the officers' quarters had mounds of ice three feet high as a result of bursting water pipes and water heaters the morning after the big freeze."

The only physical description of Truscott in the decades when the U.S. Army was at ease and at home, twenty years before he became a general in command of troops in combat, was provided by his elder son. "He was a handsome man, attractive to women, but not big, being perhaps five feet ten and about one hundred and eighty pounds when he was in good physical condition," wrote Lucian III. "But he *seemed* like a big man. He had large eyes, a prominent nose, large but not protruding ears, broad shoulders, a big chest, and huge hands, with big, square fingers. When I was young he would tell me proudly that 'they're working man's hands.' And they were, and those of a craftsman. He had an amazing talent at designing (with my mother's help) and making beautiful furniture by hand, *never* with a power tool; he made his own polo mallets; and he could repair anything with those hands. But he always kept them immaculate—originally at my mother's insistence, I'm sure. I remember watching him clean and trim his nails with his razor-sharp pocketknife, thinking that he did it because well-cared-for hands were the mark of a gentleman. And he was. A rough one, but still a gentleman."

As a captain in the U.S. Army at a time when the world was sick of war and the major powers were hammering out a treaty to limit the sizes of their navies and land forces, Truscott found satisfaction in the unchanging nature of an army post and a regimental life that was maintained by traditions and customs of the service that were the necessary measure of the conformity that any organizational system required. He recognized a natural human tendency to cling to established habits in the indoctrination that all newly joined members received in the history, tradition, and customs of military life. "Loyalty and pride in organization," he wrote, "were never difficult to create and maintain, for Americans like to be proud members of a superior organization."

Life in the cavalry involved daily riding exercises in slow trotting, squad and platoon drills, and rifle and pistol practice. Because of the postwar reorganization of the army, the reduced strength of regiments required fewer officers and resulted in a system of rotation to provide officers opportunities to become familiar with all categories of service. This meant that approximately every four years, officers departed posts for new assignments or to attend army schools. Consequently, when Truscott's regiment arrived at Camp Marfa, he and Sarah knew that it would be a temporary posting. They found the townspeople of Marfa to be similar to those of Douglas. Regarding their relationship with their military neighbors, Truscott noted, they fell into two groups. One of these was very conservative in its social outlook and viewed the social affairs of the post, such as dancing, bridge playing, and cocktail parties, with some disfavor. The other was more cosmopolitan and entered into the social activities of the camp.

While almost all of the town's ten thousand citizens were Democrats, in a contest within the party in the spring of 1923 to choose the Democratic candidate for Presidio County sheriff, a post the Democrat was certain to win, they split along the same lines as their opinions on the issue of socializing. The conservatives backed the incumbent. Liberals favored his rival. Because the Twenty-first Amendment to the United States Constitution granting women the right to vote had been ratified in 1920, the election of 1923 was the first in which the women of Marfa were able to cast a ballot for sheriff. The race was so close, and the members of the two factions were engaged in such a bitter political battle, with no quarter asked and none given, Truscott recalled, it appeared that a mere handful of votes might determine the outcome.

Believing that military men should stay out of politics, and knowing that Texas law did not permit "felons, insane persons and members of the Regular Army" to vote, Truscott spent election day as he did any other. After returning at noon to regimental headquarters from the rifle range to review orders for the next day, he went home for lunch. Entering the kitchen of his house on Officers' Row, he found Sarah putting the finishing touches on the midday meal. Turning to greet him, she exclaimed, "Guess what? I voted!"

Truscott replied, "You *what?*"

"I voted."

With her husband looking aghast, she explained that the popular wife of the rival in the contest for sheriff had come to the post that morning, pointed out that there was no law in Texas against the wives of Regular Army officers voting, and took all of them into town to the polling stations.

"And after I voted," Sarah said excitedly, "I asked the men, 'Now where is my cigar?' "

When the votes were tallied, the incumbent sheriff had lost by a margin that left no doubt that the ballots of the Camp Marfa wives had been decisive. Infuriated, the loser and important supporters among the ranchers—whose permission was needed by the army to use their land to conduct maneuvers—protested to the First Cavalry Division's commanding general and to state authorities. On the basis that army officers were not legal residents of Marfa, and therefore neither were their wives, it was ruled that their votes must be nullified.

Summarizing the episode, Truscott wrote, "For a while, all of this put somewhat of a damper on the social activities and our general relations with the town. However, we all set about mending public relations with as much charm as we possessed. Memories of distaff dabbling in local politics receded into the past, and relations were soon reestablished on the old basis. Officers stationed in Marfa during this little political storm learned thoroughly that it is not well for the military, even its distaff side, to undertake to influence the selection of candidates for political office, particularly in a local election."

Other lessons that would become professional and personal guides for Truscott as an army officer were taught by a new commander of the First Cavalry Brigade. Taking over in the summer of 1924, Brigadier General Ewing E. Booth had begun his soldiering career during the

Spanish-American War. Commissioned in the Regular Army in 1901, he graduated from the Infantry-Cavalry School (1903), Army Staff College (1905), and General Staff School (1922). The author of the textbook *Methods of Training*, he had been closely associated with General J. Franklin Bell, the prime motivator in the establishment of the army school system, which would be the most important element in shaping Truscott's career. Quiet and patient, Booth was an officer who knew what he wanted and persisted in seeking it until his troop commanders fully grasped his goals. He preached that a commander must never turn to the use of sarcasm when dealing with junior ranks, especially enlisted men, and that when a superior turned sarcastic to correct individuals of lower rank, he was taking advantage of someone who was not in a position to answer back.

"It was an illuminating concept," Truscott wrote, "coming as it did from one who had spent so many years in the service when sarcasm was almost a way of life."

After competing in the winter of 1924/25 Regimental Polo Tournament at San Antonio, Texas, Truscott returned to Camp Marfa to find his name listed with several other captains to go to the Troop Officers' Course at Cavalry School at Fort Riley, Kansas, in September 1925. In the reorganized army resulting from the National Defense Act of 1920, such training was crucial to an officer's advancement. Graduation was deemed the next step on the military ladder. In 1924, George S. Patton had completed the Command and General Staff School (C and GS), and, after serving as an instructor at the Cavalry School in the use of the saber, had established a prize in the form of a silver cup for mounted competition using the sword. When Dwight D. Eisenhower graduated at the top of the C and GS class of 245 in 1926, Patton claimed that Eisenhower had led his class because Patton had lent him his class notes.

When the Truscotts arrived at Fort Riley, they settled onto the most famous and romantic military post of the Old West. Established in 1852 to protect settlers heading west via one of two trails that took them either to Oregon or southwest to New Mexico, Arizona, and California, it had been at the heart of the Indian Wars and the home post to General George Armstrong Custer's ill-fated Seventh Cavalry. Four miles west of Junction City astride U.S. Highway 40, it sprawled over twenty thousand acres. Most of the fifty-six members of the Officers' Class of 1925 were captains. As they arrived, they were encouraged to wear a distinctive new uniform. Consisting of dark olive green blouse (long jacket), shining "Sam Browne" belt, knee-high boots with spurs, and "pink" (tan) riding pants that flared like wings from waist to knees and tapered to fit into the boots, it was adopted by American cavalrymen during the Great War from the British "Faber" riding gear made by a London tailor of that name. The outfit would become General Truscott's sartorial hallmark throughout World War II.

Half a world away in 1925, as Truscott and Sarah unpacked, a military officer who never found a conflict in dabbling in politics had installed himself as dictator of Italy. By taking power in Rome in January, Benito Mussolini envisioned himself as a twentieth-century Caesar who would create a new Roman Empire. In Germany, a former corporal during the Great War, and a leader of a failed coup by the Nazi Party in Bavaria, had just published a book that he'd written while in prison. Titled *Mein Kampf,* it was not only a tome purporting to be the life story of Adolf Hitler, but his blueprint for avenging what he considered the humiliation of Germany by the Allies through draconian peace terms. Also blaming Jews and Communists for Germany's postwar difficulties, the volume presented a plan for a totalitarian regime to be imposed once the Nazis gained control in Berlin.

The introduction of the airplane and the tank in World War I had changed the nature of the battlefield. Although Britain and France were continuing to develop the new weapons in the years following the war, the only move in the direction of adopting tank warfare in the United States took the form of articles on the subject of armor and mechanization. Truscott noted in *The Twilight of the U.S. Cavalry*, "There was not a *single* modern tank or armored car in the army at this time." In the year he arrived at Fort Riley, the minuscule Army Air Service put on a demonstration of the effect of aerial bombing against ground troops, but at the same time, the former head of the air corps, Brigadier General William "Billy" Mitchell, had been driven out of the military after a court-martial found him guilty of insubordination for criticizing the status of the nation's defenses and urging formation of an air force independent of the army.

When the War Department at last recognized the possibility of value in exploring the potential of a mechanized force in 1928, it did so halfheartedly by authorizing the conversion of frames of Dodge, La Salle, and other automobiles as the basis for vehicles in one armored car troop at Camp Meade, Maryland. The models were sent to Fort Bliss for testing, but only for a reconnaissance role. The experiment resulted in the creation, in 1930, of a second unit at Washington Barracks in the nation's capital as part of a plan to form an armored car squadron. This was a deviation from the National Defense Act, which had abolished the wartime tank corps as an independent entity that was advocated by two officers who embraced the tank during the war. While Eisenhower had chosen to concentrate on a career in the infantry, Patton remained committed to an armored force, which would be within the cavalry and had been responsible in large measure for the decision by the War Department in 1928 to test armored cars.

Another officer who saw a role for a mechanized force as part of the cavalry was second in command at the Cavalry School. Commissioned from the enlisted ranks in 1900 after serving in the Spanish-American War, Colonel Bruce Palmer had been on the General Staff from 1920 to 1924 and had come to the Cavalry School with what Truscott welcomed as an ambition to modernize the cavalry by developing tactics, techniques, organizations, and methods that would maximize the use of armored vehicles and motor transportation. In field exercises and maneuvers he converted several World War I reconnaissance cars to represent tanks. "They did not look like armored cars," Truscott noted, "but all concerned obtained some conception of the capabilities of the armored vehicles they were supposed to represent. We also learned about the appropriate employment of such vehicles."

While Palmer was introducing Truscott to the virtues of an armored force in support of advancing ground troops as men on horses had done for centuries, the Cavalry School's director of instruction, Colonel Charles L. "Scotty" Scott, introduced Truscott to the value of training men to cover a large stretch of territory in a short time. Cavalrymen of Fort Riley were expected to march one hundred miles over a measured course with full field equipment in twenty-four hours. Seventeen years later, General Truscott's soldiers were required to execute speed marches that would be cursed by footsore and exhausted infantrymen in North Africa, Sicily, and Italy as the "Truscott Trot."

Upon completing Cavalry School in 1927, the former Oklahoma schoolteacher learned that the army had been so impressed with him as a student that it chose to keep him at Riley as an instructor. The assignment would last for six years, providing Sarah with the longest time in one location since their marriage and Mary and Lucian III with uninterrupted schooling. The duty was an opportunity for Truscott to indulge in polo, cross-country riding, hunting, fishing, and social activities that were important in forging a network of friends in the officer corps, as essential to the advancement of a career as diplomas and glowing proficiency reports. Yet during the six years in Kansas, it became increasingly clear to him that the future of soldiers on horses was in doubt. "These were troublesome days for the cavalry branch," he recalled, "for it was becoming evident that there were increasing numbers who opposed the branch and did not wish it well. Some of these were among the earthbound who have ever viewed the man on horseback with obvious suspicion. Some were among those contending for limited appropriations provided for the support of the under-strength army."

Four years after the chief of cavalry, Major General Herbert B. Crosby, was directed in 1926 by the War Department to reduce the three and one-half regiments by 50 percent, he told the staff and students at the Cavalry Officers School, "There is no use beating about the bush, because there is no doubt that the cavalry is on the defensive at the present time." To those who saw the mechanization of warfare as an enemy of cavalry, he answered by predicting that it would prove to be the cavalry's greatest friend. Within months of Crosby's speech, the army's new chief of staff, General Douglas MacArthur, decreed that missions of whatever mechanized force emerged from experiments in armored vehicles would be the responsibility of the cavalry.

Although Truscott agreed that the cavalry's future lay in mechanization and welcomed the decision by MacArthur, he felt deep sadness and pangs of nostalgia as both the oldest and the youngest of the cavalry regiments turned in their horses as the First Cavalry at Camp Marfa and the Cavalry School's Thirteenth moved to Fort Knox, Kentucky. Combined with other units, they formed the First Cavalry Brigade (Mechanized).

Within a year, Truscott found himself transferred to Fort Myer in Arlington, Virginia, just across the Potomac River from Washington, D.C. He was appointed commander of Troop E, Third Cavalry in June 1931 and became part of the most visible military unit in the country. The residence of the army chief of staff, the post had long been the home of ceremonial troops. Called Brave Rifles by General Winfield Scott after the regiment stormed the Halls of Montezuma in the Mexican War in 1846, the Third Cavalry marched for presidential inaugurations and at other White House occasions, presented salutes and reviews, escorted foreign dignitaries, protected the District of Columbia, and served as honor contingents for funerals at Arlington National Cemetery. Since 1921, its soldiers had stood perpetual guard at the Great War's Tomb of the Unknown Soldier.

Despite the prestige and history associated with Fort Myer, Truscott observed, "There is always a certain amount of sameness about military posts—as there is with college campuses, and prisons!" While he mused about the most important army post in terms of visibility among the high command and influential politicians, being in Virginia was a return to Sarah's family's roots and the social milieu of her childhood. She was also pregnant. James Joseph Truscott III was born on December 26, 1930.

Seven months later, Truscott noted another auspicious arrival at Fort Myer. Appointed executive officer of the cavalry regiment, Major George S. Patton was fresh from the army's highest educational institution, the War College. Before that he'd been a staff officer in the office of the chief of cavalry and in an earlier stint served as director of plans and training in Hawaii. Although the moment that the former Oklahoma teacher who grew up poor and became a ninety-day wonder met the scion of wealth, who was a star graduate of West Point and a hero in World War I, is not mentioned in Truscott's memoirs of the cavalry, the two men who seemed to have nothing in common but their service in the islands, devotion to the cavalry, and a passion for polo would prove to be very much alike as men and battlefield commanders. Patton was ten years older than Truscott and had all of the social graces that result from having been raised to be a gentleman, yet he was able to curse as readily as any of the Oklahoma cowboys who taught Truscott how to swear. That Truscott chose not to include a description of his introduction to Patton in July 1932 is unfortunate, not only because historians have been denied an insight into such a significant moment for two forceful figures who would loom large in the campaigns in North Africa, Sicily, and Italy, but because it occurred as both were serving at Fort Myer, when the residence on the post for the army chief of staff was occupied by General Douglas MacArthur, whose assistant was Major Dwight D. Eisenhower.

Three weeks after Patton reported for duty, all of these future commanders in the greatest war of all time found themselves at the center of an episode in the history of the U.S. Army that left Truscott both embarrassed and proud, and that Patton cited as "the most disgraceful form of service." In January 1932, a sign of impending trouble took the form of an order issued by the commander of the Army Third Corps area encompassing the capital district. All officers were to be given a thorough review course titled "The Military in Domestic Disturbances."

Seeds of a crisis that was viewed as not only a possibility but likely had been sowed when Congress authorized delayed payment of a bonus to veterans of the World War. Called Adjusted Service Certificates, they were bonds that were to mature in 1945. Throughout the booming prosperity of the 1920s, the vets were content with the arrangement, but as the worst economic depression in history swept the country following the collapse of the stock market in October 1929, thousands of ex-soldiers who were suddenly cast out of work petitioned Congress to authorize immediate payment. When it failed to do so, groups of angry men took a page from the history books and emulated Coxey's Army during the Grover Cleveland administration by marching to Washington to demand redress. By May 1932, more than twenty thousand angry Americans converged on the capital, many with families in tow, and set up campgrounds in the military manner they'd learned as troops of General Pershing's American Expeditionary Force (AEF). With bitterly ironic humor, they named their army of the unemployed the Bonus Expedi tionary Force (BEF).

Recalling a feeling of anxiety in official circles and a restless, troubled atmosphere in the city, Truscott wrote, "This feeling of unease was reflected at Fort Myer, for the officers and men of the garrison were soon restricted to the limits of the post. Individual officers and men could only leave with permission of the commanding officer, and then only for brief periods for urgent reasons. Meanwhile, troops were being thoroughly trained in the tactics of riot duty and the techniques of handling riotous crowds."

The simmering situation boiled over on July 28. With squatters refusing to vacate an abandoned building on Pennsylvania Avenue that was being demolished as part of the plan to develop the Mall between the Capitol and the Washington Monument, a skirmish took place in which two veterans were killed by the city police. Within hours, Patton received an order by telephone stating that President Herbert Hoover had authorized the use of troops from Fort Myer to clear the building. In another echo of the Cleveland administration, when the president called out troops against citizens for the first time since the Civil War in order to break a national railroad strike on the basis that it interfered with the U.S. Mail, the cavalry squadron at Fort Myer mounted its horses, thundered from Arlington Cemetery, crossed the recently completed Memorial Bridge, swung past the Lincoln Memorial, and rode to the Ellipse south of the White House to await the arrival of an infantry battalion from Fort Washington. In mid-afternoon, the force, including a few World War tanks, moved up Pennsylvania Avenue toward Capitol Hill. Workers in government and private offices who gathered at windows every four years to watch troops taking part in presidential inaugural parades now watched soldiers on the move to bring force against men with whom some of the cavalrymen had fought side by side in France.

With the occupied building surrounded, MacArthur arrived along with Eisenhower and other officers. Describing Eisenhower's role in the confrontation, the biographer Peter Lyon noted that the future Supreme Allied Commander in Europe and the future American commander in the Pacific had disagreed on whether MacArthur ought to assume a visible role. "Eisenhower had urged that the chief of staff of the United States Army should be off the streets, removed from anything so vulgar as a riot," wrote Lyon. "But MacArthur had been in an epic mood. There was, he had said, 'incipient revolution in the air.'" In a news photograph taken later in the day, Lyon noted, Eisenhower stood next to MacArthur with the look on his face like that of a dog caught sucking eggs.

Remembering the day from the point of view of the cavalry, Truscott described the vets in the building as a mob that felt emboldened by the fact that the troops had taken no immediate action to evict them. He wrote, "A few bricks and stones from the rubble heaps were thrown. Several soldiers were struck, and at least two were knocked unconscious. Then word came to disperse the mob. The cavalry troops moved forward, with drawn sabers in hand. There was a hail of bricks and stones. But not one drop of veterans' blood was shed, although many felt the flat of troopers' sabers and some few were threatened with the point. Many veterans sought refuge in shacks they had built along the Mall or in trucks parked along the streets. A few blows with the pommel of a saber on the tin roofs or the thrust of a saber through cracks soon emptied the shacks and trucks, though, and the veterans continued their flight."

After retreating across the Potomac via the Anacostia Bridge to an improvised camping ground, the routed veterans were ordered to vacate. Most did so. Others replied by setting fire to shacks. By dawn's light, the almost-vacant camp was a smoldering ruin. At some point that morning, a sergeant of the Twelfth Infantry approached Patton with a bedraggled-looking veteran who had told the sergeant he was a friend of Patton.

With flushed face, Patton answered, "Sergeant, I do not know this man. Take him away, and under no circumstances permit him to return."

When the veteran was gone, Patton admitted that he had lied about not knowing the man. Joseph Angelo was a prominent leader of the Bonus March who testified before a congressional committee and pleaded for payment of the bonus money. Now he was an unemployed civilian residing in Camden, New Jersey, with a wife and child. During the war he had been Patton's wartime orderly and saved a wounded Patton's life in France by dragging him into a shell hole.

Explaining to the troops that since the war Patton and his mother has assisted Angelo on numerous occasions financially and set him up in business several times, Patton asked, "Can you imagine the headlines if the papers got wind of our meeting here this morning?"

Of his first actual military action, Truscott wrote, "Cavalry training and special training for riot duty had paid off."

The next time he rode a horse on Pennsylvania Avenue was on March 4, 1933, in the inauguration parade for President Franklin D. Roosevelt. Patton remained at Fort Myer three years. When he left to be stationed in Hawaii again, he had been promoted to lieutenant colonel. In 1935, MacArthur became military advisor to the president of the Philippines, with Dwight D. Eisenhower joining him in Manila as his assistant.

A few months earlier, Captain Lucian King Truscott, Jr., had received orders transferring him from commanding troops at Fort Myer to teaching officers at the Command and General Staff School at Fort Leavenworth, Kansas. That he was assigned to the army's most important officers' training institution clearly indicated that at the age of forty, and with sixteen years of army service, someone in the War Department high command had noticed him and marked him for advancement.

★ THREE ★

CALL TO ARMS

THE COMMAND AND GENERAL STAFF School had been founded at Leavenworth, thirty miles northwest of Kansas City, Kansas, on the west bank of the Missouri River, on May 7, 1881, by order of the army's commander, General William Tecumseh Sherman.

In General Order Number 42, the Union Civil War commander whose army had burned Atlanta and marched to the sea directed establishment of a "school of application for infantry and cavalry." Confirmed by the War Department in General Order Number 8 on January 26, 1882, it was enlarged in 1901 and developed along the lines of a postgraduate college for the officers who had demonstrated special merit and promise.

Records of the classes of 1934–1935 show that of 106 students, 1 attained the rank of general, 2 became lieutenant generals, 22 became major generals, and 39 were made brigadier generals.

Of Truscott's 1935–1936 class of 109, 3 went on to become lieutenant generals (including Truscott), 14 rose to major general, and 35 became brigadier generals.

Overseas, Mussolini's legions were advancing Il Duce's schemes to forge his new Roman Empire by conquering Ethiopia, and the League of Nations remained deaf to Emperor Haile Selassie's pleas to save his country; the Japanese were rampaging through China; and Hitler was rebuilding the German army and air force in violation of the Versailles Treaty that had ended the World War. In America, young army officers who would presently be called upon to lead a fight against these forces sat in classrooms and study halls named after the Civil War generals Sherman, Phillip Sheridan, and Ulysses Grant for 950 hours of advanced courses in offensive and defensive operations, military intelligence, reconnaissance, counteroffensives, lines of communication and supply, logistics, mechanized units, and rules and laws of war. Another 350 hours were devoted to map reading and solving problems in the two basics of combat: situation and terrain.

Friday night, Truscott recalled, was always time for relaxation among the students. "It was a common practice for friends in the same apartment building," he wrote, "to gather for a cocktail party and let off steam about various activities of the week, and more particularly to rehash the map problem of the afternoon. Later on, there were other larger cocktail parties and dinners and the weekly dance at the Officers' Club. A vast amount of talk was expended during all of these activities in the discussion of school doctrines, problems, and personalities. It might not have been at the highest intellectual level, but nevertheless it sometimes served to ease troubled minds."

Saturdays, there was golf, tennis, riding, and polo, followed by more cocktail parties and dinners, frequently in black tie or dress uniform. There were also weekend activities involving families. Wives had bridge and book clubs and riding classes. Children ranging in age from kindergarten to high school had boy and girl scout troops and attended schools on the post or went to Leavenworth High School or the parochial Immaculata High School. Kids enrolled in kindergarten and elementary school were conveyed to classes on a mule-drawn bus.

Lucian III recalled a summertime excursion when he was fifteen from Fort Leavenworth with his father and a close friend, Captain E. M. Daniels, to visit Fort Riley. "For three days," he wrote, "they relived their days there as both students and instructors by taking me as their new 'student' on every wild ride they had ever been on in those earlier years: in and out of all the canyons, down all of the slides; fording and swimming the Republican River, in the water holding on to the horse's tail and being pulled along behind him; over every type of jump known to man; galloping wildly through the mounted pistol course, the saber course, and the course that was a combination of the two; dashing through a modified stakes course; and finally a two-hour night ride rather than the six or eight of their earlier years. When it was all over they informed me that I was the only man to graduate from the Advanced Equitation Course in three days, but only because of the high quality of the instructors, not the ability of the student."

Promoted to major upon arrival at the Command and General Staff School in August 1935, Truscott completed the course in 1936 and found himself remaining at Fort Leavenworth as a teacher for the next four years. Lucian III remembered his parents studying French together. Truscott became so proficient that he translated the *French Cavalry Journal* for the Command and General Staff School library. He also found time to discuss algebra and geometry problems as Lucian III prepared for admittance examinations in the hope of qualifying to be appointed to the U.S. Military Academy at West Point.

"He had great patience and was a good teacher, of both small boys and men," Lucian III recorded. "He taught me teamwork of the polo field by letting me play on his team for many games. Then he taught me the rough part of the game by making me play on the opposite team for what seemed like forever."

The three children were expected to adhere unquestioningly to the rules. When they were too old for spankings, punishment was confinement to their rooms. Affectionate demonstrations by physical contact were rare, as was any other expression of love, but Lucian III observed that his father would seem to hesitate for fear of hurting someone's feelings. If he became boisterous in a discussion with a member of the family or friends, Sarah intervened to chasten him quietly by saying, "Lucian, you're not being very attractive."

Having missed out on combat in the Great War, Major Truscott followed the events in North Africa, Europe, and Asia with growing expectation. He knew that sooner or later the United States would be drawn into conflict with the aggressive nations that were formally allied and known as the Axis Powers. Yet the American army remained confined to strictures of the Defense Act of 1920. Mired in the Great Depression, the majority of the American people demonstrated no desire to become involved in troubles overseas.

The War Department historian Mark Skinner Watson noted that while greatly improved since mid-1932, when the army had 119,913 enlisted men, the state of the army's strength prompted Chief of Staff General George C. Marshall to state in a later review that persistent cutting by Congress of appropriations had reduced the service virtually to the status of a third-rate power, with the Regular Army having 174,079 enlisted men dispersed among 130 posts, camps, and stations and in units that were far below strength. About a quarter of the army (45,128 enlisted men by the secretary of war's annual report in 1939) were assigned to overseas garrisons, mainly in the Hawaiian Islands, the Philippines, and the Panama Canal Zone. One Regular Army cavalry division had been organized, but it was at less than half strength.

The entire tank establishment consisted of one mechanized cavalry brigade of about half strength (2,300 men), plus tank companies allotted to infantry divisions that were not fully supplied. Beginning in 1935, Congress allotted substantially larger appropriations that permitted them to improve their readiness for action. Improvements during the next three years reflected not only the increasingly critical international situation but also planning by the War Department during MacArthur's tour as chief of staff (1930–1935). Recommendations led to the reorganization of combat forces and a modest increase in their size, accompanied by more realistic planning for using the manpower and industrial might of the United States for war, if that should become necessary. For these purposes, the War Department between 1932 and 1935 created four army headquarters and a General Headquarters Air Force in the continental United States under command of the chief of staff. Beginning in the summer of 1935, Regular and National Guard divisions and other units began training together in summer maneuvers and other exercises, including joint exercises with the navy. In the same year, Congress authorized the Regular Army to increase its enlisted strength, so that by 1938 the Regular Army was considerably stronger and far readier for action than it had been earlier in the decade.

The German annexation of Austria in March 1938, followed by a Czechoslovakian crisis in September of the same year, stirred the United States and European democracies to recognize the imminence of another World War. After Hitler sealed a pact with the Soviet Union, providing for a partition of Poland and a Soviet free hand in Finland and northern Baltic states, he ordered an invasion of Poland. While Britain and France responded by declaring war on Germany, with Italy allied to Berlin, Americans continued to insist on official neutrality. But to Truscott, the United States going to war seemed inevitable. He wrote, "No one who left the Command and General Staff School in 1940 had any idea when and where war would come, but few doubted that the United States would become entangled in the European struggle in due course."

The army's increasingly urgent tempo resulted in Major Truscott's promotion on August 18, 1940. Although fifteen years had elapsed between his rise from captain to major, elevation to lieutenant colonel had taken one-third that time. With the silver oak leaf also came an order to report to Fort Knox, Kentucky, for duty as executive and operations officer, Second Battalion, Thirteenth Armored Regiment, First Armored Division. The move reunited him with a friend and mentor from the Cavalry School at Fort Riley, Charles L. Scott. Now a major general, Scott had assumed command of the headquarters of the armored force at Fort Knox after Major General George S. Patton had been given command of the Second Armored Division. Along with another Truscott mentor, Bruce Palmer, Patton, Scott, and General Adna R. Chaffee had been the prime movers in the twenty-year post–World War campaign to transform the horse cavalry into a mechanized force.

Finding Fort Knox in the autumn of 1940 a beehive of seething activity, Truscott wrote, "People were coming and going in streams—officers and men for assignment; staff officers on inspections; important visitors from Washington and elsewhere; and dozens of the idly curious. Roads and streets were filled with the incessant clanking and roar of tanks—combat cars they were called—the clatter of armored cars and half-tracks, the clamor of motorcycles, and the accompanying clouds of dust and fumes of burning gasoline and oil, caused by troops in training or on the way to training areas."

Twice a week, trains rumbled into a fortresslike building known as the United States Gold Depository. Carrying tons of bullion in blocks and hundreds of bags of gold coins sent for safekeeping for the duration of the war by European governments, the biweekly "Gold Train" attracted throngs of spectators. On Wednesday and Saturday afternoons they gathered to watch the crates of gold being shifted from freight cars to army trucks under the alert gaze of rifle-toting guards with orders to shoot to kill anybody who might dare to try a stickup.

"Considering the weight of the treasure and the mechanical problems that would have confronted any robbers," Truscott mused, "these security measures may have seemed out of proportion to the possible dangers."

Professional and personal pleasure at having been taken out of the classroom and sent to what he called the iron horses of the mechanized cavalry in the "Blue Grass" horse country of Kentucky lasted less than a year. "It was a period of change," he noted. "Since staff officers were needed for the newly organized army and corps headquarters, as well as for the divisional and other units in the process of formation, it was not surprising that the excess of field officers in the armored force at Fort Knox was gradually thinned by assignment to units of the armored force and transfer to organizations in other areas. But even a few months in the armored force brought knowledge of the capabilities and limitations of armor and some concept of views regarding missions and methods of tactical employment. These months were therefore of the utmost professional value."

The destination chosen for him by the War Department was Fort Lewis, Washington. It meant a reunion with another veteran of the rout of the 1932 Bonus March. Arriving at the post in March 1941, he discovered that the chief of staff of Fort Lewis's commander and head of the Ninth Army Corps, encompassing all of the Pacific Northwest (Major General Kenyon A. Joyce, who had headed the Third Cavalry at Fort Myer in the early 1930s) was Dwight D. Eisenhower. Transferred from command of a battalion in the Fifteenth Infantry of the Third Division and promoted to colonel on March 6, Eisenhower brought to his new assignment experience as assistant to Chief of Staff MacArthur in Washington during the Bonus March and in the same capacity in the Philippines. Truscott also observed that there was never a question about where the command responsibility at Fort Lewis rested. He recorded that Joyce dictated the policies and left the coordination and direction of the staff to Eisenhower.

Truscott's memory of Eisenhower in 1941, provided long after World War II in his book on the cavalry, presented a portrait of the Eisenhower method of leadership that he employed as Supreme Allied Commander. "When a command decision or approval of any proposal or contemplated action was required," Truscott observed, "Colonel Eisenhower, who was always thoroughly familiar with every step of the staff involved in the complicated problems, invariably had the staff officer who was primarily concerned with the problem make the presentation. Then he stood by, ready with clarifying comments, assistance, or advice as required."

When Truscott reported to Fort Lewis, the top priority for Eisenhower and his staff was a war game to be conducted on the newly designated Hunter Liggett Military Reservation on a part of the William Randolph Hearst estate near Santa Barbara, California, that the newspaper and movie magnate lent to the War Department. After four months of planning, the maneuvers on the heavily forested property were observed by a large group of officers from Army General Headquarters in Washington, D.C., headed by Brigadier General Mark W. Clark. A descendant of the colonial war hero George Rogers Clark and the son of a career infantry officer, Clark was born at Madison Barracks, New York, on May 1, 1896, and grew up in the Chicago suburb of Highland Park near Fort Sheridan. With the assistance of an aunt (Zettie Marshall, the mother of George C. Marshall), he received appointment to West Point at the age of seventeen. Often a sickly youth, he did not distinguish himself as either an athlete or scholar, and graduated 110th in a class of 139 in 1917. He was commissioned second lieutenant, and, assigned to the infantry, he became a captain in August of that year and saw action with the Eleventh Infantry in France. Wounded in action, he was decorated for bravery. He returned home in 1919, and held various posts until 1929, when he joined the Office of the Assistant Secretary of War, serving as an instructor. After he graduated from the Command and General Staff School at Fort Leavenworth in 1935, he served as deputy chief of staff for the Civilian Conservation Corps, Seventh Corps area at Omaha, Nebraska. A graduate of the Army War College in 1937, he was a longtime friend of Eisenhower.

Toward the end of the Hunter Liggett exercises in what Truscott described as "one very severe loss" to the Ninth Corps, Eisenhower departed Fort Lewis to become chief of staff of the Third Army in San Antonio, Texas, and the central planner of the largest peacetime maneuvers in the history of the United States Army. The abrupt transfer was the result of a June 11 letter from the commander of the Third Army, General Walter Krueger, to Chief of Staff George C. Marshall. The letter specified "a man possessing broad vision, progressive ideas, a thorough grasp of the magnitude of the problems in handling an army, and lots of initiative and resourcefulness," and Krueger asked for Eisenhower. Marshall responded affirmatively on June 13. Eleven days later, Eisenhower got the order, and he arrived in Texas on July 1, the twenty-fifth anniversary of his marriage.

The maneuvers at Camp Polk, Louisiana, that Eisenhower helped plan, organize, and execute for that September (15–30) also required a move for Truscott. Ordered to take part in the war game between the Second and Third armies, arriving "at such time as would enable them to report prior to 5:00 p.m., September 9, 1941," staff officers of the Ninth Corps found themselves under the command of Lieutenant General Ben Lear and acting as part of a 200,000-man "Red" Army fighting against an equal force of the Third's "Blue" Army. With two fast-moving, hard-hitting armored divisions leading the way, Lear pushed his attackers across the Red River, where Lieutenant General Walter Krueger's Third (Blue) Army lay in wait.

In a mock fight that lasted five days, the Red Army's tanks were on the defensive. Instead of keeping on the move, they waited for motorized infantry to move up from the rear. On terrain unsuited for tanks, this hesitation proved fatal. With superior manpower and superior firepower and three antitank groups, the Blues swung their main forces to a position squarely in front of the Red's armored divisions. Under the protection of Major General Herbert A. Dargue's Blue air force, the Reds endured a relentless pounding. A *Time* magazine account noted, "So ended the first phase of the Battle of Louisiana. But for weeks to come army men will be debating its lessons. Said Lieutenant General Lesley J. McNair, GHQ Chief of Staff: 'The principal weakness was deficiency in small unit training due fundamentally to inadequate leadership.' "

Although Truscott devoted only a paragraph in *Command Missions* to the maneuvers, he agreed with subsequent analyses that noted that the army recognized the urgent necessity to upgrade its armored forces. Despite the continued opposition from high-ranking traditionalists, at a meeting held in the basement of a local high school, on the day the maneuvers ended Generals Chaffee and Magruder, the armored brigade commanders, and other officers, including Patton and Brigadier General Frank Andrews, assistant chief of staff, discussed creation of an armor branch. When they sent their recommendations to Washington with Andrews for presentation to Army Chief of Staff George C. Marshall, he responded by withdrawing armor from the cavalry and assigning it to a new armored force based at Fort Knox under Chaffee's command.

Truscott found the war games "of the utmost value to those who participated and were of value to the high command in sorting out some of the commanders who were engaged in it."

Unmentioned in his account of the Louisiana excursion is that the Second Army was routed by the Third and that the exercises had exposed serious flaws in the preparedness of America's burgeoning military. Two weeks after the maneuvers, *Time* magazine reported that Lieutenant General McNair had told field commanders, "There is no question that many of the weaknesses developed in these maneuvers are repeated again and again for lack of discipline."

A later edition observed that newsmen who covered the maneuvers witnessed plenty to corroborate the general's critique. They had seen it in the casual air of some officers and in the listlessness with which many soldiers carried out orders. "Some, who had once hoped to see a 'democratic' army, where officers and enlisted men were friends in a big happy family," the item continued, "looked with dismay on isolated instances of army democracy: officers drinking off-duty with enlisted soldiers, officers soft and indecisive in their enforcement of quick, football-field obedience. There was no question about it: the U.S. Army, model 1941, had plenty of steam, but it lacked snap, dash, spit and polish." When more than two hundred reporters and photographers convened for the war games, many of them were veterans of genuine combat, including the United Press's Richard C. Hottelet, fresh from a German prison, and Leon Kay, who saw the Nazi invasions of the Low Countries and the Balkans. CBS's Eric Sevareid arrived from London with a group of observers from the British government. "At the scene of operations," *Time* reported, "all were fitted out with officers' uniforms. Each was supplied with a map of the 30,000-square-mile maneuver area about the size of a bedspread (most of them found common road maps much handier). They were also supplied with free transportation: jeeps, command cars or ordinary taxis (hired by the army at $10 a day) and turned loose to try and find out what war was like."

Sevareid told CBS listeners, "War in Louisiana is rougher on reporters than the war in Europe. Over there you sit around waiting for communiqués. Over here you go up to the front or you don't find much to report."

A good quote could be gotten from George Patton. Cited as the star of the mock warfare for his skillful use of armor, he declared, "If you could take these tanks through Louisiana, you could take them through hell." Reporters also delightedly wrote of a frustrated military policeman who was directing traffic at an intersection in a town north of DeRidder and was unable to unsnarl the jam until Patton appeared and started "cussing and raising hell." As the traffic jam began unwinding, a priest celebrating Mass emerged from the church and told Patton to "hush up." Apologizing, Patton turned the traffic control back over to the MP, saluted the priest, and headed south with the advancing Second Armored Division. During one of the mock invasions, Patton was also reported to have bought up all the gasoline along Highway 171 so that when General Krueger brought his Red Army across the Sabine River to invade Blue Army territory, there was no fuel.

Demonstrating a facet of his personality and public relations savvy as a commander that would capture the affection of war correspondents and through their stories introduce "Ike" to the American people, Eisenhower converted his tent into a kind of resort for reporters covering the maneuvers. Described by the biographer Peter Lyon in *Eisenhower: Portrait of a Hero* as "charming them with his warm friendliness," he amused them with unprintable tales about the New Orleans whores with whom some of his troops had sported. Readers of the influential columnist and radio commentator Drew Pearson's "Washington Merry-Go-Round" heard that the credit for the strategy that routed the Second Army belonged to Colonel Eisenhower.

Barely settled back into their quarters at Fort Lewis, Washington, the officers and men of the IX Corps found themselves presented with a plan for another set of war games. Conducted by the Fourth Army in an area between southwestern Washington and the Olympic Peninsula, involving troops from Fort Ord, California, and Fort Lewis, the maneuvers again showed the U.S. Army was inadequately prepared for war. Endeavoring to move southward through Olympia, troops from Fort Ord became entangled with columns of troops from Fort Lewis heading north in a traffic jam that needed hours to untie. The lesson for Truscott was the necessity for carefully planning movements of large bodies of troops whenever road nets were limited.

After eight months at Fort Lewis, and seventeen years since Truscott served with the Eighth Cavalry at Fort Bliss, Texas, he received orders transferring him to the state of his birth for duty with the Fifth Regiment, First Cavalry Division. He found the post almost unchanged, but now the division consisted of more than seven thousand officers and men and was equipped with a force of 17 "combat cars," 178 scout cars,

180 trucks, 420 motorcycles, antitank guns, scores of mortars, and hundreds of light and heavy machine guns.

The Truscott family settled into a snug but comfortable bungalow with rooms for a trio of kids on a post with a movie theater, a polo field, an Olympic jumping ring that was home to the annual El Paso–Fort Bliss Horse Show, a stadium, and a broad parade ground for troop reviews with the Stars and Stripes fluttering on a soft breeze. On a December Sunday less than a month later families were returning from church and Sunday school. Children cavorted on the lawns. Riders returned horses to stables. Midday meals were being prepared. In most houses and barracks, radios were turned on to music appropriate for the Sabbath. On a few tuned in to the broadcast of a professional football game between two New York City teams, the Giants and the Dodgers, the play-by-play description was cut off by a man's voice that seemed at the same time calm and urgent. It announced that United States Navy and Army bases in Hawaii had just been attacked by the Japanese.

No details. Only repetition of the bulletin.

"So it was that war came to Fort Bliss," Truscott remembered. "The first reaction to the dreadful news of Pearl Harbor was one of disbelief. Then shock. As fragments of information sifted in to indicate something of the magnitude of the blow we had suffered, the feeling of shock gave way to one of bitter anger at the perfidy of a government that would launch such a dastardly blow under cover of serious diplomatic endeavors then in progress in Washington, seeking to resolve the differences [between the United States and Japan]."

Truscott's memories of being stationed in Hawaii in the 1920s, the paradise where Mary and Lucian III were born, were mixed with a grim realization that as the Japanese invaders swept into the Philippines and other American outposts in the Pacific his cavalry comrades were being killed or taken prisoner, and that thousands more faced mobilization for combat in places that for most of the men to that moment had been strange names on a map.

The Pearl Harbor attack prompted President Franklin Delano Roosevelt to declare war against Japan. Germany declared war on the United States the next day. Seventeen days after the attack, Truscott was promoted. Effective on Christmas Eve, he became a full colonel, but there would be no change in his assignment for three months. On April 1, 1942, while observing a training exercise, he was interrupted by a regimental messenger, who saluted smartly and exclaimed, "Colonel, sir, the War Department's been trying to get you on the phone. Sergeant Major says it's important and they want you to call right away."

Returning on horseback to regimental headquarters at a gallop, Truscott was told by the adjutant that he was to phone the chief of ground forces. When General Mark Clark came on the line, he asked, "Lucian, how soon can you leave there for an important assignment?"

Glancing at his wristwatch, Truscott replied, "Right now, I reckon. That is, as soon as I can get transportation."

"Take what time you need to get ready, but you ought to be here within the next two or three days. Come to Washington and report to me. I can't tell you where you're going nor what you are going to do. All I can tell you is that you're going overseas."

★   **FOUR**   ★

All-American Outfit

Arriving at General Mark W. Clark's offices at the Army War College, Truscott found that it now housed Headquarters, Army Ground Forces. Located on a peninsula between the Washington Channel and the Anacostia River, the beautiful old post, formerly known as the Washington Barracks, seemed anything but warlike. Behind high walls, it consisted of a long row of two-story redbrick buildings with tall white pillars amid sheltering shade trees fronting a parade ground. On the opposite side were temporary frame buildings. At the far end stood the main, domed building. The vista struck Truscott as more like a peaceful college campus than the nerve center of gathering hosts.

After welcoming amenities and a brief recalling of the recent maneuvers, Clark startled Truscott by asking if he would like to be a British Commando. The term had been coined at the turn of the century by the British during the Second Boer War for a guerrilla force. Revived in early 1940 by Prime Minister Churchill, who had been hailed as a hero in that conflict, the unit was created to both harass Germans with hit-and-run raids and boost British morale.

Trained in physical fitness, survival, close-quarter combat, silent killing, signaling, reconnaissance, amphibious and cliff assaulting at Achnacarry, Scotland, they had carried out their first attack on the night of June 23, 1940. Called Operation Collar, it was an offensive reconnaissance on the French coast south of Boulogne and Le Touquet. A second attack, Operation Ambassador, was on the German-occupied island of Guernsey on the night of July 14, 1940, but the raiders failed to make contact with the German garrison. Following intensive training and a number of canceled operations over the following months, Operation Claymore was launched on the morning of March 3, 1941, on the practically undefended Norwegian Lofoten Islands. They destroyed fish-oil factories, fuel dumps, and eleven ships while capturing 216 Germans and recruiting 315 Norwegian volunteers. Coding equipment and code books were also seized during this operation.

In an attempt to stem the successes of Germany's Afrika Korps, a combined Middle East Commando group named Layforce (after their commander, Lieutenant Colonel Robert Laycock) carried out a raid on April 20, 1941, against the port of Bardia in Libya. While it caused little damage, General Erwin Rommel was forced to recall a brigade from the front. Commandos were then used to help defend the island of Crete and cover its eventual evacuation. Following a British invasion of Syria on June 8, 1941, they successfully led a crossing of the Litani River in Lebanon, fighting against troops of the collaborationist regime based in Vichy, France. On December 27, 1941, the minor Norwegian port of Vaagso was the main target of the first raids by Lord Louis Mountbatten's Combined Operations. Three Commando units, a Royal Navy flotilla, and limited air support inflicted significant damage to factories, storage warehouses, and the German garrison, while sinking eight ships. The raid was strong enough to persuade Hitler to divert thirty thousand troops to Norway, upgrade coastal and inland defenses, and send the battleship *Tirpitz* and other warships to Norway in a major diversion of forces in a mistaken belief that the British planned to invade northern Norway. The most recent raid was on the French port of St. Nazaire and the only dry dock on the French Atlantic coast capable of berthing the *Tirpitz* for repairs. The dock remained out of action for the duration of the war.

"In spite of my astonishment," Truscott remembered of Clark's question about being a Commando, "I was able to say that I thought I would like it very much."

Clark explained that Roosevelt and Churchill had agreed to launch an invasion of Europe in the spring of 1943. Truscott was to head a group of American officers who were to join Mountbatten's staff to learn how to set up a group of U.S. Commandos. Truscott exclaimed in *Command Missions*, "I could hardly have been more amazed."

Clark ended the meeting by telling Truscott he would be given instructions by General Eisenhower. Because of his success during the Louisiana maneuvers in August, Ike had received a temporary promotion to brigadier general. Called to Washington from Texas by Chief of Staff George C. Marshall after the attack on Pearl Harbor to review the Philippines situation, he had remained at the War Department on Marshall's orders. Named assistant chief of staff and put in charge of War Plans, he was promoted to major general (temporary) in March and appointed assistant chief of staff of the new Operations Division.

As Truscott crossed the Potomac from Clark's headquarters to report to Eisenhower, he found evidence of great change in the ten years since his regiment had rushed from Arlington to rout the Bonus Army. In four months of rapid mobilization to fight another World War, Washington—which in 1932 had been more like a sleepy small Southern town than a national capital—had been turned into a world-class city on war footing by men in uniforms left over from the First World War who had been called back to duty. Stern-looking civilians carrying

bulging briefcases were everywhere. An army of janitors, plumbers, car-
penters, painters, and electricians with tools of their trades was engaged
in the remodeling and renovation of buildings as if there were not enough
time to achieve what needed to be done. All of this activity was shrouded
in a feeling of cloak-and-dagger intrigue.

To provide office space for a burgeoning military, two dozen buildings had been taken over for a civilian workforce that at the end of 1941
had swelled from seven thousand to over forty-one thousand. Although
a new War Department was under construction on Virginia Avenue, the
secretary of war, Henry Stimson, had let it be known that he hated it
and would never move in. Ultimately, the structure in a boggy section of
Washington, D.C, known as Foggy Bottom, became the State Department. Even as the building was going up, plans were being made to
move the military into a five-sided headquarters in Arlington. At a cost
of $35 million, the sprawling home for the army and navy would be the
world's largest building. Already being called the Pentagon, it would
house thirty thousand workers. Fretting over the price tag and already
looking ahead to the end of a war that had just started, the Illinois Republican congressman Everett McKinley Dirksen speculated, "We may
not need all that space when the war comes to an end."

Twenty years later as a U.S. senator, Dirksen would joke during debate on a military appropriations bill that in spending a billion here and
a billion there, sooner or later you're talking about real money. In 1942
he grumbled that by locating the Pentagon in Virginia, a visit to the
War Department that could be made by taxi for twenty cents would
now cost him at least sixty cents each way.

When completed, the Pentagon would replace the present headquarters of the army in the Munitions Building. A remnant of World War I,
it stood on the Mall. As Truscott walked to its entrance at Twentieth
Street, he observed streams of people arriving and leaving on foot, in
taxis, buses, private autos, and government cars. Guards at the door
checked for identification papers. Corridors seemed to be thronged with

foreign military officers and Americans of every branch of the services toting important-looking briefcases and bags, folders, or rolled-up maps or blueprints. Directed by sentries placed along hallways, he arrived at the Operations Division.

Eisenhower greeted him warmly, asked about his recent activities, inquired of mutual friends, and sought his impressions of the reaction of people in the southwest who had lost loved ones in the fall of Bataan. Getting down to business, he explained that General Marshall felt that the United States and Britain should direct their first offensive against Germany, rather than against Japan. This required an invasion across the English Channel.

Logistical and other factors fixed the first of April 1943 as the earliest date. Having just returned from London with British agreement to this concept, General Marshall proposed that American forces be concentrated in England as rapidly as shipping and other factors would permit. While confident that the American troops would be well trained, Marshall expressed concern that none would have had battle experience. Therefore, he considered it vital that U.S. units have within their ranks men who had experienced battle against Germans. They would then become instructors. Accordingly, Marshall had arranged with Mountbatten to send a group of American officers to England for assignment to his Combined Operations Headquarters. Their purpose was to plan for training Americans in the hit-and-run tactics of Britain's Commandos.

It was this group, said Eisenhower, that Truscott had been selected to head. The War Department was selecting officers who would accompany him. Marshall had also arranged to assign other American officers to other headquarters in the British military to assist in planning and to facilitate mutual understanding between the British and the Americans.

The U.S. Navy, Eisenhower noted, was cold toward this plan. They favored operations in the Pacific, where the navy would have the dominant role. The naval authorities thought that commitments in the Pacific would absorb all of their resources and were unwilling to provide the landing craft and to organize and train the crews to operate them, which would be required in large numbers. Therefore, Army Ground Forces headquarters in England would organize special engineer units to operate and maintain landing craft and establish bases.

Meanwhile, Eisenhower added, Truscott would study the information available and talk to the officers who had accompanied Marshall to London for the conferences with the British.

As Truscott listened attentively while Eisenhower unfolded this plan, he realized that he had no battle-experience and had not taken part in large amphibious operations. Only twice in his life had he been in a small boat on salt water. His cavalry background provided little familiarity with mechanized forces and less with the air force. He had studied theory in the service schools, and had been an instructor at both the Cavalry School and the Command and General Staff School, but assignment to a staff of British battle-seasoned veterans of ground, air, and naval battles, and being actively engaged in the planning and conducting of operations against a real enemy, seemed to call for an expert.

"This I definitely was not," Truscott noted.

As if reading Truscott's mind, Eisenhower said, "I consider that your background as a cavalry officer, your experience with the Armored Force, your experience as an instructor at Fort Leavenworth, your experience on a corps staff, and even your experience as a polo player especially fit you for this assignment." He paused a moment, then asked, "Did you know that Lord Louis wrote a book on polo?"

With the decision to send him to England having been made, Truscott learned that the officers who had accompanied Marshall to London were old friends. Colonel John E. Hull was now chief of the European Section, and Lieutenant Colonel Albert C. Wedemeyer was assigned to the Plans Section, Operations Division. They had been Truscott's classmates at the Command and General Staff School in the 1934–1936 class.

"We spent many hours discussing the plans which had been agreed upon," Truscott recalled. "They described various British personalities, outlined some of the differences in British organization and methods which they had observed, and suggested some of the problems that might arise. Wedemeyer provided copies of all the documents relating to the subjects considered during the London conferences."

These included original proposals for the invasion presented by General Marshall, minutes of numerous meetings, notes by British staff officers on items such as landing craft, shipping, engineer organization, and the concentration and training of American troops in England. He perused Commando tables of organization, the organization of various British headquarters, and many other documents.

"There was more than enough," said Truscott, "to further confuse and to challenge an already well-confused cavalry colonel."

During this learning process, Eisenhower talked with Truscott about his assignment and about the problems of the war effort in various theaters. At Ike's suggestion, Truscott spent many hours listening to discussions of problems and studies brought to Ike by officers of the Operations Division, other sections of the War Department, naval officers, congressmen, committees, and a seemingly endless chain of visitors. Truscott observed that Eisenhower's methods had not changed from those he had witnessed at Fort Lewis in the previous year. "Every view was considered," he recalled. "Each problem was carefully analyzed. There was the same extraordinary ability to place his finger at once upon the crucial fact in any problem or the weak point in any proposition. There was the same ability to arrive at quick and confident decisions. And the same charming manner and unfailing good temper. In retrospect, I think the most valuable hours of my preparation were those I spent in General Eisenhower's office. More than anything else these hours enabled me to appreciate the magnitude of our national undertaking and the vast complications involved in the direction of worldwide warfare. Viewed in this perspective, my problem, however confusing it might seem to me at the moment, did not loom so large."

It was now time for Truscott to meet George C. Marshall.

Truscott wrote, "His calm and dignified personality was most impressive. He shook my hand in a quick firm grasp, indicating a chair beside him. Leaning back slightly in his own chair, he gazed at me steadily."

Without change in expression, Marshall said slowly, "You are an older man than I wanted for this assignment. I looked you up. You are forty-seven. Mountbatten is forty-three. Most of his staff are younger. All of them are battle-experienced. They are even now engaged in planning and conducting raids against the Germans."

Truscott could think of nothing to say and wrote that it was just as well because his mouth was too dry for him to speak.

Marshall continued, "Some of your friends assure me that you are younger than your years, and that your experience especially fits you for this assignment."

When Truscott attempted to explain his lack of qualifications, Marshall disregarded him and went on to describe Mountbatten, the organization he headed, the activities in which they were currently engaged, and the part they would have in making preparations for the projected invasion. He expressed concern because Americans would be committed to their first battle. He had no fear that they would not be well trained, but there could be no substitute for actual battle in readying men psychologically to meet the nervous tensions and uncertainties of combat. While the nature of the proposed operations would preclude battle experience on any large scale for U.S. divisions, as was done in World War I, it still would be possible to give such experience to a limited number of men in Commando raids. A few experienced men in every assault unit would be able to counter the uncertainties that imagination and rumor always multiplied in combat. These men would then be equipped to disseminate practical information among their comrades.

It was primarily for this reason, Marshall continued, that he had arranged with Lord Mountbatten to send Truscott's group to London. Raids against German-held territory would be increased in scope and in frequency until the time for the invasion in 1943. As many American soldiers as possible would be given an opportunity to participate in these operations. Truscott's task would be to arrange for this participation and for the dissemination of this battle experience among assault units. He would work with members of Mountbatten's staff and would assist in every way possible in the training of American troops and the preparations for the invasion. General Eisenhower would see that the necessary instructions were issued and that proper facilities were provided in England. He wished Truscott "every success," and said he would see him in London.

"This interview made an everlasting impression upon me," Truscott wrote. "General Marshall had removed any confusion in my mind as to what was expected of me. For the rest, it was up to me."

Returning to General Eisenhower's office, Truscott recounted his meeting with General Marshall in detail. Ike summoned a stenographer and dictated a letter of instructions intended to guide the operations of Truscott's group in England. He also dictated a letter of instructions to the commanding general, U.S. Army Forces in the British Isles (USAFBI), on the topic of War Department representation at British headquarters. The letter explained that Truscott and others to accompany him were directed to report to the USAFBI for their attachment to the staff of the commander of Combined Operations. They would work with members of that staff and perform all duties allotted to them that were not in conflict with their missions. Those tasks were to study the planning, organization, preparation, and conduct of combined operations (especially of Commando type), and to keep the War Department Operations Division informed as to developments in training, technique, and equipment pertaining to these and related operations. They would also initiate plans for participation by American troops in the operations to the fullest practicable extent with a view to affording battle experience to maximum personnel, and to plan and coordinate the training of detachments designated for such participation, and to provide information and recommendations relative to techniques, training, and equipment involved in these and related operations.

Eisenhower turned next to the touchy topic of British pride and sensibilities to the fact that the once-mightiest military and economic power on earth found itself in dire need of help from a former colony. Foremost in his concerns was that the unit to be formed by Truscott not be called Commandos. Asserting that the name belonged to the British, he urged the choice of a name that would be unmistakably American.

After hastily made travel arrangements and a weeklong journey that included a transatlantic flight plagued by stormy winter weather, Truscott and his team arrived in bleak, bomb-shattered London on May 17, 1942. Shocked at the sight of the ruins, he wrote, "Londoners, we were told, had to wait in queues for everything from transportation and theater tickets to articles of food and clothing. Shop windows displayed little for sale, prices were high, and all essential items were strictly rationed. We were surprised at the drab and untidy appearance of the women we saw on the streets and in the shops, for we had just come from an America in which the rough hand of war had not yet swept aside the luxuries, much less the necessities, of life. Nor did we appreciate the psychological change that results from continued exposure to danger, denial of the ordinary amenities of life, and from conditions of existence that could offer only blood, sweat, and tears. We were not prepared for the numbers of women in uniform and in military formations. While it was new to us, this mobilization of women brought home to us the strain which war had placed upon British manpower."

Truscott's first obligation was to present himself and his mission's purpose to the commanding general, U.S. Army Forces in the British Isles, Major General James E. Chaney, Army Air Force. With a group of ground and air officers, he had been in London for more than a year with orders to organize the European Theater of Operations (ETO). Its headquarters was in Grosvenor Square. Chaney glanced briefly at Truscott's letter of instructions, but gave no indication that he had any previous knowledge of his assignment or any interest whatsoever in Truscott's mission.

Promoted to brigadier general to allow him to deal on par in terms of rank with the British high command, and having been tutored by Sarah in how to behave like a gentleman, Truscott was ready to meet royalty. Born at Windsor Castle, as *His Serene Highness Prince Louis of Battenberg*, Admiral Lord Louis Mountbatten was the second son of Prince Louis of Battenberg and his wife, Princess Victoria of Hesse and the Rhine. His maternal grandparents were Ludwig IV, Grand Duke of Hesse, and Princess Alice of the United Kingdom, the daughter of Queen Victoria and Prince Albert of Saxe-Coburg and Gotha. Mountbatten's father had been England's First Sea Lord at the outbreak of the First World War, but the prevailing extreme anti-German feelings obliged him to resign. When the Royal Family stopped using their German names and titles in 1917, Prince Louis of Battenberg became Louis Mountbatten, and was given the title Marquess of Milford Haven. Having served in the Royal Navy during the First World War, he went to war at sea at the outset of World War II and commanded the Fifth destroyer flotilla. His HMS *Kelly* was famous for daring exploits. In early May 1940, he led a British convoy through fog to evacuate the Allied forces participating in the Namsos Expedition. After his ship was sunk during the Crete Campaign, he was the inspiration for a wildly popular and over-the-top film, *In Which We Serve*, written, directed, and starring Noël Coward as a Mountbattenesque hero. A favorite of Prime Minister Churchill, Lord Louis became chief of Combined Operations early in 1942.

Prepared to some degree by the various accounts he'd been given by Marshall, Eisenhower, and Wedemeyer, Truscott found the relative of King George VI to be as described. Tall, slender, perfectly straight but graceful, with dark eyes, high brow, and rather curly dark hair, Mountbatten seemed extremely easy and natural in manner of speech, with more personality and force than in any other Briton Truscott had met. In a letter to Sarah, Truscott confided, "He is quite a person. I see in him a hardness and perhaps a selfishness or overweening ambition that I have heard no one mention."

Describing meeting Mountbatten, he also reported to Sarah, "He welcomed us gracefully and he hoped that we would like them [the British], and assured us that they were grateful for having us with them. I replied that General Marshall desired that we be members of his staff and expressed the hope that we would not be too much in the way while we were learning. He was sure that we would not and that they would have much to learn from us."

Mountbatten informed Truscott that the Combined Operations Command had been organized from personnel of the three services and described the functions of the organization. He said that it would have an important part in planning, training for, and carrying out the invasion.

Truscott found Combined Operations Headquarters (COHQ) to be like no other headquarters he had known. Not only were British staff organization and procedures different from those in the U.S. Army, but there were also differences resulting from combining three services in a single staff, and still others resulting from the personality of the man who was chief of Combined Operations. A few weeks elapsed before the Americans became so familiar with the organization and procedures that they felt they could go about their work with confidence. One of the problems was opposition to the Commandos among British army officers who resented losing their best men to the elite unit. Further resentment was caused by the fact that only Commandos had the opportunity for active operations, while the regular formations endured the monotony of defensive organization and training for operations in a distant future. Many British officers thought the publicity accorded the

Commandos adversely affected the morale of other British forces. Others thought that Commando operations could have been carried out by regular formations.

Nine days after setting foot in England, Truscott griped in a letter to Sarah, "Everything is done by committee."

Recognizing that American soldiers were to be transported in British craft and supported by naval elements, operating under control of COHQ, Truscott decided that it was logical to form a purely American unit. Consequently, on May 26, 1942, he sent to Marshall proposals that he be permitted to base it on the Commando concept, but adapted to U.S. Army tables of organization and equipment. These proposals were approved by the ETO and the War Department in a cable two days later. Truscott also drafted a letter of instructions to the commanding general, United States Army Forces in Northern Ireland, informing him of the purpose and directing him to proceed with the organization of the unit.

Truscott next dealt with Eisenhower's requirement that it be given a uniquely American name. While several appellations were proposed in discussions with aides, he found the solution to the dilemma in the name of a band of irregular fighters during the French and Indian War. Formed by Major Robert Rogers and known as Rogers' Rangers, they'd moved from the annals of history into American popular culture in 1937 in the Kenneth Roberts novel *Northwest Passage* and a 1940 movie adaptation starring Spencer Tracy and Robert Young. Truscott decided it would be fitting that the organization destined to be the first U.S. ground forces to do battle with Germans on the European continent in World War II be named Rangers, as a compliment to heroes in America's early history who exemplified high standards of individual courage, personal initiative, ruggedness, determination, fighting ability, and achievement.

Although Lord Mountbatten also claimed to have come up with the designation, a Truscott aide and former reporter for the *New York Times*,

Captain Ted Conway, who was present at a meeting where the name was chosen, confirmed in an article for the paper on August 20, 1942, that it was Truscott. The name appeared officially for the first time in a letter drafted by Truscott and sent to General Russell Hartle, commander of the Thirty-fourth Division in Northern Ireland. Over the name of General Chaney, it stated that the designation would be "First Ranger Battalion" and also directed Hartle to organize the "Commando-like unit" within the Thirty-fourth as soon as possible. Only fully trained soldiers of the highest possible type would be sought. Requirements were natural athletic ability, physical stamina, skills in self-defense, scouting, use of firearms and knives, mountaineering, boating, electrical engineering, and operation and repair of radios. Physical specifications were twenty-twenty vision without eyeglasses, normal hearing, normal blood pressure for a man of twenty-five, no cardiac defects, no dentures, and no night blindness. Officers and noncommissioned officers were to possess qualities of leadership, initiative, judgment, and common sense.

The battalion would be formed at a site in Northern Ireland of General Hartle's choice and attached to the British Special Services Brigade (Commandos) for training and tactical control, but adhering to American methods and military doctrines as much as possible. Authorized to choose its commander, Hartle picked a young West Pointer who had been one of his aides since the Thirty-fourth Division had arrived in Northern Ireland a few months earlier. From Fort Smith, Arkansas, thirty-three-year-old William Orlando Darby had graduated from the U.S. Military Academy in 1933. As an artillery officer, he had gained experience in conducting amphibious assaults during a week of combined operations in training exercises in Puerto Rico. Hoping to be put in command of a combat outfit in the Pacific, he had been disappointed, frustrated, and outspoken about his dismay at being assigned to an administrative post as Hartle's aide in Northern Ireland. By coincidence, Truscott's letter directing Hartle to organize the Ranger Battalion had been written on the same day that Darby was promoted to major. When

Hartle offered him the job of setting up, training, and leading the Rangers, he saw "a rugged future in a job where a man could call his soul his own." Suddenly in charge of forging a battalion from nothing more than a bare-bones concept in a letter for an irregular outfit drawn from volunteers, he was given ten days to achieve it.

The first decision was the selection of his executive officer. The same age as Darby, Captain Herman W. Dammer had graduated from Curtis High School on Staten Island in 1928. A National Guard cavalry lieutenant, he'd been called to active duty in July 1941. The adjutant of an antiaircraft battery protecting Belfast, he volunteered to join the Rangers because he preferred to be in the infantry. As second in command, he would have responsibility for organizing an officer staff and serving as plans and training officer. Assisting him would be Captain Roy A. Murray. A reserve officer, hiker, and runner with boating experience from California, he possessed excellent analytical and communication skills. In selecting twenty-nine officers, Darby chose eleven from the infantry, four from the field artillery, three combat engineers, two cavalrymen, and one each from the Quartermaster, Signal, Ordnance, and Medical Corps. Sixty percent of the enlisted men were to come from the Thirty-fourth Division and thirty percent from the First Armored Division. The selection criteria were personality traits and their motivation in volunteering. Looking beyond the physical demands, Darby attempted to determine whether a volunteer had good judgment and if his desire to be a Ranger was genuine. The object, Darby said, was weeding out the braggart and anyone expecting to be a swashbuckling hero who could live as he pleased if he exhibited courage and daring in battle. These determinations were made during interviews with two thousand men over a two-week period in which Darby and his officers chose 575 men. Darby described them as all types of Americans. Ages seventeen to thirty-five, they ranged from boyish soldiers just out of high school to an occasional grizzled old soldier and hailed from nearly every part of the United States.

As civilians, the prospective Rangers had worked in heavy industries, as coal miners, on farms, in offices, and in a variety of offbeat jobs. One had been a lion tamer in the Frank Buck circus. One claimed to have been a bullfighter. Another had kept the books of a burlesque house. Each believed he met the definition of a Ranger given in the official appeal for volunteers. It sought a "high type of soldier" with an excellent character, who was not averse to seeing dangerous action, was athletically inclined, and mentally adapted for making quick decisions in unforeseen circumstances.

After being assembled at Carrickfergus, North Ireland, the incipient battalion moved to the Commando headquarters and training center on the grounds of an ancient castle at Achnacarry, Scotland. Officially designated the "School for Unconventional Warfare," it was run by the British officer who almost single-handedly forged Winston Churchill's concept of a Commando force into reality. Lieutenant Colonel Charles E. Vaughan, Order of the British Empire (OBE), was a veteran of World War I and had participated with distinction in the Commando raids in Norway and elsewhere in 1940. Barrel-chested, six feet two, with a ruddy face and a grin that could change from sunny to stormy in an instant, he devised a one-month training regimen to transform American civilians into U.S.-style Commandos by means of dawn-to-darkness training, seven days a week. While participating in, observing, and criticizing, he insisted on discipline. Noting that the schedule would have delighted the heart of a Napoléon, Darby saw the training as a trilogy of physical conditioning, weapons training, and battle preparedness. This included speed marching, increasingly difficult obstacle courses, practice with all types of firearms, using bayonets and knives, learning how to stalk and kill a sentry, the techniques of scouting, gathering information behind enemy lines, taking out German fortifications, and street fighting. Speed marches began with three-mile hikes and soon worked up to courses of five, seven, ten, twelve, and sixteen miles, with an average of more than four miles an hour over various terrains, with full equipment.

Finding northern Scotland ideal for such training, Darby extolled the rugged, scenic terrain of mountains, valleys, bogs, and heavily forested country with stout heather undergrowth. Augmenting these natural advantages were man-made devices, including high walls, ladders, ditches, and hedges positioned around the Command Depot. Looking back on the period spent at Achnacarry (July 1–30, 1942), he proudly reported, "We marched swiftly, swam rivers or crossed them on bridges made of toggle ropes—a length of cord with a wood handle at one end and a loop at the other. Each man carried one. There were cliffs to climb, slides to tumble down, and when all that was not quite enough, we played hard games."

On June 6, 1942, Truscott had written to Sarah, "I am going to Ireland tomorrow on the first leg of my job—the first real active part anyway." The destination was the Ranger camp at Carrickfergus in Nothern Ireland. On subsequent occasions when he found himself able to briefly break away from his responsibilities at Lord Mountbatten's Combined Operations Headquarters, he dashed up to Scotland to check on the progress of training and took great delight in observing Americans demonstrating their newly learned skills in hand-to-hand fighting. Clad in cavalry togs and standing next to Darby and Colonel Vaughan, he watched them either jousting with one another or bettering Scottish instructors. At the end of July, Vaughan reported, "The stay of the First Battalion, U.S. Rangers, in the Commando Depot has been a very pleasant one. They are now just getting over their teething troubles and have gained good knowledge of the basic training in Commando tactics." He found Darby "the ideal Commando leader," possessing energy, keenness, and a personality that produces the best out of those under his command.

From Achnacarry Darby's Rangers shifted their training from the basics to a series of exercises in conducting amphibious operations. These were practiced on the islands of Mull, Rhum, Eigg, Canna, and Soay in western Scotland in conjunction with the Royal Navy. Describing the most miserable stretch of training so far, the Ranger James Altieri recorded that about twice a week His Majesty's sailors arrived in a flo-tilla of assault craft to convey Rangers for landing exercises "opposed" by Commandos with Bren guns and mortars. With bullets whizzing above their heads and mortar rounds landing six yards from the landing craft, the Rangers reached the beach, tumbled out of the boats, and streaked for their beach objectives. "After blowing up coast guns," said Altieri, "we would withdraw, still under fire. We often made landings at night against rocky cliffs from boats lashing about precariously in huge swells, and often a Ranger would miscalculate his leap from the boat and fall into the waves, narrowly missing being dashed to bits against the rocks."

Participating with the troops and his officers, Darby found the site an excellent assault area in which machine guns were nestled in the cliffs overlooking a rocky beach. As exercises became more and more specific in terms of the Rangers' targets, the Rangers realized that they were practicing for assaults on two kinds of objectives. One was a beachhead defended by a coastal artillery battery situated in a hilltop blockhouse that was surrounded by rows of barbed wire. The other was a small port protected by a gun installation. Returning from training to settle down for the night in two-man pup tents, Rangers speculated on where the real targets were located. Most picked the west coast of France. A few thought they'd head for the southern French coast, or perhaps Greece. Some thought they might be sent to help the British defend Egypt.

No one mentioned Algeria.

★ FIVE ★

REHEARSAL

WHEN COLONEL LUCIAN KING TRUSCOTT, JR., arrived in England, the possibility of an invasion of French North Africa did not appear on the American agenda. The goal that had been set by President Roosevelt and Prime Minister Churchill was France. Meeting for the first time in a secrecy-shrouded conference on an American cruiser off the coast of Newfoundland four months before the Japanese attacked Pearl Harbor, they agreed that U.S. entry into the war was inevitable. Although Roosevelt had been constrained in providing direct assistance to Britain by a strong isolationist movement and a law that required U.S. neutrality, he had given a series of speeches to make a case for American intervention and at the same time had done all he could to bolster the British. During their shipboard conference, the two leaders agreed that once the United States was in the war, priority should be given to defeating Germany first, and that the earliest date for an invasion of Europe would be in 1943, with the code name Roundup.

Immediately after this decision, movement of U.S. troops to the United Kingdom began under the code name Bolero. Early in June 1942, Major General John C. H. Lee arrived in London to create an organization to support the force. On June 5, Prime Minister Churchill sent the British chiefs of staff a memorandum setting forth his ideas on how Roundup should be conceived and executed. The operation, he said, would require "qualities of magnitude, simultaneity, and violence." It should comprise at least six heavy assaults in the first wave, with at least half a dozen feints from Norway to Spain to mystify the enemy. At least ten armored brigades should land in the first wave "to penetrate deeply inland regardless of losses to rouse the populace and to spread confusion among the enemy." Simultaneously, four major ports should be seized. If, in two weeks, 700,000 men were ashore, air supremacy gained, the enemy in considerable confusion, and the Allies had four workable ports, he said, "we shall have got our claws well into the job." In his concluding remarks he warned, "Unless we are prepared to commit the immense forces comprised in the first three waves to a hostile shore with the certainty that many of our attacks will miscarry, and that if we fail the whole stake will be lost, we ought not to undertake such an extraordinary operation of war under modern conditions."

Less than three weeks after Truscott's arrival in London, the combined commanders expressed their opinion of the proposed invasion. In a memorandum to the British chiefs of staff, they asserted their conclusion that unless German morale deteriorated by the spring of 1943, invading France would not be a feasible operation of war.

When Eisenhower arrived in London to replace General Chaney as commanding general, European Theater of Operations on June 24 and found that British authorities did not fully share the American enthusiasm for Roundup, discussions started on an alternative site that would relieve pressure from the Soviet Union for a second front and meet Roosevelt's demand that U.S. forces engage the Germans as early as possible. In urging an invasion of French North Africa, Winston Churchill envisioned an occupation of Morocco, Algeria, and Tunisia that would trap Rommell's Afrika Korps between Anglo-American forces in the west and the British Eighth Army in Egypt. Insisting that "it is of the highest importance that U.S. ground troops be brought into action against the enemy in 1942," Roosevelt approved the North Africa invasion plan in July. In early August, American and British officers met at Norfolk House in St. James's Square, London, to begin planning Operation Torch.

On September 5, 1942, the Allies agreed that landings would be made by Americans and British out of Great Britain around the coastal cities of Algiers and Oran in Algeria and at the same time in Morocco by Americans sailing from the United States under the command of General George S. Patton. To work with Patton on the planning and execution of the invasion from the Atlantic Ocean, Truscott was to be sent back to the States. But before he left for home, he would participate in an action that would give him and a handful of Rangers their first taste of combat.

In pursuit of Winston Churchill's desire for a British victory on the continent, and the demand by President Roosevelt that Americans get into battle against Germans as quickly as possible, a raid on the French port of Dieppe that Mountbatten's Combined Operations had planned for the fourth of July (Operation Rutter) had been canceled and pushed back to August 19. Code-named Jubilee, it would involve 250 ships, including 9 destroyers, 1 gunboat, 9 landing ships, and 73 personnel landing craft (LCT) crossing the English Channel to take a combined force of Commandos, Royal Marines, Canadians, and Rangers, totaling 6,086 men, to Dieppe. The Americans were to be divided between two Commando groups in attacking four beaches on the flanks of the assault, with Canadians attacking at the center.

With an all-out invasion of Europe ruled out, and planners at work on the problem of invading French North Africa, Roosevelt felt increasing agitation in the American press for a second front to help the Russians, as well as mounting pressures for some kind of action by American troops. Adamant that the U.S. Army go on the offensive as quickly as possible, he welcomed a second try at Dieppe. With a detachment of U.S. officers assigned as observers, forty-four men from the First Ranger Battalion were to accompany the Canadian and Commando units. Truscott was designated to go along as the chief U.S. observer. When he informed Patton of what was in the works, Patton said that he wished he could go along on the operation himself. The reaction of General Mark Clark was the opposite. Considering Truscott's role in Torch planning essential, he refused to permit Truscott to go. Taking the issue to their boss, Truscott succeeded in getting Eisenhower to give him the green light.

Arriving at Portsmouth, he was assigned to the HMS *Fernie*. As the destroyer joined the invasion convoy, he could see landing craft filled with men and tanks, infantry assault ships with landing boats at the davits, and decks crowded with men, assault landing craft loaded with the Commandos and the small group of Rangers, motor gunboats, and launches. "It was a novel and thrilling experience," he wrote, "and I hated to go below even to be briefed on the plan for the operation. A small wardroom had been converted into an operation room for the assault. Walls were covered with maps. On a table was a model in relief of that portion of the French coast where the operation would take place. All about were the radios which were to be the means of communication with troops onshore and other elements of the landing force afloat."

The primary purpose of such raids was to harass the enemy. It was thought that a raid on a larger scale than any previously attempted would not only harass the enemy and destroy many valuable military objectives, but would also test German defenses in the west and provide the Allied staffs with valuable information concerning their effectiveness and the means for overcoming them. In addition, it was thought that an attack in broad daylight might provoke a reaction by the Luftwaffe and bring on an extensive air battle, which the Luftwaffe had for many months avoided with the Royal Air Force. This was considered especially desirable at this time because much of the German air force was concentrated against the Russians. Heavy losses over France might divert German aircraft from the Russian front. This aspect of bringing on an air battle was considered the principal objective by the higher command levels, Truscott noted, although it was not considered important by the officers of the ground and naval forces actually engaged in the operation.

Truscott appreciated that Dieppe was selected as the objective because it was typical of defenses that would be encountered in ports along the French coast. A harbor used by German convoys on which the Germans were compelled to rely in ever-increasing degree for supplying their far-flung garrisons, it was also a base for submarines that had been attacking shipping to Britain. There were marshaling yards, a pharmaceutical factory, oil dumps, power stations, and an airfield—all of which it would be desirable to destroy. The port was just within the range at which aircraft based in England could provide effective fighter cover.

The voyage passed without incident for hours, with hopes mounting that the Germans would be caught by surprise. Suddenly, at nearly four o'clock in the morning, off to the left front and distant some two or three miles, a star shell flared into the sky and illuminated the sea below. Intense flashes and streaks of red and white and green lit up the sky like a display of fireworks.

Whatever surprise the raiders hoped to achieve had been scuttled seven miles from the coast because they'd been spotted by a convoy of German gunboats escorting a tanker.

As dawn broke, the former Oklahoma schoolteacher got his first sight of France as squadrons of Royal Air Force Spitfires circled and wheeled, crossing and recrossing the sky at high altitudes, then dove low into the smoke with flashing guns to emerge off to the east in steep climbs, turning toward the sea amid the great puffs of gray and black smoke of bursting antiaircraft shells. Bright flashes appeared along the cliffs and great clouds of smoke drifted over the scene of action as Spitfires and

Hurricanes made low-level attacks. With the battle area obscured by smoke, Truscott went below to see what he could learn in the operations room. He asked the force commander how things seemed to be going and was told that while the attack had not developed as well as he'd hoped, it appeared to be doing better than might have been expected in view of the loss of surprise. Back on deck, with the *Fernie* moving shoreward, Truscott observed assault craft returning from the initial landing.

"Toward the town there was the crash of bursting bombs and shells and the distant rattle of machine gun fire," he wrote. "A few hundred yards from the beaches, we could see through drifting smoke a blasted tank landing craft with lowered ramp swinging to and fro with the tide and with only dead men visible within. Closer to the beach there were assault craft half sunk and aground with the ebbing tide. On the beach itself, there was a confusion of broken landing craft and burning tanks. Standing near the companionway and watching the scene through glasses, I was thrown against the rail by a sudden crash which almost knocked me flat. The whole ship quivered. Something struck my boot and clattered to the steel deck. I picked it up. It was a nut torn loose from the *Fernie*'s superstructure by a shell which had just struck aft. Sixteen men were killed or wounded. Then the *Fernie* sought the sheltering smoke to seaward laying a smokescreen as she went."

Returning to the operations room, he was told that Lieutenant Colonel Lord Lovat had just reported that Commando Number 4 was re-embarking, its mission accomplished in full. The battery that was their target was destroyed and two hundred Germans were killed. Canadians were through the town. On the main beaches, a casino on the esplanade was taken, Allied tanks were over the esplanade, and a tobacco factory and other buildings in the center of the German defenses were now on fire. The force commander thought there was a chance of seizing the town by employing reserves.

This confidence was soon shattered. Alerted to the landings, Germans concealed in cliff-top positions and in buildings overlooking the promenade laid down machine-gun fire. As the Essex Scottish forces assaulted an open eastern section named Red Beach, all attempts to breach the seawall were beaten back with heavy losses. The Canadian Royal Hamilton Light Infantry, landing at White Beach at the west end of the promenade opposite a casino, received withering fire and were pinned against the seawall. The landing of the tanks of the Calgary Regiment, timed to follow an air and naval bombardment, was fifteen minutes late, leaving the infantry without support during the first critical minutes of the attack. As tanks came ashore, they met an inferno of fire and were brought to a halt not only by enemy guns, but by the seawall. After fifteen of the twenty-nine tanks breached it, they were blocked by concrete obstacles that sealed off the narrow streets. With sappers who could have cleared barriers dying on the beaches behind them, the immobilized armor continued to fight, supporting the infantry as they scrambled to withdraw. Most of the tank crews became prisoners or died in battle.

The last troops to land were the reserve, the Canadian Fusiliers Mont Royal Battalion and part of the Royal Marine "A" Commando. Lured by a report that the Canadians had secured the casino and were into the town, they also fell into a trap.

Monitoring the unfolding disaster from the *Fernie* radio room, Truscott learned that in the final act of the tragedy of panicky attempts to withdraw, miscommunications, and a change in the planned withdrawal time from 10:30 a.m. to 11:00 a.m. had resulted in massive confusion. The Saskatchewans and Camerons were meant to withdraw from the main beach, but remained stuck at Pourville. By the time four boats tried to evacuate them at 11:00 a.m., the tide was out, turning more than two hundred yards of exposed beach into a killing ground. At the main beach, the boats that approached the shore met storms of enemy fire, with the result that none got near the main beach before noon. By one o'clock, most attempts at rescue had ended in failure and the evacuation had to be called off. All that remained was for the German troops to collect the wounded and collect prisoners. Of the 4,963 Canadians who embarked for the operation only 2,210 returned to England, and many of these were wounded. There were 3,367 casualties, including 1,946 prisoners.

"General," said the grim commander to Truscott, "I am afraid that this operation will go down as one of the great failures of history."

Back on deck, Truscott watched destroyers and gunboats covering the withdrawing troops. "It was a bloody business," he recalled. "Fire was intense. Craft were hit, yet others ploughed their way forward to the water's edge under withering fire. Some craft took on men and came away again. Others remained on the beach. Yet on and on they came, a marvelous display of courage. The final effort to bring men off was made about one o'clock. The *Fernie* was now in close to shore and well inside the sheltering smoke that shrouded the transport area, so close that machine gun bullets from guns onshore were spattering against the ship's armor. Nothing but derelicts and the wreckage of war was now visible on the beaches. Spreading smoke, the *Fernie* turned again to seaward."

The battle of Dieppe was over.

"The return across the channel was a sad and wearisome journey," Truscott wrote. "On board the *Fernie* every nook and cranny filled with wounded, for we had taken on board from landing craft all that we could carry. The medical staff and medical supplies were inadequate to give more than bare first aid. It was a grim ship."

Pursued almost to the English coast by German planes, the ships reached Portsmouth at midnight. Truscott took a train to London. He described himself as "a sadder and wiser man."

During the battle and in the initial attempts to land troops, Truscott's Rangers suffered their first casualties. Three enlisted men were killed. As First Lieutenant Edwin Loustabout dashed across a field of poppies to attack a German automatic weapons position, he became the first American officer killed on French soil. Twenty-three-year-old Lieutenant Joseph H. Randall of Washington, D.C., never made it ashore. He was killed at the water's edge.

Despite the disappointing result, Truscott felt that much was learned about the German coastal defenses. While others have described Dieppe as a disaster, the Allies gained knowledge of the conditions to be met in any large-scale assault of a German channel port. They'd also gained experience on how to plan and conduct large-scale assaults, and what weapons and equipment such assaults would require. These were lessons successfully applied to the invasions of North Africa, Sicily, Italy, and at Normandy in France on June 6, 1944. The Dieppe raid also gave the German General Staff cause for alarm as to where the next blow would fall and forced them to fortify the entire coast of France. Analyzing Dieppe, Truscott said in his memoir, "I am not among those who consider the Dieppe raid a failure."

He added correctly, "It was an essential though costly lesson in modern warfare."

Although Truscott made history as the first American general of World War II to see combat in Europe, he wrote modestly to Sarah, "I spent that day off Dieppe watching the whole thing, and getting a pretty good picture of what was going on."

On August 24, knowing that she would have read press reports of the raid, he cast aside protective restraint and informed her, "I will have to admit that I have seen war—and have been in danger—and have seen men die on the land, in the sea, and in the sky."

The day after his return from Dieppe, General Clark advised him that it was necessary to have someone in London to represent General Patton in order to ensure coordination of the various assault plans for Torch and to keep Patton current on developments in the planning. Consequently, Eisenhower had directed that Truscott should remain in London for the time being as General Patton's deputy to represent him during planning meetings. In a letter to Patton about the change in the plan for him to leave immediately for the States, he said, "The Dieppe raid was a great experience which I would not have missed for the world."

★　　　　SIX　　　　★

TORCH

As the result of happenstance in the structure of the U.S. Army and its procedures for advancing its officers throughout the 1930s, and the designs of George C. Marshall and Dwight D. Eisenhower in the summer of 1942, planning for the Allied invasion of North Africa had brought together two generals of similar personality and temperament. Their professional lives and personal fates would become so intimately linked over the next three years that they stand in the chronicles of the Second World War as inextricably as Caesar and Antony in Roman history, Washington and Lafayette in the American Revolution, Napoléon and Wellington at Waterloo, and Robert E. Lee and Stonewall Jackson in the Civil War.

Ironically, it had not been the West Point graduate and heroic veteran of France in 1918, who had glorified war as an enterprise unsurpassed by any other human endeavor, who became the first American general under German fire in 1942, but a former ninety-day wonder who'd worked his way up to a star primarily as a teacher in army schools. On the eve of the landings on the coast of Morocco, Patton would confide to his diary, "I am just a little worried about ability of Truscott." He would add the afterthought, "It may be nerves."

In a letter to Sarah two weeks earlier, Truscott's primary concern about leading men into battle was not about whether he would measure up to what Patton expected of him. Addressing her as "Beloved Wife," he wrote, "My greatest ambition is to justify your confidence and to deserve your love."

When Truscott left England for the United States in September 1942 to become Patton's deputy, the master plan for the North African invasion had gone through a number of changes and consisted of three stages.

The Western Assault Force under Patton would consist of 35,000 American troops with the objective of taking Casablanca in French Morocco and a key airfield at Port Lyautey. The armada would be made up of three battleships, five aircraft carriers, seven cruisers, thirty-eight destroyers, eight minesweepers, and five tankers. Under the command of Rear Admiral H. Kent Hewitt, they were to be accompanied by an assault force of ninety-one vessels, including twenty-three landing craft.

The Central Task Force, commanded by the U.S. major general Lloyd R. Fredendall, consisted of 18,500 Americans with the mission of capturing Oran in Algeria. Among the troops hitting the beaches would be Darby's Rangers. Tasked with spearheading a pair of landings at the port of Arzew, they were expected to knock out two large coastal artillery installations to clear the way for troops led ashore by Major General Terry de la Mesa Allen, while his deputy, Theodore (Ted) Roosevelt, Jr., led a landing at Oran. The ships under Commodore T. H. Troubridge of the Royal Navy were the flagship, HMS *Largs*, two carriers, two cruisers, two antiaircraft ships, thirteen destroyers, six corvettes, eight minesweepers, and troop carriers.

The Eastern Task Force under the British lieutenant general K. A. N. Anderson included 20,000 troops in the first wave, half American and half British. The objective was the city of Algiers. Under command of the British vice admiral Sir Harold Burrough aboard the *Bulolo* were two carriers, three cruisers and three antiaircraft vessels, thirteen destroyers, three submarines, three sloops, seven minesweepers, seven corvettes, and troop transports.

Final operational orders were to be issued between October 3 and 20, 1942, in eight parts. These outlined the strategic plan, routing, and scheduling of the three convoys, instructions for landings, descriptions of submarine screens to cover the assaults, and convoy arrangements for the period after the landings. The last of the task forces was due at Gibraltar on November 4. Three days later, RAF reconnaissance patrols were to operate between the eastern coast of Spain and the Bonifacio Strait between Sardinia and Corsica in order to detect any threatening moves by the Italian fleet; and north and west of Dakar in French West Africa to give early warning of any northern movements toward the task force by French warships. British Coastal Command aircraft would fly antisubmarine operations and reconnaissance sorties over Italian and French bases.

The Torch landings would be opposed by Vichy French forces with an estimated strength of 120,000, but the men were mostly native rank and file with French officers, supported by five hundred aircraft and a sizable fleet at Toulon. Although the troops and the air force suffered from obsolete equipment, the French navy's firepower was able to wreak havoc on any landing. The Italian fleet also presented a threat, but it suffered from low morale, poor leadership, and a lack of fuel oil. The most serious challenge was from the Luftwaffe based in Italy and North Africa. Noting that planners hoped that the French would offer only token resistance to satisfy the demands of "French honor," Truscott recorded that the plans had to be based on the assumption that the French might bitterly resent being attacked because they were deemed to be allied with Germany.

Hoping to persuade the French authorities in Morocco and Algeria to cooperate in the invasion, the planners arranged a secret mission to be given to Mark Clark. In an effort to assure nonresistance from the French forces, he would be sent into Algeria on the British submarine *Seraph* to meet with French officers to coordinate details of the invasion. In another attempt to gain French compliance, Eisenhower would meet at Gibraltar with the French commander General Henri-Honoré Giraud to persuade him to cooperate. Giraud responded by demanding to be put in charge of the invasion. The plan also anticipated that the chief American diplomat in Morocco, Robert Murphy, would cajole French officials in Casablanca to refrain from resisting the invasion.

Of the initial investigations of the Casablanca operation, Truscott recorded that the planners considered a direct assault on the city, but came to the conclusion that the seaward defenses, together with the strong French naval forces that were based there, might make such an assault costly and could result in destruction within the port area, which would interfere with its subsequent use. Then they considered making landings immediately north and south of the city just beyond range of the defenses, seizing the city and port as well as the airfield by attack from the landward side. But studies of the beaches and weather conditions in the area showed that beaches immediately adjacent to the city were difficult and that the whole of the exposed coast was subject to those unusual conditions of swell and surf that might make open beach landings impossible except for a few days in each month. Such conditions might interrupt landings at any time and thus might jeopardize the whole operation.

There were a few small ports at widely separated points on this coast where landings might be effected except under the most violent conditions of weather. Such ports were Fedala, a few miles to the north of Casablanca; Port Lyautey, some 80 miles to the north; and Safi, about 130 miles to the south of Casablanca. Rabat was midway between Fedala and Port Lyautey, but its small port had fallen into disuse and was closed by sandbars. While there was a landing field near Rabat, beaches in the area were difficult. The city was also the residence of the

Muslim sultan of Morocco. Because he was the spiritual and political symbol for all of the Arab tribes, any injury to him or to his holy city might set the Arabs against the invading force, which was a risk to be avoided.

"Our outline plan," Truscott wrote, "therefore provided for the main landing to be made on beaches in the vicinity of Fedala to seize that port. Here one division with an armored regimental combat team would seize the port and then, assisted by naval and air forces, would capture Casablanca."

A second operation under Truscott's command would land at the Sebou River near Port Lyautey to open the river and capture an airfield located inland. Air forces established on this field would assist in the attack on Casablanca.

Original drafts of this outline had been taken by Patton to the United States in August. Revised drafts together with assembled intelligence were forwarded to him from Truscott by courier on September 6. On the same date, Patton sent his initial estimate and outline plan for the Casablanca operation to Eisenhower. This estimate analyzed the various ports on the Moroccan coast as possible assault objectives. The Patton version indicated that the main landing would be made at Fedala by a division less one regimental combat team with an armored regimental combat team attached. A secondary landing would be made at Rabat by two battalion combat teams and one armored battalion combat team with the objective of capturing and stocking one airport. Another landing would be made at Safi with one infantry battalion combat team and one armored battalion combat team to capture the port and set up a beachhead, after which a seagoing railroad ferry, if one could be obtained, would unload additional armor to attack Marrakech, about sixty miles inland, or, if resistance to the other landings proved formidable, to attack the enemy rear.

When this estimate and plan were referred to Truscott for comment, he pointed out that he did not believe an attack on Marrakech would have any effect on the early capture of Casablanca. It was his opinion that the success of the Western Task Force depended upon the early capture of at least one airfield and the neutralization of French aircraft. Studies showed that the best chance of capturing an airfield quickly was in the Port Lyautey area, and that neutralization of French aircraft would have to be accomplished by carrier-based planes, parachute troops, and sabotage.

The final plan for the assault of the Western Task Force retained the landing at Safi to provide armor to assist in the assault on Casablanca and substituted the Port Lyautey assault for the one proposed against Rabat. Given the designation "Sub-Task Force" and the code name Goalpost, the attackers under Truscott's command would consist of the Sixtieth Infantry Regimental Combat Team of the Ninth Infantry Division and an Armored Battalion Combat Team of the Second Armored Division. Their mission was capturing the airfield.

On the afternoon before Truscott's departure from England, he went to bid good-bye to Eisenhower. While he was sitting in his office talking with him, an aide announced that a French officer was outside with a message from Charles de Gaulle, the self-anointed leader of the Free French. Truscott started to leave. Eisenhower told him to stay.

The French officer entered, saluted smartly, and said that he was de Gaulle's chief of staff. Eisenhower greeted him and offered a chair. The officer remained standing. In fluent English he declared, "Sir, I am directed by General de Gaulle to inform General Eisenhower that General de Gaulle understands that the British and Americans are planning to invade French North Africa. General de Gaulle wishes to say that in such case he expects to be designated as Commander in Chief. Any invasion of French territory that is not under French command is bound to fail."

With no change in expression, Eisenhower replied, "Thank you."

The French officer again saluted smartly and departed.

Eisenhower turned to Truscott and asked, "Now do you suppose there has been a breach of security somewhere?"

All of the Torch planning, Truscott answered, had taken place without consultation with the Free French. The Combined Chiefs of Staff had decided that they should be kept in ignorance of Torch planning. While the visit by the French officer suggested there'd been some breach of security and de Gaulle had information about Torch, Truscott ventured, because of all the activity in London in the preceding weeks, anyone might deduce that something was in the wind. Truscott surmised that de Gaulle's man had been simply fishing.

Early the next morning (September 20), Truscott departed for Patton's headquarters in Washington, D.C., and a reunion with Sarah after the longest period of separation since their marriage in 1919. During his absence, twenty-year-old Lucian III had begun his plebe year as a cadet at West Point. Among his classmates in what would be the graduating class of 1945 was Eisenhower's son, John. Hoping to follow Lucian III to the Military Academy, eleven-year-old James was in junior high school. Twenty-one-year-old Mary Randolph Truscott was married to cavalryman Robert Wilburn.

While their father was en route from England, George Patton had met with President Roosevelt at the White House and vowed to the bemused commander in chief, "I will leave the beaches either a conqueror or a corpse."

For the first invasion by the U.S. Army in the fight against Nazi Germany, in which it would not confront Germans but Frenchmen, Patton's and Truscott's soldiers would have to travel farther than any invasion force of World War II. The last time Americans had sailed from a U.S. port and plunged directly into combat had been in the Spanish-American War. The journey then from Tampa Bay, Florida, to Cuba had taken only a few days. For the Western Task Force, the journey to Morocco across the Atlantic that started on October 23 would take almost two weeks. Because there were insufficient berths at Hampton Roads, Virginia, to permit all of the ships to load and embark simultaneously, Truscott's sub–task force would have to load early, a full week before the date of sailing. The advance parties were to report to Hampton Roads on October 7. Loaded transports were to clear their berths on October 16. Meanwhile, there were detailed plans to be prepared for the debarkation and assault in every assault echelon, and all of these had to be coordinated. On October 14 at a final conference of commanders with Patton in Washington, it was realized that the plan had not provided for a countersign for identification purposes during the invasion. Discussing the oversight, everyone agreed that it should be one that was easy to remember and pronounce, but difficult for Arabs, French, or Spaniards to repeat. Someone with a delicious sense of humor suggested "George Patton." The challenger would call out "George." The challenged, if a friend, would answer "Patton."

On the night before the armada sailed from Hampton Roads, Patton wrote to his wife, Beatrice, "This is my last night in America. It may be years and it may be forever. God grant that I do my full duty to my men and myself."

Truscott wrote to Sarah, "This great convoy is quite a sight—it looks far more like a Hollywood interpretation of going to war than the real thing. Right now I feel just like I've always felt before tournament polo games."

Remembering his thoughts about the impending odyssey in *Command Missions*, he wrote,

Men like Columbus, Drake, John Paul Jones, Farragut, Nelson, and Dewey had pitted their strength against the sea in high adventure. What names to stir the hearts and fire the ambitions of American youth! There are few who have not felt the majesty of the ocean and at one time or another responded in some way to the appeal of the sea. There is always something of romance about a sea voyage, and how especially is this true of a first one. For the vast majority of the soldiers on board the transports of our division when we slipped out through Hampton Roads and past the Virginia capes onto the broad Atlantic, this was a first sea voyage.

More, it was a voyage that would end for them in their first battle—and a battle on foreign soil two thousand miles from the homes they had no wish to leave. As we watched the dim outlines of the American shores dip below the western horizon, I was sobered by the thought that for many of these on board this would be their last view of our native land.

During the crossing there were occasional unfounded reports of contacts with enemy submarines and a report of an intercepted merchantman that proved far beyond Truscott's view. The crossing was so peaceful that he found it difficult to realize that it was more than a pleasure cruise. When the convoy separated into three components on Saturday, November 7, and Truscott's portion bore off to the north on its own, the ocean seemed strangely empty.

In a "Dear Jamie" letter dated November 7 and inscribed as being written "at sea," he wrote to his youngest child, "I do wish that you could have been with me on this trip. You would have loved watching all the ships—battleships, cruisers, destroyers, minesweepers, tugs—one hundred ships all told. It has been a wonderful sight. In less than twelve hours now we begin our landing. But you will know all about it before you read this."

Noting the splitting of the convoy in his diary, he wrote, "Now we are on our own. We can only hope that our plans are good and click as they should."

At ten o'clock that evening, with zero hour for the invasion approaching, word was flashed that lights had been seen onshore. "We were sliding along silently in darkness at reduced speed under a star-studded sky," he wrote. "Off to starboard glittered the lights of a good-sized town only a few miles distant. Lights were encouraging, for lights meant that we were not expected. But what town?"

Neither the armada's commodore nor any navy officer on the quarterdeck hazarded a guess. Some thought that it was Rabat, some twenty miles south of the objective area. There was a silence of intense concentration on the quarterdeck of the *Henry T. Allen* as it glided along through the calmest seas Truscott had experienced. When the ship stood so close to shore that outlines of cliffs and sand dunes beyond the beaches could be dimly discerned, he asked the naval commander, "Well, Commodore, where are we?"

He replied, "Well, General, to be perfectly honest, I am not right sure exactly where the hell we are."

Truscott recalled, "We had been steaming northward too close to shore and had turned seaward to reach our transport area some eight miles off. Some of the ships had either not received, or had misunderstood, the signal. As a result, when we entered the transport area where everything depended upon every ship being in its prescribed location, no one ship knew the position of any other, or was certain of its own. And we were already an hour late."

Truscott noted that Port Lyautey lay about nine miles upstream from the mouth of the Sebou River. It was a broad stream with a depth ranging from thirteen feet at lowest tide to nineteen feet at the highest. Below the town, the river formed a wide loop open to the south, with the airfield in its center. The beaches were suitable for landing all along the coast, but the exits inland were few and difficult because of commanding ridges that paralleled the coast close behind the beaches. A coastal defense battery situated in an old fort called the Kasbah (or Casbah) protected the channel to the river and blocked the principal roadway from the coast to the town. Another roadway inland passed around the southern end of a lagoon along the foot of the high ridge for three or four miles southward from the Kasbah. The road connecting Port Lyautey with Rabat, roughly twenty miles to the south, and with Casablanca between fifty and sixty miles farther on, paralleled the coast. Just below the Kasbah, the French had stretched a cable or net across the river to prevent unauthorized craft from proceeding upstream. The airfield was protected by antiaircraft defenses.

If Torch were going as planned while Goalpost unfolded at Port

Lyautey and Patton's force stormed ashore at Casablanca at dawn on November 8, 1942, the group of men whom Truscott had named Rangers were following Colonel Bill Darby ashore at Arzew in Algeria to clear the way for Terry Allen's First Division. Ted Roosevelt was to be leading his men ashore at Oran. Americans and British were landing at Algiers. Awaiting reports of the outcome at Gibraltar and chain-smoking Camel cigarettes, Eisenhower had sent a letter to Marshall that said, "If a man permitted himself to do so, he could get absolutely frantic about questions of weather, politics, personalities in France and Morocco and so on." He added a postscript that applied to everyone involved in Torch. "To a certain extent," wrote Ike, "a man must merely believe in his luck."

All across the United States it was the middle of the night. If a majority of Americans who went to the movies were awakened and asked what they knew about Algiers, they would have answered that it was a mysterious place in a 1938 movie with Charles Boyer. Mention Casablanca, and only those who kept up with Hollywood by reading the fan magazines and the columnists Louella Parsons and Walter Winchell would know that Warner Bros. studio was about to release a movie with Humphrey Bogart and Ingrid Bergman in a love story set in an exotic and romantic place with that name. A proposal to any American who followed reports about the war that they would be reading in their morning papers and hearing news reports on the radio that American soldiers were fighting in both places, and that Casablanca would soon be the site of a conference between Roosevelt and Churchill, would have been greeted with an expression of incredulity.

Off the coast of Morocco as the command ship *Henry T. Allen* began lowering boats at half past twelve for troops that were to begin disembarking just before dawn, Truscott wondered what the men on other ships were doing. In the confusion, would their commanders wait for orders? Would they proceed with the plans for landing in darkness? Radios were silent. He had to find out.

Leaving one aide on the *Allen*, he and another assistant clambered down the nets and into a landing craft. "We found ships everywhere," Truscott recalled, "but each one was reluctant to identify itself, for they were suspicious of this unexpected visit. When we were finally able to identify ourselves, none could tell us in what direction to find the ships we sought. But from one to another we went until I had found and boarded each of the assault ships and had verified plans with troop commanders and ship's officers. We were late, but all hoped that with luck we could still reach the shore before daylight."

By half past three, he was back on board the *Allen*. An aide met him at the rail and took him to the communications room. On the radio in a rebroadcast of a recorded message to the French people, General Eisenhower was announcing the invasion. Half an hour earlier, President Roosevelt had been on the radio in a recorded proclamation to the world that stated the purpose of the landings. Unfortunately, the broadcasts had been sent out too early, alerting the French to an invasion that had not yet begun.

A few minutes after Truscott heard the rebroadcasts, five French warships in column, each brightly lighted, came from the river's mouth and moved slowly westward through the U.S. fleet. One passed so closely that Truscott could read the name *Lorraine*. A signal lamp blinked a message that a young naval officer standing beside Truscott translated. "Be warned," said the French ship. "They are alert onshore."

At 0550, in the Moroccan predawn, guns onshore opened fire.

As the debarkation of troops proceeded and landing craft carried a battalion from the *Allen* there was an eerie quiet on board. Shoreward, a red rocket flared into the air and burst like a shooting star. To the south, seven chains of red balls streaked through the darkness toward the shore. Seconds later the sound of firing drifted across the water as destroyers opened fire. The battle was on.

Presently, a message from shore stated, "At mouth of river. Being shelled by enemy and our own navy. Going to land on Green Beach." A little later, another message reported, "Troops landed and moving inland. Proceeding on mission."

Truscott had expected to follow events onshore by radio reports, by observation, and by reports from aircraft. In spite of planning and preparations, communications with shore proved almost nonexistent. Confused and fragmentary reports indicated that two battalions had landed by dawn and moved inland. One report said that a battalion was in the fort. Deciding to go ashore to see for himself, he found the beach command post dark and silent, with only a sleepy operator listening for radio signals that he could not hear. No officers were present. Several enlisted men were sleeping. Others were stumbling about the beach and sand dunes in the darkness. There were shouts and oaths and calls of "George" and "Patton." Sending two aides to check on the situation elsewhere, he sat down on a sand dune to wait. As their figures disappeared into the gloom, it occurred to him that even with hundreds of soldiers all around, he felt utterly alone.

Out to sea, signal lamps were flashing between the ships. As far as he could see along the beach, there was chaos. Landing craft were beaching in the pounding surf, broaching to the waves, and spilling men and equipment into the water. Men wandered aimlessly, hopelessly lost, calling to each other and for their units, swearing at each other and at nothing. There was no beach party or shore party anywhere in sight.

Chilled and feeling lonely, Truscott felt in need of a cigarette. Disregarding his own order banning smoking during the landing because troops lighting cigarettes onshore in the dark could attract enemy fire, he lit up. When glowing tips of cigarettes appeared as other lonely and uncertain soldiers smoked, he was amused by the realization that their commanding general had been the first to violate the blackout order.

With his cigarette half smoked, and wondering what he was going to do next and how, he saw out of the gloom a figure approaching from the shoreline with uncertain steps and peering nervously from side to side. Stopping in front of Truscott, he demanded, "Gimme a cigarette."

Drawing one from his pack and handing it to him, Truscott saw that he was Asian.

The soldier said, "Gimme a light, too."

As Truscott gave him a book of paper matches, one of Truscott's aides returned. As he approached, he gave the identifying code word "George."

"Georgie, hell," snapped the soldier. In the exaggerated mixture of Chinese and English featured in *Charlie Chan* movies, he continued, "Me no George. Me Lee! Me Cook! Company C, Five-hundred-fortieth Engineers."

An official U.S. Army history of Goalpost recorded that with support units, Truscott had a force of 9,079 officers and men. Their main objectives were airfields at Port Lyautey and at Sale, twenty-five miles to the south, near Rabat. To reach them the troops would first have to take the village of Mehdia and Port Lyautey. While the coastline was smooth, the Sebou meandered in a sharp S shape to form two peninsulas. Port Lyautey airfield was in the larger. An advance from Mehdia was the most direct route to it, but Truscott's troops would have to advance through a narrow marsh between the river and a lagoon while under the guns of the Kasbah. From bluffs between the two towns, heavy artillery dominated all points. Truscott had landed his troops at five beaches along ten miles of shoreline. Two battalion landing teams, going ashore south of the river, would advance on separate axes while a third would move from the north toward Port Lyautey.

If all had gone as planned, the airfield and towns should be under American control by sundown on D-day. But a string of problems had thwarted the plan. Approaching the coast the previous night, navy transports had lost formation. H hour was then delayed to allow boat crews to improvise assault waves. Heavy seas slowed debarkation. Only the first three waves of the Second Battalion Landing Team had reached shore before dawn. Later waves were not only late but off course. Two missed their assigned beaches by twenty-eight hundred yards and five miles. Opposition had caused more confusion and delays. At dawn French planes had strafed the beaches and bombed transports and the strong coast artillery at a fortress near Mehdia rained a heavy volume of fire on transports offshore. The First Battalion Landing Team had struggled in the sand for more than five hours to regain its beach, to go around a lagoon, and to start toward the airfield, only to be pinned down by machine-gun fire the remainder of the day. To the rear, French reinforcements from Rabat fired on landing team outposts. When the Second Battalion Landing Team stopped to await naval gunfire support, it was hit hard by a French counterattack, and pushed back almost to the beach with heavy losses. While the navy fired on the Mehdia fortress, troops ashore did not have enough artillery to silence the French batteries. Their fire kept tanks from being landed and forced transports to move out of range, lengthening the distance to the shore. By nightfall, Truscott's men held precarious positions that were miles from the airfield.

The second day brought both success and frustration. While naval gunfire dispersed the enemy, the troops made good progress toward the airfield. But unidentified artillery and U.S. naval aircraft dropped ordnance on the First Team, and the Second Team could do no more than hold position only a mile inland against a French unit that had been reinforced. The Third Battalion Landing Team succeeded in placing troops and artillery north and east of the airfield but stalled under fire from Port Lyautey.

On the night of November 9–10, the navy boosted Truscott's spirits. On the Sebou River the destroyer-transport *Dallas* pushed aside a barricade and sneaked upstream with a detachment of raiders to spearhead the assault on the airfield. While some French units gave up the fight, the Foreign Legion continued to resist. As Truscott followed reports, he read one that triggered a laugh. Bypassing a French machine-gun position, three companies of the First Team became disoriented and found themselves at a building that they thought housed the airfield garrison. Bursting in, they discovered that they'd captured a French café. The startled patrons put down wineglasses and surrendered.

At daylight on November 10, the First Team launched a new drive with tanks. By 1045 they'd reached the west side of the airfield. On the

river, the *Dallas* ran a gauntlet of artillery fire and debarked raiders on
the east side of the airfield, giving Truscott's forces three sides of their
objective. But the Kasbah held out. Although naval gunfire had silenced
its larger batteries earlier, machine-gun and rifle fire exchanges continued. Navy dive-bombers were called in, and after only one bombing run
the garrison gave up. After claiming the fort and gathering prisoners, the
Second Battalion Landing Team moved on to close the ring around the
airport. By nightfall the American victory was assured.

Sometime after midnight, a group of French officers arrived at Truscott's command post in an open car. They had arrived at one of the outposts with lights on and a bugler standing on the running board sounding
the French bugle call for a cease-fire. They stated that General Mathinet
had arrived in Port Lyautey during the evening with instructions from
Admiral Jean Louis Darlan to cease all opposition because an armistice
had been agreed upon. Now Mathinet wanted to meet Truscott in the
morning to arrange for cessation of hostilities in the local area.

Soon after this, Truscott received a message from Patton saying that
French resistance had ceased all through North Africa, but American
troops would remain in place and prepare for further action. Truscott
hoped to receive further instructions during the night from Patton that
would guide him in the meeting with the French commander, but there
was no word beyond that first brief message.

Escorted by a company of tanks to lend what Truscott called "something of military display to the event," he went to the main gate in the
high walls of the Kasbah that his soldiers had blasted open and met the
French commander and his party. With a blue cape thrown back over
one shoulder and its scarlet lining gleaming in the sun, General Mathinet was accompanied by seven or eight French officers in trim uniforms,
gleaming belts, and boots that contrasted with Truscott's rumpled cavalry attire and his men's battle-stained uniforms.

At this point, Truscott did not have to use the French he'd learned
with Sarah years ago. In excellent English, the French general said that

he had received orders to cease all opposition by direction of French Commander in Chief Admiral Darlan. Mathinet desired to arrange details for ending the hostilities. Truscott replied that so far as the American government was concerned there was no question of a French surrender. He stated that the United States desired cooperation with the French and had sought it by every means. America's single purpose was to strike the common enemy and all who stood with them. Mathinet said that he was powerless to agree on any terms without reference to higher authority. Truscott informed him there was no question of terms. He would indicate what must be done, pending further instructions from General Patton. French troops not now prisoners could retain their arms and could return to barracks in areas not occupied by American troops, pledging only that they would not fight again against us. American prisoners in French hands would be returned at once.

Truscott's force would occupy the port area in Port Lyautey, but otherwise American troops would remain generally in their present areas, which no French troops would enter. The French civil officials would continue their normal functions but would take no action prejudicial to American forces. The Americans would not interfere with the civil economy of the area, and whenever it was necessary to requisition property, it would be paid for at fair prices. Unarmed French search parties would be permitted to locate and retrieve their wounded and dead.

The parley ended with an interchange of stiff salutes.

At 0400 on November 11, the twenty-fourth anniversary of the armistice that had ended World War I, a cease-fire went into effect in French North Africa. Goalpost had achieved all of its objectives. During the fighting, Eisenhower followed the progress of Torch from Gibraltar. While two reinforced U.S. divisions fought along the Atlantic coast of French Morocco under Patton and Truscott, the Center Task Force landed one reinforced division at Oran and the Eastern Task Force put ashore two regiments and one battalion of landing teams at Algiers. On November 9, Ike sent this letter to Truscott:

Dear Lucian:

You can well imagine with what eagerness we are watching every report coming in from the battlefront. It is not that I have the slightest doubt concerning the skill and devotion to duty that all our soldiers are applying to their task; it is merely that I am anxious to get this phase completed, so that we can start fighting Germans. At no place along the front have I got greater confidence in what the Commander will do with the means he has than I have in your locality.

Algiers is ours completely. At Oran some fighting is still going on, where one fort on a big promontory gives us a lot of trouble. We know very little about the situation on the West Coast because communications have been poor, but it does appear that you fellows are gradually making progress against the opposition. I do not for a moment doubt that we will quickly have this whole thing cleared up—the sooner, of course, the better.

I hope you understand the depth of my appreciation to you and your gallant men for the effort you are making. The same to George Patton, if you should happen to see him.

God bless you and prosper you, and here's to quick VIC-TORY!

As ever,
EISENHOWER

In his hand below was: *"With warmest personal regards."*

On November 12, Truscott wrote to Patton, "We had a hell of a war up here, primarily due to the fact that the navy was one hour and forty-five minutes late in landing us and had some confusion as to beaches." Abandoning what he'd been taught as a young officer about using sarcasm, he went on, "Further, when we failed to take the battery by assault, owing to the loss of surprise, the navy took station about halfway to Bermuda and consequently the unloading progressed very slowly."

The letter continued, "I am trying to conduct my Force in accordance with what I believe you would desire. I have not entered Port Lyautey and I am not advancing beyond the ground I held when hostilities ceased in order not to embarrass you in any way. I am not going to allow the French to return to the barracks that are located within areas now occupied by my troops until I know your desires relative to my movement beyond ground I now hold."

The report ended, "With kindest regards and a toast to the Patton luck."

Operation Torch involved 125,000 soldiers, sailors, and airmen, of which 82,600 were U.S. Army personnel. Ninety-six percent of the 1,469 casualties were American, with the army losing 526 killed and 837 wounded. The Eastern Task Force had the fewest killed in action (108). The Center Task Force lost 276. The Patton-Truscott Western Task Force had 142 killed. Addressing troops at a wreath ceremony at an improvised cemetery on November 22, 1942, Truscott noted that in the greatest amphibious expedition ever undertaken, and with the combined efforts of the U.S. Army, Navy, and Air Force, they had landed in North Africa not for the purposes of aggression, not to seize either land or matériel, but to obtain a route in order to come to grips with the most evil forces ever known—the Axis Powers.

Speaking for the first time to survivors of a fight he had commanded, he told them, "There can be no doubt that Divine Providence has spared us in this, our first battle, to carry on. Let us, therefore, bid adieu to our brave and gallant comrades and pledge that we shall never fail them, that we will carry on the battle until evil forces are defeated, and Liberty, Justice and Freedom are restored to all men."

★ SEVEN ★

CHASING THE FOX

ON SATURDAY, DECEMBER 19, 1942, PATTON informed Truscott that because of Truscott's successes in the planning for Torch and his triumph in the capture of Port Lyautey, Truscott was being promoted. On December 21, he would become a major general. As his staff held a champagne dinner for him on the evening of the nineteenth and gave him an engraved plaque to commemorate the awarding of two stars, Patton was confiding to his diary, "His promotion has been well deserved and he has invariably done a good, though never brilliant, job. I am very proud of him."

With a demonstration of a modesty and tact that was typical of the characterizations of individuals depicted in his war memoir, Truscott did not speculate in *Command Missions* that his elevation to the same rank as Patton created an ego problem for Patton. He wrote only that Patton made it clear that as a result of the new rank, Truscott would have "no berth" in the Western Task Force. Patton also stated that he had no objection if Truscott chose to go to Algiers to ask if Eisenhower intended to retain him in the North African theater or to send him to the United States for reassignment.

Eager for another combat command, Truscott traveled with his primary aide, Major Theodore J. Conway, by plane to Algeria. Grounded at Oran by bad weather, they borrowed a car from II Corps headquarters. Arriving at Ike's headquarters in the St. George Hotel in the city of Algiers late on Christmas Eve, they were told that Eisenhower was at the front and was expected back the next day. After he and Conway spent what he termed a cheerless night before Christmas in the Alleti Hotel in Algiers, Truscott returned to the St. George to enjoy a reunion with Mark Clark, also a major general and Eisenhower's deputy. They also met with Ike's chief of staff, Major General Walter Bedell Smith, known to everyone on Ike's personal staff as "Beetle." Neither knew what Eisenhower might have in mind for Truscott. Because Ike did not return from the front until very late that night, Truscott could not confer with him until the next morning.

"When I told him I had come to Algiers," Truscott recalled, "he said he was glad I had done so. He wanted me to wait around a few days. He was considering an operation, and if it materialized, he would have a job for me. The staff was studying a problem, but it would be several days before there would be any decision. While I was waiting around, I could occupy my time making a study of his headquarters. It was growing too large. Perhaps I could suggest something that might help."

When Truscott saw Eisenhower again on December 29, Ike expressed disappointment that an Allied drive into Tunisia had been stopped before capturing the vital port of Tunis. During the month of December, the British general Harold R. I. G. Alexander had attempted to mount an attack that was thwarted by poor weather conditions. On a trip to the front, Ike had postponed the attack to wait for better weather. He had also discussed with commanders the feasibility of an operation farther south, where the countryside was more arid and the climate was much friendlier. The idea was to use the U.S. First Armored Division and a regimental combat team of the First Infantry Division to cut the German line of communication with Tunis. Staff studies showed that the plan was practicable and that forces could be assembled in the vicinity of Tebessa by January 22. Truscott's job would be in connection with this operation. The British First Army had been designated to control all operations in Tunisia. When the French, occupying a wide sector of the front, refused to serve under a British command, they forced Eisenhower to exercise control of all Allied forces in his capacity as the commander in chief. For this purpose, he intended to set up a small command group near the headquarters of the First Army at Constantine. Truscott was to organize it as Eisenhower's deputy chief of staff. Thrilled by the assignment, Truscott phoned Patton at Casablanca, informed him about his new post, and asked him to have Truscott's staff fly to Algiers. They arrived the following day.

Eisenhower's objective was to clear Germans and their Italian allies from Tunisia and capture the port of Tunis. His forces had taken defensive positions in mountains between the Mediterranean Sea on the north and the Sahara Desert on the south. Moving east into Tunisia as Germans moved west, they would face the enemy on a curving front from Medjez-el-Bab in the north to El Guettar in the south called the Mareth Line. With Italians operating in the fore, and Colonel General Hans-Jurgen von Arnim's Fifth Panzer Army poised near Tunis, the Panzer Army Africa stood ready to rush from Libya under the command of the German general who had become as well known in the United States as Eisenhower, Patton, and MacArthur.

A year younger than Ike, Erwin Rommel had become Adolf Hitler's favorite general by excelling in the invasion of Poland, spearheading the conquest of France, and chasing the British in North Africa back into Egypt and threatening the Suez Canal. Since a defeat at the hands of a vastly reinforced British force at El Alamein, he had demonstrated his brilliance by fashioning a withdrawal into Libya to protect the port cities of Tunis and Bizerte, which were now at the top of Eisenhower's list of objectives.

The headquarters of the American II Corps under Major General Lloyd Fredendall was at Tebessa, Algeria, in a region called Speedy Valley located west of a mountain range known as the Grand Dorsal. With the bulk of his troops committed to the protection of extended lines of communication, Eisenhower had decided to detach II Corps, of which the First Armored Division was the nucleus, from the Center Task Force at Oran in order to concentrate it in Tunisia. On January 1, 1943, he appointed Fredendall to command II Corps, including a French force at Constantine and a British paratroop brigade. He was to concentrate these forces in the Tebessa and Kasserine area to prepare for an offensive action against the enemy's lines of communication. Having completed this concentration in mid-January, II Corps was to be ready to launch an attack by January 23. Success depended on perfect coordination with the British in order to contain von Arnim's forces. Intelligence estimated that he was receiving 750 men a day and that his forces numbered about 65,000.

Before II Corps arrived in the south in late December 1942, Ike learned that Rommel had correctly analyzed the strategic situation. Although his force was in full retreat from the British Eighth Army, in a captured document dated December 16, 1942, he posited that the Allies suffered from weaknesses inherent in a combined command and proposed to hold the British Eighth Army with a minimum force and use the remainder to attack and cut off the Allied lines of communication in Tunisia. Calculating that two divisions could either hold the Eighth Army or delay its pursuit of the German withdrawal, he proposed to advance the bulk of his force against vulnerable Allied lines of communications in the south. Arnim's mission would be to keep a corridor open for Rommel's advance northward from Libya along the coast of the Gulf of Gabes to link up with Arnim's panzer army and form a front from which to push west to keep the Allies from taking both Tunis and the port of Bizerte. Each was to figure importantly in an invasion of Sicily, the planning for which had been given to Patton.

Arriving at Constantine on January 2, 1943, with a bad cold, Major General Truscott's immediate role in an operation against Rommel code-named Satin was to find an advanced command post for use by Eisenhower that was closer to the front than Algiers. The personnel would be drawn from Algiers and rotated to give others experience at the front.

One of the principal cities of Algeria and the headquarters of the British First Army, as well as the center of both British and French lines of communication, Constantine teemed with refugees from the Algerian battle zone and Tunisia. After conferences with representatives of the First Army and French and British line of communications commands, Truscott selected an almost empty American orphanage as a suitable location for the advanced command post. It had a villa next door that was deemed suitable as quarters for Eisenhower. On January 14, the command post was open for business. During the second week of the month, there were conferences between various staff sections dealing with the organization of the advanced command post and Satin planners.

Truscott learned that Fredendall's plan was to strike eastward from the Feriana-Gafsa area with the First Armored Division and one regimental combat team of the First Infantry Division. They would seize a bottleneck in Rommel's line of communications at Gabes on the eastern coast. With minefields laid to protect the U.S. right flank against any reaction by Rommel, he planned to swing north to capture Sfax. These operations would be supported by U.S. tactical aviation operating from airfields at Tebessa, Feriana, Thelepte, and elsewhere in Algeria and Tunisia. Fredendall hoped to achieve all this in about ten days. The date chosen for commencement of the offensive was January 30. Meanwhile, the primary force facing the Germans would be the French. Their commander, Truscott learned, was the general to whom he had defined the terms of the cease-fire at the Kasbah.

On January 17 (the day before Eisenhower was due at Constantine), General Mathinet reported that the Germans had launched an attack against his force at Pont du Fahs, outside the British sector. In a hasty conference with the British lieutenant general Kenneth Anderson, Truscott agreed with Anderson's estimate that the French would not be able to contain the situation alone. This surprise German attack at Pont du Fahs, Truscott recalled, began a chain of events that would explode in unexpected places and result in the Allies dancing to German tunes, with considerable discomfiture to the Allied command and American troops.

Drawing on official records, his diary entries, and a keen memory of his role as deputy to Eisenhower at the front, Truscott provided in *Command Missions* a singular perspective of the first clash of Americans and Germans. His analyses of the two central figures at the start of battle illuminate not only flaws in their nature that contributed to what became a military disaster, but an insight into virtues in Truscott that had been discerned by both Marshall and Eisenhower and catapulted him to prominence at the outset of the war.

Of the British lieutenant general Sir Kenneth Anderson, Truscott wrote, "Personally bold and fearless, he nevertheless usually took a pessimistic view of military operations. Although stubborn in his opinions, he was always completely loyal to General Eisenhower. All in all, General Anderson was not easy for American officers to know and understand, nor was his personality one to inspire them with confidence."

Truscott found that U.S. II Corps commander Lloyd Fredendall was endowed neither by nature nor training with qualities that would have simplified the problems of inter-Allied cooperation and command relationships. He wrote, "He rarely left his command post for personal visits and reconnaissance, yet he was impatient with recommendations of others who were more familiar with the terrain and other conditions. Fredendall had no confidence in the French, no liking for the British in general and for General Anderson in particular."

Describing the strategic situation at this time, Truscott noted, "From Tebessa, one of the main roads leading toward Sfax on the Tunisian plain passed through the easternmost mountain chain at the village of Faid [and a vital pass that was essential for any Allied advance toward the German line of communications at Sfax]. In German hands it would expose the forward airfields at Feriana and Thelepte to attack by German ground forces and would facilitate a German advance toward Tebessa and to the northwest."

When the French were attacked at Faid Pass on January 28, Anderson ordered General Fredendall to restore the situation. As German forces cut off and overwhelmed two battalions of American infantry placed too far apart for mutual support, and panzers reversed attacks by U.S. reserves, including elements of the First Armored Division, the Americans evacuated airfields and supply depots on the plain and withdrew to the western arm of the mountains. Digging in at the town of Sbeitla, infantry and armor managed to hold off the Germans until February 16. When defenses began to disintegrate during the night, the town was abandoned and troops retreated through the Sbiba and Kasserine passes.

"That was the bitter picture which I had to convey to Eisenhower," Truscott recalled. "More than one hundred American tanks destroyed in two days, along with two battalions of artillery overrun, and two battalions of infantry lost, and no one knew how much more."

Eisenhower, newly promoted to four-star general, received more bad news from Truscott the next day. Fredendall had reported that his troops were retreating through the Kasserine Pass. Relating having had an argument with Anderson, Fredendall complained that Anderson wanted him to hold on. He griped, "They [the British] not only want to tell you what to do, but how to do it. Anyway, we are going to get our tail out of the door all right."

Truscott noted, "We did succeed in getting our tail out of the door during February 17, and we were hopeful that the doors—Kasserine

Pass and the Feriana Gap—were shut and barred so that we could lick our wounds and repair some of the damage."

By February 21, the Germans had pushed through both passes and were poised to seize road junctions leading to the British rear. Meanwhile, Allied reinforcements rushed forward. The First Armored Division turned back German probes toward Tebessa, but British armor met a more powerful thrust toward Thala, where four battalions of field artillery from the U.S. Ninth Infantry Division arrived just in time to bolster the sagging defenses.

"From all along the front and from the rear," Truscott recorded, "every gun and tank which could be brought to bear upon the enemy was being rushed to the critical area. And the whole weight of Allied Air Power in North Africa, including B-17s, was brought in to support our hard-pressed troops. At nightfall, no one knew what would happen next."

On the night of February 22, the Germans began a pullback.

That day, Eisenhower had arrived at the advanced command post. In discussions with Anderson in the afternoon and by phone with Fredendall, likely German intentions were debated. Eisenhower thought the Germans had lost their momentum and Fredendall should counterattack at once. Fredendall believed he should wait at least one more day. Eisenhower was right. The Battle of Kasserine Pass was over. In the first test of American fighting ability against Germans, the United States had lost 2,546 men, 103 tanks, 280 vehicles, 18 field guns, 3 antitank guns, and an entire antiaircraft battery.

Truscott wrote that the general who had earned the nickname "Desert Fox" had achieved little in the way of gaining elbow room in Tunisia and had sustained losses that could not be replaced. "He had thrown a scare into every headquarters in North Africa," Truscott went on, "and he had taught us much."

On the morning of February 3, the U.S. lines were still holding and the situation was looking better. That afternoon at Tebessa, Eisenhower,

Fredendall, General Terry Allen of the First Division, other officers, and Truscott met for a conference. Along the front, conditions had vastly improved and there was a note of optimism. Eisenhower insisted that every effort be made to destroy the Germans before they could escape.

Late in the day, Eisenhower told Truscott to have his sedan brought from Constantine that night to take him back to his quarters. Truscott told an aide to leave Eisenhower's usual driver behind. Thirty-five, Irish, attractive, and with a divorce pending, Kay Summersby had been assigned as Ike's driver by the British Motor Transport Corps shortly after his arrival in London in 1942. Assuming that Ike would not want her exposed to the possibility of an air attack, Truscott blundered. "It was the only time in our associations," he wrote, "that General Eisenhower showed irritation." Ike explained that Summersby was the only driver in whom he had confidence for blackout driving at night.

In conferences with Eisenhower and members of the staff on March 4, Truscott found himself asked to assess General Fredendall. He replied that he felt he had lost the confidence of his subordinates and that II Corps could never fight well under his command. He also asserted his belief that Fredendall both disliked and distrusted the British and would never get along well under British command. He proposed that Ike relieve Fredendall from II Corps and give its command to Patton. By the time of his arrival in Algeria, Truscott was on his way to take over the Third Infantry Division.

★ **EIGHT** ★

Truscott's Trotters

"Every person who is given a new task takes stock," wrote Lucian King Truscott, Jr., in the most introspective of the chapters of *Command Missions*, "and measures himself against its requirements as best he can."

When he and a few aides boarded a C-47 transport plane in Algeria on March 5 to head westward toward Morocco, he appreciated that he had been given command of a distinguished division. Activated in November 1917 at Camp Greene, North Carolina, the Third Infantry Division had gone into combat for the first time eight months later in France. On July 14, 1918, during the Aisne-Marne offensive, as it was protecting Paris with a position on the banks of the Marne River and other units retreated, it stood its ground and earned the nickname "Rock of the Marne." As the new commander of the Third, Truscott replaced Major General John Porter Lucas. Born in West Virginia on

January 14, 1890, he'd ranked fifty-fifth of eighty-two in the West Point class of 1911 with a commission in the cavalry. Wounded in World War I while serving with the Thirty-third Infantry Division, he eventually transferred to the field artillery. Known as Old Luke, he'd graduated from the Command and General Staff School in 1924.

Truscott had gotten to know the Third Division while he was a member of the Ninth Army Corps staff at Fort Lewis, Washington, in 1941, when he prepared and conducted the training exercises and tests that had been given to the divisions of the corps that summer. During the fighting in Tunisia, he had recommended to Eisenhower that the Third be called upon to provide thirty-five hundred men, almost one-fourth of its strength, to fill the ranks of the First and Thirty-fourth infantry divisions. As a cavalry officer, he'd come to his new post with an appreciation that few men in the Third Infantry Division would have had much experience with cavalrymen. He also understood that there had always been branch jealousy in the army and was keenly conscious that both brigadier generals in the Third Division, two of three regimental commanders, and probably other officers had been senior to him before his wartime promotion.

"I had formed strong views concerning the standards which should be expected of American infantry divisions in war," he noted. "From my previous military training and experience, particularly at the Command and General Staff School, I believed that I was as familiar with the theory of the organization and employment of an infantry division as any other American officer, and more so than most. I had long felt that our standards for marching and fighting in the infantry were too low, not up to those of the Roman legions nor countless examples from our own frontier history, nor even to those of Stonewall Jackson's Foot Cavalry."

As he left Algiers, he had known for some time that the Third Infantry Division was to play an important part in Operation Husky. In a conference at Casablanca in January, Roosevelt and Churchill had determined that the next objective in the Allied strategy for defeating

Germany was knocking Italy out of the war. The first step in that direction would be an invasion of Sicily under the overall command of Eisenhower. Ground forces commanded by General Alexander were to consist of a British field army under General Sir Bernard Law Montgomery and a U.S. task force commanded by General Patton. Alexander's planning headquarters was designated Force 141; the British field army, Force 545; and the American task force, Force 343. Initial planning envisaged landing the British forces in the southeastern corner of Sicily and the American task force in the northwestern corner, with capturing Palermo as its immediate objective.

Looking down on his first battlefield on the short flight to Casablanca, Truscott picked out landmarks and ruminated about the soldier's life he'd chosen. During the past year, he had acquired an intimate knowledge of invasion plans and personalities involved in the conduct of the war in Europe that few division commanders could hope to have. He observed modern war at Dieppe and experienced it in command at Port Lyautey. He had been closely associated with American troops in the first battles against veteran Germans.

With the Rangers in Commando training, he observed what could be achieved in the physical and psychological preparation of men for battle. While Rangers were selected according to relatively high standards, it had not seemed to Truscott that they had been markedly superior in physique to the average man. What he did not know was whether the average American soldier, even though free from physical defect or weaknesses, would bear the rigorous training required in the physical and psychological preparation of Rangers and Commandos. Most young Americans of the present generation had been born during and immediately after World War I. They had gone to school in a period when pacifism and isolationism were rife in the schools and colleges. They had grown to manhood during the Great Depression and during a policy of appeasement of Hitler. Their lives had been far easier in the way of physical comforts and conveniences than had been those of any preceding generation. "For the most part," Truscott wrote, "their feet were far more at home in sport shoes on the way to a game or dance than in combat boots lugging the impedimenta of war along the road to battle."

While he believed the average American soldier should be able to approximate the Ranger and Commando standards in preparation for battle, he felt that to require such standards for an entire infantry division and then fail to attain them would result in a lack of confidence, affect relations within the command, and be generally harmful. He wrote, "A wise commander does not demand results which are beyond capabilities of his troops, or issue orders which he cannot enforce or can only enforce by that tyrannical and arbitrary authority which is so repugnant to Americans."

From observation and experience, he was convinced that tactical principles and training methods were sound. Most difficulties were the result of faulty execution and inadequate standards. Throughout his service, he had heard young officers being blamed for everything that went wrong, and combat had been no exception. Personally, he'd found junior officers were usually willing and enthusiastic. Most were much better trained than their superiors. If they failed to respond with ingenuity and initiative, the fault was not entirely their own. Either they had not been trained properly, or the reins on them were held so tightly that they were like a horse who could not use his head.

"Rank carries with it certain prerogatives," he wrote, "but more important, it carries also certain responsibilities."

On March 8, 1943, Truscott signed the order assuming command of the Third Infantry Division and had his first conference with division staff: Lieutenant Colonel Albert Connor, Major General Grover Wilson, Lieutenant Colonel Ben Harrel, Colonel Charles Johnson, Lieutenant Colonel Karl Glos (inspector general), and Colonel Matthew Pugsley (surgeon). In the afternoon, he met subordinate commanders.

In most divisions at the time, Truscott recalled, the division commander and the staff ate together in a headquarters mess operated by the headquarters commandant. The practice had certain disadvantages for both commander and staff. The commander had to adjust his hours to those prescribed for general mess or cause inconvenience to both staff and mess personnel. The presence of the division commander at meals put some constraint upon juniors. This was accentuated whenever a division commander entertained senior officers. Consequently, Truscott decided to establish a separate mess for the division commander, chief of staff, and aides. After a search, Don Carleton found a Chinese cook named Lee (the same Lee who had bummed a cigarette from Truscott on the landing beach in Morocco) and three orderlies, Hong, Dare, and Vong. They remained with Truscott through the war. Their mess with the Third Division became known as the Canton Restaurant.

During daily inspections of training and in visits with troops, Truscott saw much but said little. After a week of observations, he seized the occasion of a movement by a battalion on outpost to a new position about ten miles north of Port Lyautey to issue an order that the shift be done with the men marching at four miles an hour. The startled colonel said, "But, General, infantry marches at two and a half miles an hour."

"Yes, Colonel, I know," said Truscott, "but I want those battalions to march at four miles an hour."

Believing that physical exertion was one of the most important aids in the physical and psychological preparation of men for battle, Truscott felt that training of infantry battalions should approximate Ranger and Commando marching standards. The basis of this regimen was the speed march, described in this Truscott order:

> Full advantage will be taken of movements to and from training areas, and exercises and other opportunities to train individuals and units in traversing given distances at maximum rates and arriving fit for combat. Officers and men will be instructed in techniques of speed marching and in methods of pace setting and checking for various rates of march:

104 steps (30 inches) per minute—three mph
123 steps (34 inches) per minute—four mph
146 steps (36 inches) per minute—five mph

Truscott observed that attaining the standards caused no difficulty and almost every battalion reported greater speeds in the first two weeks. They eventually reached five miles an hour, four miles an hour for twenty miles, and three and a half miles an hour for distances up to thirty miles.

The strenuous pace quickly became known in the ranks of both the enlisted men and the officers as the Truscott Trot.

★ NINE ★

Footrace to Messina

The final three weeks of training by the Third Division for Operation Husky culminated in a full-scale dress rehearsal called Copybook that was so realistic, Truscott noted, that most of the troops thought the invasion of Sicily was actually under way. In his estimation, the practice had generated full confidence among his soldiers in the ability of their naval comrades to land them on the right beaches. When the intensive training ended, drill hours were shortened and more time was allowed for rest and recreation, although the speed marching and physical conditioning continued.

"Never was any division more fit for combat and more in readiness to close with the enemy," wrote Truscott proudly, "than the Third Infantry Division when it embarked for Sicily."

The mission of General Patton's newly created Seventh Army in Husky was to assault the southeast portion of Sicily in conjunction with the British Eighth Army under Montgomery and capture it as a base for later operations. The Americans were to take airfields close to the small ports of Gela and Licata, and prepare for operations by the British. Under General Alexander's plan, Patton's Seventh Army was to conduct simultaneous assaults under cover of darkness on D-day at Sampieri, Gela, and Licata, capture and secure airfields and the port of Licata by D-day plus two, extend the beachhead and establish contact with the British in the vicinity of Ragusa, then move to high ground to keep the Germans from counterattacking out of the northwest.

Assaults called Cent and Dime under General Omar Bradley's II Corps were to capture and secure an airfield at Ponte Olivo by daylight of D-day plus one, the airfield near Comiso by daylight on D-day plus two, an airfield near Biscari by dark, and make contact with Truscott's Third Infantry Division on the left. The Third's Operation Joss called for capturing the port and airfield at Licata by dark of D-day, extending the beachhead and making contact with II Corps. Because there were no suitable major ports to handle oceangoing shipping, the invasion forces were to be supplied and maintained over the assault beaches and through the smaller ports for a period of at least thirty days.

As the command ship *Biscayne* dropped anchor a few thousand yards off the shore between Yellow and Green beaches, Truscott could see little of the target, but assumed that the troop flotillas were in their proper areas and preparing to disembark.

"All was quiet on the quarterdeck of the *Biscayne*, with each man lost in his own thoughts," he wrote. "Mine turned back to other transport areas in the last moments before Dieppe and Morocco. In Goalpost, our plans had been hastily prepared, our troops inexperienced, and confusion had surrounded all of our preparations. Here we had planned carefully and the troops were experienced and in a high state of training."

Off to the east in the direction of Gela, there was a flashing of guns and the flare of exploding shells as searchlights probed the dark. When one moved slowly inward and came to rest on the *Biscayne*, someone yelled, "Stand by to shoot out searchlights!" Truscott protested that they should wait until the enemy guns actually fired at support and landing craft moving shoreward. Rear Admiral Richard Connolly agreed and rescinded the order. No shots came from shore. One by one by one the searchlights went out.

With the exception of a slight delay in the hour of landing occasioned by bad weather, the Joss assault went almost exactly as planned. Careful planning and preparation, rigorous and thorough training, determination, and speed in execution had paid dividends. Battalions had landed before they were discovered and quickly cleared the beaches of all resistance. In little more than an hour, ten infantry battalions, including the Rangers with supporting tanks, had landed. In seven hours, they seized the first day's objectives and were pushing reconnaissance far out to the front. The airfield, town, and port were in American hands, the beaches and the port were organized, and additional troops and supplies were flowing ashore. Resistance had been smothered by the speed and violence of the assault and more than a thousand prisoners taken. U.S. casualties numbered a little more than a hundred.

By nightfall on July 10, contact had been established between all elements along a fifty-mile front and every unit was pressing reconnaissance to make and maintain contact with the withdrawing enemy force.

Other than protecting the left flank of the operation against German interference from the northwest, Truscott recorded, his instructions did not extend beyond the Yellow Line, nor did General Patton's, but they had established a firm base.

Late on the third day (July 12), all vehicles would be ashore, all units reorganized, more than seven thousand tons of supplies unloaded, a supply depot in full operation, and more than four thousand German prisoners evacuated to North Africa.

He wrote that his pride in the Third Infantry Division knew no bounds.

Knowing that even the best troops sometimes needed prodding, he went ashore on July 11 to see how the advance toward the town of Campobello was progressing. He found a column of the Fifteenth Infantry Regiment hunkered down in the roadside gullies. Locating a noncommissioned officer, he asked, "Why are you hiding in the ditch?"

The sergeant answered sheepishly, "Sir, I don't know."

Finding a company commander, Truscott repeated the question. The captain explained that they had been fired on from the woods off to the right and had taken cover.

"How much firing?" demanded Truscott.

"Well, sir, not very much. We heard three or four shots."

Had he not sent out patrols to see what was there? Why wasn't he advancing?

"Sir, I was waiting for orders."

"Battles," Truscott advised, "are not won by lying in ditches."

With the patrol out of their ditches and on the way to scout the woods, and all the men under way again, Truscott walked about a mile farther. Almost on the outskirts of the town of Campobello, he found an advance party of about a dozen men. Roughly a hundred yards to the left, the rest of the company had deployed to clear out resistance. Firing was brisk. To the east lay an open field between the town and a woods to the south that was broken only by a few scattered trees. Looking across this field and hoping to see a battalion going on attack against Campobello, he watched a column of about seventy soldiers come from the woods. Using field glasses, he realized they were not Americans. A machine gun opened fire. A few Germans fell. As others started to run and some scattered and sought cover, Truscott thought they looked like a startled covey of quail. Those nearest buildings reached the cover of the town and the action was over as quickly as it had begun.

At that point, a sergeant drew Truscott's attention to the fact that while Truscott stood in the middle of the road, the Germans had also been shooting at him.

When the Americans continued their patrol, he explored the battle scene and found more than a dozen dead Germans, several wounded being cared for by U.S. medics, and the prisoners being marched off. Although he had been at Dieppe, had led an invasion in Morocco, and had been involved in the Battle of Kasserine Pass, it was the first time he saw Germans killed by infantry fire in frontline action.

During a visit to the Third Infantry Division command post at noon on July 14, Patton told Truscott about having been present in Gela during an attack by a column of tanks in which Colonel Bill Darby's heroic manning of an antitank gun inspired the Rangers to drive back an assault that imperiled the First Division's beachhead. Patton also reported that on the east coast of Sicily, Montgomery's Eighth Army had taken Augusta and was advancing against only moderate resistance. For the next phase in the operation, Patton said, he believed that the Seventh Army should shift to the north toward Palermo, the largest and most important seaport in Sicily, but he was advised that the honor of taking the city had been reserved for Montgomery. The Seventh Army was to protect his left flank.

With sublime understatement, Truscott wrote that this was a passive mission that did not appeal to Patton. When Patton remarked to Truscott that the Allies would need to take the port of Porto Empedocle for the drive toward Palermo, and that he had orders not to do so because a heavy battle might risk exposure of the flank of the Eighth Army, Truscott replied that he was confident the mission could be done without too much trouble. All Patton had to do was give the word.

With a cunning smile, Patton repeated that he had orders not to launch an attack on Empedocle. Truscott suggested that the high command would surely have no objection to Truscott making a reconnaissance in force toward Agrigento on his own responsibility. Of this conspiratorial conversation between generals, Truscott wrote, "Patton, with something of the air of the cat that had swallowed the canary, agreed that he thought they would not."

When Patton left, Truscott set the wheels in motion. In his plan, a reconnaissance in force would move to Agrigento to "clear up an uncertain situation." On July 14, the Ranger Battalion would circle around Agrigento during the night and seize the port. If all went well Truscott could report to Patton by noon the next day that Agrigento was his. Following the progress of the mission from a forward command post, Truscott learned at mid-afternoon that the attackers had isolated the port. After some street fighting, the Italian defenders gave up. To Truscott's surprise and amazement the improvised and officially illicit maneuver ended with heavy enemy casualties, six thousand Italian army prisoners, and the capture of hundreds of their tanks, vehicles, and artillery pieces. Of this bold maneuver Patton later said that had it failed he (Patton) would have been relieved of command.

When General Alexander learned of the capture of Porto Empedocle on July 18, he issued Field Orders Number 1, giving Patton permission to form a provisional corps, including the Third Division, to head west to take Palermo. Describing the capture of the port as Patton's lodestar, and saying that Patton hated playing second fiddle to Montgomery in Sicily and anywhere else, Truscott depicted the champion of tank warfare looking ahead to a spectacular sweep into Palermo as the first great exploit for American armor.

Noting in *Command Missions* that the mission was daunting, he wrote of the terrain, "Palermo was a hundred miles to the north and west. Our first forty or so miles led through rugged mountains which rose to a height of more than 4,000 feet around Cammarata and San Stefano di Quisquina. Our three tortuous roads northward had steep grades, numerous hairpin turns, and many bridges which would be rendered more difficult by enemy demolitions and delaying actions. Once through the mountainous belt at Prizzi, there would be easier going for another four miles across the central plateau, bringing us to the range of rugged hills which encircled Palermo. Since these demolitions would constitute our greatest obstacle, it seemed to me that the faster we could traverse the distance, the less time the enemy would have for demolitions and destruction."

After explaining the challenge to his combat team commanders at a conference on July 18, Truscott told them he expected them to be in

Palermo in five days and be the first to arrive. With that, they broke out a bottle of Scotch and toasted the "American Doughboy."

Taking time out from planning the attack, Truscott answered a complaint from the commander of the Eighty-second Airborne on the topic of uncontrolled Italian prisoners at Realmonte. Major General Matthew B. Ridgway had written to Truscott that prisoners and members of the Third Ranger Battalion were indulging in local wines with possibly serious consequences. He added a request that Truscott issue instructions to the Rangers and other elements of the Third Division to evacuate the prisoners forthwith.

Truscott caustically replied that because Ridgway had already relieved the Third Ranger Battalion in the vicinity of Realmonte and that the battalion would be withdrawn from the region, Ridgway had authority to issue his own instructions.

The next day, the drive for Palermo began.

After three days of house-to-house fighting, the city fell and fifty-three thousand Italian soldiers were captured. With this stunning victory, the Allies controlled half of Sicily.

Patton slapped Truscott on the back and said, "Well, the Truscott Trot sure got us here in a damn hurry."

Truscott wrote to Sarah, "You will have guessed where I am and what I have been doing. The censor will permit me to say that I am now in Sicily, and you will guess that the division has been in the forefront. It has done well. I do not believe the equal of these men has ever existed in our army, though I may be somewhat prejudiced! Anyway, it has been a grand experience and we have opened lots of eyes."

The mention of censors referred to a previous occasion when a letter from Truscott to Sarah that gave his location had been returned. Written on a form known as V-mail and sent unsealed so the contents could be examined, it was rejected with a censor's admonition, "Not permissible to disclose geographical location." Recounting this episode in his next letter to Sarah, Truscott wrote that even generals get censored.

Whenever possible thereafter, he chose to avoid the use of V-mail by sending letters to Sarah by way of message pouches carried by a courier to the War Department.

With Patton having set his sights on beating Montgomery to Messina, the plan called for an attack from the west along the northern coast of Sicily. Strongly defended by four of the best German divisions, the city was surrounded by mountainous terrain. The Seventh Army would advance along Highway 113 with the First and Forty-fifth Infantry Divisions in the lead and the Third Division in support. After the Forty-fifth captured a ridge outside Santo Stefano, the Third was to be brought forward to take over the advance. As the plan unfolded, the Third faced its greatest opposition from the Twenty-ninth Panzer Grenadier Division, dug in on a steep ridgeline at San Fratello. When a series of attacks proved unsuccessful, Patton decided to mount an amphibious landing to flank the German position.

During the afternoon of August 6, a landing force under the command of Lieutenant Colonel Lyle W. Bernard began loading on boats for the invasion on the following morning. After a German air raid sank one of the craft while loading was in progress, the operation had to be delayed until another boat could be brought up from Palermo. Truscott decided to put off the landing again, explaining that he did not believe that a support force for the landing could reach the landing beach in time to assist Bernard's force. Patton's deputy, General Geoffrey Keyes, expressed his feeling that Patton would want the operation to go on. He also pointed out that because arrangements had been made for a large contingent of war correspondents to witness the landing, Patton might be subjected to a storm of criticism if the operation had to be postponed. In a call to General Bradley, Truscott's direct commander in Sicily, Truscott succeeded in winning agreement that the landing should not proceed unless it were properly timed with the operations of the rest of the division.

With that, Keyes phoned Patton and mistakenly reported that Truscott did not want to carry out the landing. Grabbing the phone, Truscott attempted to explain his reasoning.

Patton blared, "Dammit, that operation will go on."

An hour later, Patton stormed into Truscott's command post. Truscott depicted him as screamingly angry as only Patton could be and giving everybody hell, from military police sentries at the entrance right on through to Truscott. "Goddammit, Lucian," he thundered, "what's the matter with you? Are you afraid to fight?"

Bristling, Truscott answered, "General, you know that's ridiculous and insulting. You have ordered the operation and it is now loading. If you don't think I can carry out orders, you can give the division to anyone you please. But I will tell you one thing, you will not find anyone who can carry out orders which they do not approve as well as I can."

Throwing an arm around Truscott's shoulder, Patton said, "Dammit, Lucian, I know that. Come on, let's have a drink of your liquor."

The language in the entry for Tuesday, August 10, 1942, in a diary kept on Truscott's behalf by an aide was less melodramatic:

Gen Keyes arrived at 1900 and was told amphibious operation scheduled for tonight was postponed because it was almost impossible to get artillery up to support the 15th and the surprise element of the troops. Keyes advised Gen T to go. Gen Bradley was phoned. He agreed with Gen T, stating it was unwise to execute the movement unless the timing was exactly right. Gen Keyes called Patton, who ordered the amphibious operation be consummated. Gen Patton arrived at 2100 and personally indorsed the orders to go ahead with previous plans.

Assessing the situation, Truscott noted that Bernard's battalion had been reduced in strength by previous losses and the beach at Brolo was not ideal for a landing. The exits to the inland were made difficult by way of an olive grove and steep banks onto the coastal highway. Bernard's men were to take Mount Cipolla, a steep spur that overlooked the coastal highway, and the town of Brolo, a short distance to the east. This objective was not far behind German lines that ran from Cape Orlando south through Naso. The Germans' route of escape was along the foot of Mount Cipolla. Because Bernard's objective lay miles across difficult terrain with a bitterly defending enemy, the battalion would be hard-pressed to maintain itself until joined by a Ranger Battalion that would have to fight its way through to assist Bernard's battalion.

On August 8, the Second Battalion, Thirtieth Infantry, reinforced with batteries of artillery and a platoon of tanks, landed at Saint Agata, cutting off escape by some of the Germans. Learning that the bulk of their force had withdrawn the previous night, Patton insisted that if he'd had more landing craft and more troops, he would have caught all of them. He noted in his diary that he had a sixth sense about war and was willing to take chances. "I may have been a little bullheaded," he wrote, "but I truly feel that I did my exact and full duty . . . and demonstrated that I am a great leader."

Truscott believed that if the operation had been delayed by one day, as he'd proposed, most of the German force would have been captured. "Nevertheless," he reflected twelve years later in *Command Missions,* "we had gained important time."

Although the Truscott-Patton confrontation over the timing of the Brolo operation would provide an exciting scene in the film *Patton,* it was not the last contest of wills between them on the way to Messina. After ordering Colonel William Darby to lead his Rangers in climbing the mountain heights overlooking it on the afternoon of August 15 in expectation that they would be in the city the next morning, Truscott returned to his command post and found General Keyes waiting. Keyes informed him that Patton had directed a landing by a combat team of the Forty-fifth Infantry east of Cape Milazzo at daylight the next day. Astounded, Truscott countered that such a landing could serve no useful military purpose and was almost certain to have dire and unfortunate consequences. Keyes stated that he was reluctant to cancel it, adding that Patton was not averse to profiting from such a spectacular operation.

When Truscott threatened to halt the Third Division's pursuit of the

Germans and move all his men to the west of Cape Milazzo to support the proposed landing, Keyes conceded that the operation was not practical.

On August 16, the Seventh Infantry overcame the last German resistance and by nightfall was on the heights overlooking Messina. After one hundred rounds of artillery were lobbed onto the mainland of Europe as the Germans escaped into Italy, Rangers entered the city. On the heights above, Truscott accepted the surrender of Messina by civil functionaries. When the senior Italian military official, Colonel Michele Tomaselle, presented his Beretta pistol to Truscott as a symbol of capitulation, Truscott told him to go back into the city and wait to make the formal surrender to Patton.

Directed by Keyes to delay entering Messina until Patton arrived, Truscott arranged for transportation with motorcycles and scout car escorts. When Patton appeared the next day with characteristic flurry, he barked, "What in the hell are you all standing around for?"

Truscott replied, "We were waiting for you, General."

As the lengthy cavalcade moved down a winding road into Messina in plain view of the Germans on the mainland across the Straits, it was accompanied by German artillery fire. A Patton aide seated with Keyes in the car behind the one in which Patton and Truscott were riding was wounded by a shell fragment.

"Just after we arrived in the city," Truscott recorded, "a British armored patrol entered it from the west. General Montgomery had no doubt been anxious to beat General Patton into Messina, for he had landed a patrol a few miles down the coast for the purpose of being there before us."

With the footrace to Messina ended in an American triumph, Truscott and his staff celebrated that night at his command post with cocktails and a buffet supper. An aide noted in the diary, "A very nice time was had by all. Scotch highballs, cognac and champagne enjoyed after the mad dash to Messina."

★ TEN ★

Mountains and Mud

ON JULY 25, 1943, THE TWO-DECADE Fascist dictatorship of Benito Mussolini ended with a coup d'état. Count Galeazzo Ciano (the foreign minister and Mussolini's son-in-law) and others in the Fascist Grand Council revolted. King Vittorio Emanuele III called Mussolini to his palace and stripped him of his power. The man who called himself Il Duce was arrested and confined at Gran Sasso, a mountain resort in central Italy. He was replaced by General Pietro Badoglio, who immediately declared, "The war continues at the side of our Germanic allies." Secretly, the government began talking with the Allies about an Italian surrender to coincide with the planned Allied invasion. Although Truscott had not been involved in the formation of the design of the operation named Avalanche, he learned that the broad concept was to have the British Eighth Army cross the Straits of Messina and advance up the Italian boot in conjunction with a later assault somewhere in the vicinity of Naples by the newly organized U.S. Fifth Army, under Mark Clark. The Allies would then sweep up to take Rome.

Once the Italian campaign was well in hand, some U.S. units were to be transferred from reserve in Sicily to England as part of preparations for the invasion of France. Because of the Third Division's experience in the conduct of amphibious assaults, and in part because of his expertise in the planning and execution of combined operations acquired at Mountbatten's headquarters in London, Truscott expected his division to be shifted to England as part of the cross-channel operation known as Overlord. Unhappy at the prospect of his men, and himself, being taken out of action, if only temporarily, he was relieved to learn that Clark persuaded Eisenhower to leave the Third Division in the Mediterranean theater.

He was also feeling confident about his judgment as both combat commander and in evaluating the performance of junior officers. In a letter to Eisenhower on August 25, 1943, that addressed Ike as "Dear Chief," the forty-eight-year-old major general wrote to the fifty-two-year-old four-star general and Supreme Allied Commander, "As a result of my Sicilian experience, I am firmly of the opinion that any man fifty years old is much too old to command a modern infantry regiment in modern war."

Perhaps thinking about thirty-two-year-old Colonel William O. Darby's leadership of the Rangers, he wrote, "I would really like to have regimental commanders of about the [West Point] Class of 1930 or later."

Possibly with fifty-eight-year-old George Patton in mind, he allowed that there might be exceptions to his age-limit preference. The Truscott-Patton partnership had been contentious at times, and although Truscott had experienced the fury of Patton's wrath if he suspected a man of cowardice, he was shocked to learn that Patton had slapped two soldiers and called them cowards. Encountering them while inspecting field hospitals, and told they were suffering from combat fatigue, he'd exploded with rage. When the incidents were recounted in stories by war correspondents in newspapers at home, the result was an outburst of public indignation that compelled Eisenhower to remove Patton from command and abandon plans to place him in charge of ground forces in Overlord. Left with no troops to lead into battle, he could only observe from the island of Malta as General Omar Bradley got the Overlord job and Mark Clark planned the invasion of Italy.

The assault envisaged landing the Thirty-sixth Infantry Division, freshly arrived from the United States, on the beaches at Paestum, while the British X Corps landed two divisions on beaches farther to the north opposite Salerno, with the port of Naples being the ultimate objective. Because the new Italian government promised to announce their surrender at the exact time of the Salerno landings, Clark assured Truscott that the invasion force would meet no opposition. "Clark told me to be prepared for landing farther north," Truscott recalled, "and said that he might even have it land as far north as Rome, which was already looming large as an objective with General Clark and others. However, I had already had enough experience with the Boche to believe that the landing at Salerno would bring a violent reaction of some sort even though the landing itself might be unopposed."

According to the plan, the Italians were to fly their air force to U.S. bases in Sicily and sail their navy to Allied ports. Remaining in reserve in Sicily, Truscott's troops were to guard six airfields "to prevent any trickery on the part of the Italians," or in case the Italians should be followed in by German planes. Truscott reinforced each of the six airfields and placed a strong reserve in readiness. But after Italian radio announced Italy's surrender on the ninth of September and Allies revealed that landings were under way at Salerno, no Italian airplanes appeared. "It was obvious," Truscott said, "that the Germans interfered with Italian plans."

In the three weeks that had elapsed since the capture of Messina he'd done everything required to prepare the Third Division for further action. While it was under its authorized strength, he was confident it was fit and ready. Studying reports from Salerno that Clark's headquarters were established onshore, he recognized that there was desperate fighting and discerned that events were not going well. Sending a message to Clark that he was coming to Salerno, he requested that a guide meet him and his aides at the beach to provide transportation. As a landing craft taking him to Salerno approached the beach, he saw the shoreline stretched before him in a wide semicircle and lit by the flare of bursting shells.

"Knowing little or nothing of what had transpired onshore," he recalled, "we were prepared for the worst. There was little activity on the beach where we landed. No craft were beaching, nor was there any congestion of men, vehicles or supplies as we were prepared to expect. There was no one to meet us, but we found the shore party command post, where we obtained transportation to take us to the army command post, which we found about a mile inland well concealed in a dense thicket, ensconced in vans, trailers and tents."

Finding General Albert Gruenther, Clark's chief of staff, he was told that Clark was on a visit to the British X Corps, a trip that enemy activity had compelled him to make by sea. Gruenther reported that the invasion had been "a near thing." It had been met on the beaches not by Italians but by a German panzer division and had to fight in to shore. Also in the battle were the Twenty-ninth Panzer Division and elements of the Hermann Göring tank division. Striking in a gap between the British and Americans, Germans had overrun a battalion of the Thirty-sixth Infantry Division near Persano, surrounded another at Altavilla, and forced back a regiment of the Forty-fifth Infantry Division. Desperate measures had been necessary to establish a new defense line.

Truscott learned that in the British sector, the X Corps had been unable to clear the heights back of Salerno and Battipaglia and secure the Montecorvino airfield. Because of the German counterattacks, the situation on the front of X Corps was so serious that Clark had ordered the drop of a parachute battalion in mountain passes to the north in order to interrupt the communications of German forces opposing X Corps.

Farther to the north, Darby's Rangers had seized mountain passes lead-ing from Salerno toward Naples, but Clark had been forced to send a battalion from the Thirty-sixth Infantry Division to reinforce them.

"It had been expected that the Eighth Army would advance more rapidly than it had done and that its approach would have reduced the threat to the beachhead," Truscott noted. "As a matter of fact, the ad-vance of the Eighth Army probably had this effect, albeit a somewhat tardy one, for the hard-pressed Avalanche forces. While we were talking with General Gruenther, two correspondents were brought into him. They had made the trip overland from the Eighth Army then some forty miles to the south by the coastal road. They had encountered no enemy and had only slight delay avoiding a few scattered demolitions. It was obvious then that the worst was over, even though the Germans renewed their attacks on the following day."

The next morning (September 15), Truscott saw Clark, found him encouraged, and told him the Third Division was in Palermo and ready to load as soon as craft were available. Clark replied that he was anxious that the division arrive as soon as possible. It would be assigned to VI Corps. Truscott proposed to leave at once to expedite the move.

Early on the morning of September 17, as the first convoy sailed and the next began to load, Truscott boarded a PT boat to return to Salerno, accompanied by several members of the division staff, to arrange for the unloading and assembly of the troops upon their arrival. The first con-voy appeared on September 18 and moved to assembly areas north of the Sele River. The Seventh Infantry disembarked the next night and the Fifteenth Infantry during the day of September 20. At a conference at Clark's headquarters at which future plans were discussed, the consen-sus was that the situation was vastly improved by the advance of the Forty-fifth Infantry Division in the area north of the Sele River. It was known that the Germans were withdrawing, but it was expected that they would hold the difficult mountain terrain as long as possible in order to give them time to destroy the port of Naples to prevent its use by the Allies. There were indications that the Germans were preparing defenses farther north along the Volturno River.

Truscott viewed the plan for the American advance northward, dictated largely by the availability of roads, as "simple enough." The VI Corps, with his Third Infantry Division in concert with the Forty-fifth, would proceed abreast on the two available roads to drive into and through mountains. Because the British Eighth Army had not yet come up abreast of the beachhead forces, the right flank of VI Corps was to advance northward beyond Teora as the Eighth Army advanced on its right. Meanwhile, the British X Corps was to attack northward from Salerno through the two passes where Rangers maintained a foothold. After moving into the Naples plain, the Allies would capture the port and drive the enemy north of the Volturno.

Truscott felt that because the Third Division was fresh from its experience in Sicily, it was as well prepared for the task that lay ahead as any division could hope to be. "We had learned much of German delaying methods and how to overcome them," he wrote. "The term 'supermen' applied to the Germans was now a term of derision."

Depicting the terrain that his division would have to traverse as enormously difficult, with narrow valleys broken by cultivated plots and mountains rising to elevations of more than three thousand feet, he anticipated crossing numerous bridges and troops clinging precariously to cliffs in many places. Off the roads, occasional cart trails led to villages nestled among the mountains. A few mule paths led to their tops and along ridges. These difficulties were made worse by rains that began on September 26.

"When lines of action are limited, military decisions are not difficult," Truscott wrote, "and the formulation of operational plans is relatively easy. So it was in this case. Our plans followed the general pattern of our Sicilian operation. It was the execution which proved to be difficult. One regiment with the bare minimum of vehicles required for transport of weapons, ammunition, and for communications advanced along the main route, brushing aside light enemy resistance. When the advance was stopped by enemy demolitions defended by the enemy, one battalion remained on the axis of movement to maintain contact and protect the deployment of the division artillery, while other battalions took to the mountains on either side to outflank the enemy positions."

During this challenging maneuver, a rumor spread through a part of the division that the Germans were using poison gas. A wire-laying party had sustained severe burns from contact with wet foliage along a road. The discovery of containers nearby led the men to believe that the Germans were using mustard gas. Informed of this, Truscott did not believe that the Germans would dare to turn to chemical warfare, but he appreciated that under the circumstances little imagination was required to picture the harm that would result from the spreading of such a rumor. Accordingly, he issued orders to isolate the wire-laying party and to stop all talk of the incident while the report was investigated. The result of an analysis of the suspect containers was that they contained tear gas for use by the Germans to control Italian mobs that formed to harass them as they retreated. "The casualties recovered quickly," Truscott wrote, "and were back at their assigned tasks within a day or so. So ended the only gas scare which I was to encounter throughout the war."

In a shock that was almost as severe as learning the fate of George Patton, Truscott received word that VI Corps commander, Major General Ernest J. Dawley, who had established the Salerno beachhead, was judged by Clark to have lost control of a combat situation and had been reduced to his permanent rank of colonel and fired. His replacement as the VI Corps commander was to be Major General John Lucas. Brought over from II Corps in Sicily, he was to capture Benevento and secure crossings of the Calore River. As soon as the crossings were secured, one division was to move by roads northwest of Benevento while the remainder of the corps, moving to the northwest by road between Benevento and the VI Corps boundary, went forward with all speed in the corps zone of action. Because the Forty-fifth Division was still farther to the east, Lucas decided that the Thirty-fourth Infantry Division would continue the advance to seize the crossings at Benevento. Truscott's Third Division would continue to the Volturno. With torrential rains doing more to delay the advance than German demolition teams working frantically to delay the Allies, Truscott's men found that along main highways, piles of trees that the Germans had felled had been booby-trapped and mined. In many places in the mountains, the road passed through ancient towns where the Germans had demolished entire blocks of old stone buildings to block the narrow streets. Bypasses were rarely possible and removal of the rubble was impossible.

Up to this time, Truscott wrote, neither General Clark nor Lucas had anticipated much delay in crossing the Volturno and continuing the advance. Orders issued on October 2 had directed the British X Corps to push its attack up to the Volturno, force the crossings of that river, and continue the advance to the first phase line of the plan without waiting for the VI Corps. Advancing through the mountains, it had a longer distance to cover. Since this latter provision referred to the part of the corps zone in which the Third Division was operating, Truscott expected to clear German patrols from the south bank of the Volturno on October 7, make necessary reconnaissance and preparations, and cross over the following day, assuming that dispositions could be completed in time.

On October 6, Lieutenant General Richard L. McCreery, in command of the British X Corps, visited Truscott and told him that McCreery's troops could not be ready to cross the river for several days. He said he was planning to make his main crossing in the vicinity of Capua with the Fifty-sixth Division, with others crossing farther down toward the coast. He was concerned because the area around Capua was dominated by German observation on the heights north of Triflisco. There was also a mass of German artillery north of Capua. He said that he thought that VI Corps should cross first and seize the heights before his troops began to cross. Because these heights were in the sector of the Third Division, Truscott felt the plan would leave the Germans free to concentrate against his troops. He told McCreery it would be better for all concerned if the two divisions crossed the river at the same time. In a later conversation, Lucas expressed confidence that the Third Division could cross the river with little difficulty.

While the VI Corps crossed two divisions above Triflisco, Truscott noted, the X Corps was to cross two divisions. McCreery's plan was to have the Forty-sixth Division make the main crossing near the sea. The Seventh Armored Division was to make a demonstration near Grazzanise while the Fifty-sixth Division made a secondary attack with one battalion at the town of Capua, assisted by a demonstration force in the hills to the east. Landing craft for tanks were to land forty of them north of the mouth of the Volturno. All attacks were to be preceded by intense artillery preparation.

Truscott wrote:

> The problem in forcing a river crossing is to put infantry across in sufficient numbers and with adequate supporting weapons to clear crossing sites so combat power can be built up on the enemy side of the river to attain the objective regardless of the enemy opposition. Assault boats, rafts, swimming, wading, foot bridges were all means for crossing men with the weapons they carry under appropriate conditions. More difficult is the problem of crossing tanks and anti-tank weapons to support infantry in the early fighting, and crossing artillery so that it will be within effective range to support its infantry closely, and crossing trucks and heavy equipment to transport ammunition, supplies, communications, materials and equipment for repair of roads, bridges and the like. Properly waterproofed for assault landings, tanks and tank destroyers can wade depths of six feet or more if banks are in such condition that vehicles can enter and leave the water. But to cross artillery, armor and heavy equipment in quantity and to maintain adequate supplies, bridges are essential and must be constructed early. Ferrying is much too slow.

Noting that under ordinary conditions the Volturno was fordable at many places, he found that continuous rains had transformed it into a major obstacle. With few assault boats available to carry the assault battalions, he had to improvise by obtaining life rafts from the navy in Naples, extra water and gas cans from U.S. and captured stocks, a large quantity of Italian life jackets found in storage in Naples, and other material from which to improvise rafts and ferries for crossing men, mortars, and machine guns, and even a few light vehicles. Where reconnaissance indicated places that men could wade across the stream, his men found miles of rope for use as guidelines.

"Our plan was simple, as all good tactical plans must be," he wrote. The aim was to clear enemy fire from the river line to permit the building of bridges so that the entire division could cross over in the shortest possible time. First to cross were infantry battalions with tanks and tank destroyers supported by artillery to the south of the river. Opposite Triflisco, where the Germans expected to be attacked in force, Truscott planned a full-scale feint that would be timed and coordinated with the British making a crossing at Capua. He hoped that the action would lead the Germans to believe that it was the main attack. While the Germans were preparing to meet it, his boats would ferry the infantry regiments with the intention of advancing rapidly to the north and gaining the heights in the rear of the German defenses.

Fire was to begin at midnight and continue thereafter to shroud the heights in smoke until they were finally cleared. The Second Battalion, Thirtieth Infantry, was to be held in readiness to cross immediately if there were any sign that the Germans were withdrawing. Five minutes before the crossings began, these positions and the bank of the river on the enemy side would be obscured by a smoke screen.

"Every officer and man knew the part he was to play," Truscott wrote. "All the preparations had been completed with great secrecy. All bridging, ferrying, and fording materials were in readiness in concealed positions near the river banks."

Because VI Corps was in much better position to continue the advance than X Corps, to expedite the crossing of the X Corps, General Clark decided to change the boundary between the two corps in order to give the British Fifty-sixth Division the bridge that Truscott's men had built at Triflisco. Truscott and Lucas agreed that this was a logical measure. Since the objective of the Third Infantry Division was given to the British, Lucas issued orders directing the Third to turn northeast toward Dragoni and continue the advance northward to Mount Delli Angelli and Pietramelara while the Thirty-fourth Infantry Division advanced up the valley of the Volturno to cross over east of Dragoni and continue the advance northward to Raviscanina. The Forty-fifth Division would revert to reserve when it reached Piedmonte d'Alife.

Rain was now almost continuous. Mud rendered all movements difficult and frequently made movements of vehicles off roads impossible. Heavy rains washed out bypasses, often making them impassable, and bridging operations became a major problem. Cold and wet caused extreme discomfort and was beginning to affect the health of the command.

"While losses in battle had not been excessive," Truscott recalled, "the daily total was beginning to mount, and losses from non-battle causes such as sickness and injury were even larger and were affecting the combat effectiveness of every battalion. My men were clad in woolen clothing as they had been for the Sicilian campaign, but the barracks bags and squad rolls were still in Palermo. Except for what men could carry, there were no changes in clothing, no heavy underwear, no extra shoes, no overcoats, and far from enough blankets to keep men comfortable."

On October 4, he wrote to General Gruenther:

> Numerous requests have been made to your headquarters to have the Third Division Administration Center and baggage shipped from Sicily, a situation that is now becoming critical both from the standpoint of essential administration

and the health of the command. Morning report extracts and graves registration reports have been accumulating since September 18. However, no battle casualty reports have been submitted, nor can they be prepared until the Administration Center arrives with the individual records and necessary information for proper processing. The losses to the Division through casualties and sickness are averaging 130 men per day and a terrific back log of work is piling up.

The Division APO [post office], an integral part of the Administration Center, is badly needed to handle and process mail, which is arriving daily. Properly handled and efficient mail service is a decided morale factor for these troops. The Division baggage consisting of bed rolls, clothing and equipment, is essential to the successful operation of this command. The lack of sleeping rolls and shelter halves contained in this baggage has not only caused actual suffering among the men concerned, but it is jeopardizing the health of the Division.

Truscott recorded that while army and theater service and supply agencies were making strenuous efforts to obtain the winter clothing and equipment for the troops, many weeks would pass before anything like adequate supplies would be on hand.

Conditions on the mountaintops were appalling. All supply was by man and mules, much of it by man. Casualties had to be carried out on stretchers, which often required hours. Hot food was out of the question. Incessant cold rain not only added to the discomfort but reduced visibility almost to nothing, interfered with air support, and vastly increased the difficulties of attacking. Companies were seriously reduced in strength by casualties and sickness. It was during this period that the bane of men who had served in France in the First World War, trench foot, began to plague their soldier sons in the second.

"Morale suffers under long-continued exposure to battle and the exertion of campaign," Truscott wrote. "The Air Force had been able to combat this by rotating men home to the States after a certain number of missions or a certain length of time. No such policy was considered practicable for ground forces on any large scale, but the theater arranged to rotate limited numbers of men on a quota basis. This policy, even with the limited numbers which could be rotated, was an important morale factor, for even with only a few men being rotated, there was always an element of hope that one's turn might come."

On November 2 while the battle was in progress, he wrote to Gruenther:

> I am forwarding to your headquarters through normal channels recommendations for rotation of officers and enlisted men of this command for the months of August, September, and October. My Adjutant General informs me that there is some question as to whether the recommendations for the months of August and September will be considered under the Fifth Army quota (whatever that may mean). I hope that you will look these over and see that my outfit receives due consideration. You are familiar with the difficulties incident to getting my Administration Center over here, which accounts for the delay in submitting these recommendations. We are still plugging away and apparently getting on all right. I wish you would come up and have dinner with me and see how a field soldier lives.

Having recognized for some time the urgent need to give men in combat a chance to rest in an area away from the battle zone, Clark had authorized a rest center for the Fifth Army in the Naples area to which divisions could send quotas of men for periods of five days. The first eight hundred left the Third Division area for Naples on November 5. When they were assembled for departure, Truscott spoke to them.

Gazing at haggard, dirty, bedraggled, long-haired, and unshaven men with tattered clothes and boots worn out, he found their appearance appalling. He told them to enjoy themselves to the fullest, but to uphold the division's honor. He promised that when they returned, they would make the Germans pay for the hardships they'd forced the division to endure. A week later, the eight hundred who'd lounged and played amid all the city's abundant entertainment amenities and pleasures of the city's bars, restaurants, and other carnal resorts returned looking rested, clean, and trim in new uniforms.

"The effect of this rest camp program on the morale of the battle-weary men of the command," said Truscott, "was of inestimable value, and saved many men who otherwise would have broken under the strain."

When Gruenther paid a call on November 5 to spend the night with Truscott's division and to visit the front, Truscott told him that while on that day going had been slow, they were making progress and he was optimistic. They had just finished dinner when Truscott was called to the telephone.

In an urgent tone, General Lucas said, "You are to move the Third Infantry by motor tonight through the zone of the Forty-fifth Infantry Division to Rocca Pipirozzi and attack northwest early tomorrow morning to capture Mount Lungo."

Truscott protested that the order meant a sudden move of about twenty miles with no prior reconnaissance and inadequate artillery support over difficult terrain by men who were not ready to launch an attack.

Lucas replied, "Yes, Lucian. I know that. But I can't help it. This is Clark's order. He's been trying to get the British to move against Camino and he told McCreery that you could do this. McCreery didn't think you could. I tried to explain to him that this isn't the time or place yet. But he wants it done."

"Well, General, let me talk to Clark."

"No, Lucian. Dammit, you have just got to do it."

"Okay, General, we will do the best we can. I still think it's wrong. It will take the Third two days to get across those mountains to reach Lungo. There will be no surprise. I think our chances of taking it are damn slim."

"Yes, Lucian. I know all that. I agree with you. But do the best you can."

Some way or other, Truscott wrote, his men reached the objective and the attack got under way at half past five the following morning. Fighting their way across spurs along the north slopes of Mount Cesima, one battalion came in sight of Rotundo on the first day. It was not until the afternoon of November 7 that the Second and Third battalions were in positions to make any coordinated effort, but without properly organized artillery and other supporting fires. When that effort proved unsuccessful, the entire division attacked. After bitter fighting, it gained a foothold on the southern end of Mount Lungo and held the position against strong counterattacks. Relieved by the Thirty-sixth Infantry Division ten days later, they began to refit and rest in preparation for the next operation.

Instead of a rapid sweep from the Salerno beaches up the Italian boot in September for a triumphal entry into Rome, the invaders had been stalemated in mountains amidst the worst winter weather in recent Italian memory. The British had been unable to clear the Germans from Mount Camino and were compelled to give up some of the gains they'd made. The Thirty-fourth and Forty-fifth divisions had been able to do little more than gain a foothold on the heights north and west of Venafro. Accordingly, on November 5, General Alexander called a halt, and Mark Clark set about regrouping the Fifth Army and affording divisions an opportunity to rest and refit.

With the Third Division pulled off the front line Truscott stoically wrote, "So ended our fifty-nine days of mountains and mud."

★ ELEVEN ★

DOGFACE SOLDIERS

IN A LETTER TO TRUSCOTT dated November 18, 1943, that lamented the detachment of the Third Division from VI Corps, General Lucas lauded Truscott's leadership during fifty-nine days over the most difficult terrain imaginable to fight a determined and skillful enemy. "The courage and resourcefulness of all officers and men of the division, their endurance of hardships, and their rugged soldierly duties," he wrote, "have excited the admiration of all who have knowledge of the facts."

Two days later, Truscott issued a message to be read to the men of the division at their first formation after its receipt. Summarizing their history in Italy, he said to them, "This record is one in which every officer and man can feel just pride. It has been made possible only because of your sound training and discipline, your unexcelled physical condition, the splendid leadership of the officers and noncommissioned officers, and most important the magnificent loyalty and determination which has driven you to every objective regardless of hazard and difficulty." Writing to Eisenhower on November 24, 1943, he hailed the "ability of the American soldier" in a protracted campaign.

During the Sicilian campaign, the most famous reporter to have emerged in the war filed an account of a group of Third Division combat engineers laboring to fill in a hole in a road on the way to Messina that had been blasted by retreating Germans. Born on August 3, 1900, on a tenant farm near Dana, Indiana, Ernest Taylor Pyle had taken journalism classes at Indiana University but did not graduate. Instead, he found work on a small newspaper in La Plante, Indiana. Moving to Washington, D.C., he soon became the country's first aviation editor, then managing editor of the *Washington Daily News*, and finally a columnist. In 1935 he went to work as a roving correspondent for the Scripps Howard newspaper chain. Stopping in out-of-the-way places for visits with locals, he wrote about them in the folksy style of a letter to a friend in columns that appeared in two hundred papers and were later collected in a book, *Home Country*. Venturing to England in 1940 to report on the Battle of Britain, he witnessed a fire-bombing raid on London and wrote that it was "the most hateful, most beautiful single scene I have ever known." A book of his experiences, *Ernie Pyle in England*, was published in 1941. A year later he began covering America's involvement in the war, reporting on the Allied operations in North Africa and Sicily.

After observing the attempts to fill the hole in the Messina road, Pyle included in the column he wrote on the subject this glimpse of the Third Division's boss:

> During the night Major General Lucian Truscott, commanding the Third Division, came up to see how the work was coming along. Bridging that hole was his main interest in life that night. He couldn't help any, of course, but somehow he couldn't bear to leave. He stood around

and talked to officers, and the men. After a while he went off a few feet to one side and sat down on the ground and lit a cigarette. A moment later a passing soldier saw the glow and leaned over and said, "Hey, gimme a light, will you?"

The general did, and the soldier never knew he had been ordering the general around.

General Truscott, like many men of great action, has the ability to refresh himself by tiny catnaps of five or ten minutes. So, instead of going back to his command post and going to bed, he stretched out there against some rocks and dozed off. One of the working engineers came past, dragging some air hose. It got tangled up in the general's feet. The tired soldier was annoyed, and he said crossly to the dark, anonymous figure on the ground, "If you're not working, get the hell out of the way." The general got up and moved farther back without saying a word.

From Tunisia, Pyle had written of foot soldiers, "Now to the infantry—the God-damned infantry, as they like to call themselves. I love the infantry because they are the underdogs. They are the mud-rain-frost-and-wind boys. They have no comforts, and they even learn to live without the necessities. And in the end they are the guys that wars can't be won without."

Another observer among men of the Fourth Estate who liked Truscott and frequently dropped in on him to chat and drink his liquor was not a writer but a cartoonist. Born in Mountain Park, New Mexico, in 1921, William Henry Mauldin had a grandfather who was a civilian cavalry scout in the Apache Wars and a father who had served in the artillery in World War I. Discovering that he possessed a talent for drawing cartoons, Mauldin took courses at the Chicago Academy of

Fine Arts and became a friend of another future Truscott journalistic pal, Will Lang of *Life* magazine. Joining the army in 1940, Mauldin had wound up among the men of the Forty-fifth Division and started to draw funny and often bitter cartoons that depicted regular guys who called themselves "dogfaces." When he invented two such creatures named Willie and Joe and they appeared in the army's newspaper *Stars and Stripes*, they were seen by soldiers all over the Mediterranean and European theaters, and by the people at home in newspapers. The pair of gritty, unshaven GIs made Mauldin so famous and popular among the folks at home that in 1943 *Time* did a story about him with Willie on the cover.

Patton was not amused by Mauldin's black humor at the expense of generals and lesser officers. He was offended that a Willie and Joe cartoon made fun of his order that all soldiers must be clean-shaven at all times, even in combat. He ordered Mauldin into his office and threatened to "throw his ass in jail for spreading dissent." When Eisenhower heard of this, he told Patton to leave Mauldin alone, explaining that the cartoons gave soldiers an outlet to vent their frustrations. Mauldin would later tell an interviewer, "I always admired Patton. Oh, sure, the stupid bastard was crazy. He was insane. He thought he was living in the Dark Ages. Soldiers were peasants to him. I didn't like that attitude, but I certainly respected his theories and the techniques he used to get his men out of their foxholes."

A Pyle column written in Italy on January 15, 1944, began, "Sergeant Bill Mauldin appears to us over here to be the finest cartoonist the war has produced. And that's not merely because his cartoons are funny, but because they are also terribly grim and real." The profile continued, saying that the cartoons weren't about training camp that people at home were acquainted with. They were about the men at the front. "His cartoons are about the war," he wrote. "Mauldin's central cartoon character is a soldier, unshaven, unwashed, unsmiling. He looks more like a hobo than like your son. He looks, in fact, exactly like a doughfoot who has been in the lines for two months. And that isn't pretty. Mauldin's cartoons in a way are bitter. His work is so mature that I pictured him as a man approaching middle age. Yet he is only twenty-two, and looks even younger."

This maturity, said Pyle, came from a native understanding of things, and from being a soldier himself for three and a half years.

As with Ernie Pyle, it was Truscott's unpretentious, self-effacing manner that attracted Mauldin and other reporters of the war to the two-star general. A writer for *Time* described him in 1943 as a hell-roaring cavalryman who turned the Third Division into one of the greatest combat outfits in the war. Mauldin had such a high regard for Truscott's sense of humor that when Truscott asked him to add his signature to an oversized autograph book crammed with inscriptions by the war's most famous and important military personalities, Mauldin not only signed it but filled a page with a drawing. Flanked by two generals in what is clearly their headquarters, a grimy, scruffy-faced, and weary GI with a helmet at a rakish angle and rifle slung on a sagging shoulder mutters, "Geez, what a joint!"

Correspondents, generals and other officers, War Department and civilian government officials, and anyone else with a reason to visit Truscott at whatever house his aides located for him when he was not at the front found themselves enjoying meals prepared by his Chinese-American kitchen staff. Entertainment after dinner was often provided by army musicians. On one of these occasions at his command post at San Felice in the Pietravairano area of Italy, three soldiers from the Seventh Infantry band provided music with a violin, accordion, guitar, and a few vocals. One of the tunes they sang amused Truscott so much that he asked them to sing it over and over again. A musical salute to the infantry, it was titled "Dogface Soldier." Written by two GIs before the division sailed from the United States for the invasion of North Africa, but never published, the song was a salute to the men of the Third Division.

Truscott, having been ordered to join in the morale-boosting sing-alongs at Camp Douglas in 1918, had occasionally mused as to why he'd not heard his men singing as their fathers had done in World War I. There were no war songs, no new catchy tunes going the rounds in bivouacs, although British soldiers had taken to singing the melancholy German song "Lili Marlene." While he had no desire to hear American soldiers singing as they tramped along into battle, he felt that good ballads were healthy for morale and the souls of men.

Fascinated by "Dogface Soldier" and aware that steps were being taken to combine regimental bands to form a division band, he had the song performed for the regimental band leaders so that it could be scored for the divisional band. By the time the division moved to Pozzuoli near Naples at the beginning of 1943, the division band was formed and ready to try out the tune for him. When the first effort did not sound quite right, he tried to explain what he was seeking. "They were vastly amused," the raspy-voiced general said, "when I sang the ditty for them and with them, as I did each morning for several days."

The only song known to have been promoted by a U.S. Army major general, it had been written by Corporal Bert Gold and Lieutenant Ken Hart, both of Long Beach, New York. Adopted as the division's marching song, it was known only inside the division until it was featured in the 1955 film *To Hell and Back*, based on the autobiography of the Medal of Honor recipient Audie Murphy, the most decorated American soldier of World War II and a member of the Third Division. Sales of a recording of the song would reach more than 300,000. Its last lines proclaimed:

> *I'm just a dogface soldier*
> *With a rifle on my shoulder*
> *And I eat a Kraut for breakfast every day.*
> *So feed me ammunition,*
> *Keep me in the Third Division,*
> *Your dogfaced soldier boy's okay.*

Truscott was so proud of the song that he included the lyrics and music in his wartime memoir. He also noted that when the Third Division boarded ships for its next operation and he stepped onto the headquarters ship *Biscayne* in the Bay of Naples, with the volcano Vesuvius in the background, the division band struck it up and men of the division bellowed out the words.

"It may not have been in the best tradition from a security point of view," he wrote, "but it was one of the most inspiring things that ever happened to me."

The Third Division's destination on that day was a small seaport that Mark Clark saw as the key to breaking the stalemate in the mountains, opening a path to Rome, and ending the war in the Mediterranean theater.

★ TWELVE ★

SHINGLE

IN THE MUSLIM CITY OF TUNIS on the second Christmas that General Lucian King Truscott, Jr., missed spending with his family since the start of the war, General Eisenhower, the British general Sir Harold Alexander, and Prime Minister Churchill agreed that an early capture of Rome would require landing at least two divisions at a point between the Eternal City and the stubborn German defensive position in the southern mountains known as the Winter Line. To accomplish this, Churchill consented to delay transporting landing craft from Italy to England that would be needed for the upcoming invasion of France. The date for commencement of the operation called Shingle would be January 20, 1944.

Three days after the Tunis conference, members of Truscott's staff joined a VI Corps delegation and the U.S. Army Planning Board at Caserta, Italy, to begin developing details of a landing by the Third Division at Anzio. The purpose of the assault was to weaken the Winter Line by forcing the Germans to withdraw a large force from there to Anzio. As the planners met on December 28, Truscott's Third Division was moving to the region of Pozzuoli, near Naples, to begin training and rehearsals. In the first week of January 1944, Truscott and VI Corps commander John Lucas agreed to advise General Mark Clark that the landing would require two divisions to succeed. Clark replied that because the decisions about the Anzio operation had been made "on the very highest level," making changes was out.

The assault force under Lucas's VI Corps headquarters consisted of the Third Infantry Division; Major General W. R. C. Penney's British First Division; the First, Second, and Third Ranger battalions under Colonel William O. Darby; the Eighty-third Chemical [mortar] Battalion; the 504th Parachute Infantry; and two British Commandos. If necessary, one regimental combat team of the Forty-fifth Infantry Division would join the beachhead forces within about three days, to be followed by the First Armored Division (less one combat command) as rapidly as landing craft could be made available.

An earlier Clark directive had provided for the successive concentration of forces on several objectives, each one to be supported by a mass of artillery and Mediterranean Allied Air Forces. In the first phase, the British X Corps and II Corps were to capture passes west of Highway 6 and south of the Rapido and Garigliano Rivers. The X Corps would relieve elements of the II Corps in that area. The VI Corps was to make harassing attacks to hold the enemy on its front. In the second phase, the II and VI Corps were to clear the Mignano Gap by capturing Mount Lungo and heights east of Highway 6. The X Corps was to assist the II Corps by fire, and continue offensive action along the Garigliano River. The third phase would constitute the main push into the Liri Valley. The II Corps was to attack northwest along Highway 6 and develop the defenses in front of Cassino, after which it would employ additional troops to force a crossing over the Rapido River below Cassino through which the First Armored Division could initiate its drive up the Liri Valley toward Frosinone.

As the attack of the II Corps progressed, the X Corps was to force a crossing over the Garigliano and advance northwest to protect the left flank while the II and VI Corps continued attacks to seize heights north and northwest of Cassino. If boats were available, the landing of Truscott's Third Division would soon follow. If not, it would receive another mission.

Truscott had learned that landing operations depended on complete mutual understanding and wholehearted cooperation between the military and naval forces involved. For this, full-scale rehearsal was the only way in which understanding and cooperation could be put to the acid test. Consequently, he and Lucas insisted that a rehearsal was essential. The practice (code name Webfoot) would be staged at Pozzuoli and Naples, after which the fleet would put out to sea to gain sufficient distance to approach the rehearsal beaches at Salerno in proper formation and in time for the first waves to land. As the Royal Navy commander sailed on the *Biscayne*, Lucas elected to wait on the beach in order to watch the troops come ashore. Truscott sailed on a landing craft designated by the navy to be his headquarters ship.

"It was a rough night for men packed on board the flat-bottomed light craft," he wrote. "Even when we came into the transport area, we could see nothing, and had no means of knowing whether or not the assault waves were disembarking and proceeding toward the beaches in accordance with landing plans. At daybreak we were a dozen miles offshore, and we learned from returning craft that the assault battalion had hit the beaches."

On the beach, he found that the battalions had already gone inland toward their initial objectives, although not without confusion. They'd been disembarked so far at sea that few had landed on their proper beaches, and all had landed late. No artillery tanks or tank destroyers were yet onshore at eight o'clock, although all should have been ashore by daylight with the infantry battalions. Then in fragments came the appalling news that through an error in navigation, the transport area had been many more miles farther from the shore than it should have been. In darkness, the tank landing craft opened their doors, lowered their ramps, and discharged DUKWs (swimming trucks), which carried the artillery into the rough seas, with twenty or more swamped and sunk. Incomplete reports indicated that artillery pieces and communication equipment of two battalions had been dumped into the sea. A few pieces straggled ashore during the latter part of the morning, as did a few tanks and tank destroyers. Beaches were in a chaotic condition, and the entire landing plan was disrupted. Only the infantry battalions were on their initial objectives, and then only because of the energy and experience of the regimental and battalion commanders. Against opposition, the landing would have been a disaster.

Looking for Lucas, Truscott was told he had returned to Caserta after observing the infantry land to inform Clark that the rehearsal was successful. To correct this erroneous account of the practice, Truscott prepared a report recounting all that had gone wrong. He wrote that no battalion landed on time or in proper formation or even on its proper beach. No artillery tanks or tank destroyers reached shore by daylight. He cited the loss of DUKWs with much of the division artillery, lack of control and of training on the naval side, and failure of communications. He concluded that if his division were to land at Anzio as it had during the rehearsal, and if the Germans counterattacked with tanks soon after daylight, the operation would be a disaster. He recommended another rehearsal.

Delivering the report to Lucas in person for Lucas to present to Clark, he discovered that because Lucas had a history of poor relations with Clark, Lucas was unwilling to do so. When Truscott went to Clark, he found that the commander of the Fifth Army already had a copy of the report. "Well, Lucian," Clark said, "it's bad. But you won't get another rehearsal. The date has been set at the very highest level. There is no possibility of delaying it even for a day. You have got to do it."

As in the fight with Patton on the way to Messina, Truscott objected, though he was not unwilling. Like then, he simply wanted a little more time. If a delay of one or two days to get in a second practice meant the difference between success and failure, he reasoned, the high authorities would certainly grant it if the request were presented to them.

Clark said this was not so. He asserted that Churchill himself had stated at the Tunis conference that experienced troops did not need a rehearsal. The plan called for the operation to go on without it. There had been trouble enough arranging one. Any further delay would be flatly refused. As for the lost artillery and equipment, Clark would replace it from other divisions if necessary. Truscott was to let him know the full extent of the losses as soon as possible.

With a second practice vetoed, the plan for ships of Operation Anvil to sail on the chosen date stood. Recourse to Eisenhower was impossible. To take charge of the planning for Overlord, Ike had been shifted to London and replaced as commander in chief of the Mediterranean theater by General Sir Henry Maitland Wilson, with U.S. Lieutenant General Jacob L. Devers as his deputy. Neither possessed the stature that Eisenhower had earned to argue with Churchill and come out the winner.

Because Truscott expected to encounter strong opposition on the beaches and the Germans to counterattack with armor within a few hours after landing, his plan emphasized establishing a beachhead force to repel attacks even as the division advanced to establish itself farther inland. A regimental combat team of the Forty-fifth Infantry Division was to follow in about three days. This force was to be followed if the situation required it by one combat command of the First Armored Division and the remainder of the Forty-fifth as rapidly as the transportation permitted.

Concluding that the poor performance during the rehearsal had put the Royal Navy on its mettle, he noted that immediately upon arrival in the transport area, landing craft were lowered away on schedule and headed for beaches already marked by naval scouts, exactly as planned. On schedule, navy rocket craft launched a short but effective barrage on the beaches where the battalions were to land. "After the almost disastrous performance during the rehearsal," he wrote, "our navy comrades gave us one which was almost unbelievably smooth and accurate."

As described by Truscott in his account of his third amphibious assault of the war, Anzio and the nearby town of Nettuno were small ports about thirty miles south of Rome that were said to have been favored by Roman emperors. A good road and railroad led practically due north along a ridge through Aprilia and Campoleone to Albano eighteen miles inland on the slopes of Colli Laziali (the Alban Hills), where the road joined a coastal road (Highway 7) from the south to Rome. Another road followed the coast northwest to Ostia and along the south bank of the Tiber River to Rome. North of Anzio, adjacent to the Albano Road, the country was broken by numerous deep ravines. A few miles inland, the area was covered with dense pine woods that had been planted in a reforestation project promoted by Mussolini. About eight miles north of Anzio, ravines led westward from the Albano Road and into the Moletta River. This flowed westward to the sea and marked the corps beachhead line in the sector of the British First Division. Five miles east of Nettuno, a creek known as the Asturia River drained from southern slopes of Colli Laziali to the sea. There were patches of woods along it near the coast, but for the most part the whole area to the north and east of Nettuno was farmland that had been reclaimed from the Pontine Marshes in another of Il Duce's reclamation projects. A main drainage canal began near Padiglione about six miles north of Nettuno and cut west between high dikes across drainage lines to a point near the village of Sessano, where it joined an eastern tributary to flow southward to the sea nine miles east of Nettuno. Called the Mussolini Canal, it and its western tributary marked the VI Corps beachhead line in the sector of the Third Infantry Division, with the boundary between divisions lying east of the Albano Road.

The area of reclaimed marshland was passable in dry weather, but the water was usually within two feet of the surface. When rains fell or the pumps stopped working, the area became so marshy that movement off roads was almost impossible. One road followed the coast eastward from Nettuno through Littoria and joined Highway 7 farther on down the coast. Still another road led northeast from Nettuno through Cisterna and Cori to Artena and Valmontone on Highway 6, the main road from Cassino to Rome. The beachhead area was roughly seven miles in depth and fifteen miles in width at its broadest part.

Leaving Naples in the early morning hours of January 21, the invasion armada set a devious course designed to avoid mines and deceive the Germans as to its destination. As the fleet got under way, Truscott knew that the British X Corps had succeeded in crossing the lower Carigliano River and was making good progress. The X Corps had launched its attack across the Rapido River the previous day, but he knew little of its progress beyond the fact that no bridges were crossed during the first day.

"We spent a quiet day in a calm sea in balmy weather," he wrote, "but I think few among the commanders and staffs of the VI Corps, Third Division and the Royal Navy crowding the *Biscayne* were in any frame of mind to enjoy the beauties of a Mediterranean cruise."

During the evening, he wrote to Sarah, knowing that she would hear about the invasion on the radio and read of it in newspapers long before she got the letter. In the two years since he'd last seen her, he'd risen from colonel to major general, planned and taken part in three historic invasions, witnessed seemingly numberless skirmishes and full-scale battles, and counted hundreds of young men wounded and killed in action. For his efforts with the Western Task Force the U.S. Army had awarded him the Distinguished Service Medal (DSM) on December 15, 1942. For his success in working with the British high command in developing a plan for Anglo-American combined operations, including the groundwork for Torch, and creating the Rangers, he'd received the Legion of Merit in August of 1943. In gratitude for the capture of Agrigento that had opened the way to taking Palermo and Messina, George Patton had recommended a second DSM. Given command of the proud and illustrious Third Infantry Division, he'd found himself standing shoulder-to-shoulder and at times toe-to-toe with brilliant and inspiring generals of two nations that history had allied in a noble cause to wage the greatest war of all time on two continents.

As a general and before that as an instructor in army schools he'd learned that no greater mistake could be made in military leadership than clinging to outmoded concepts, methods, and equipment. To a high degree the measure of success in battle leadership was the ability to profit by the lessons of battle experience. In London, he learned much from British associates, especially in the preparation of staff papers and the technique of planning. Somewhat to his surprise, he found British staff papers were far more thorough and much better expressed than corresponding American papers.

British planning techniques through the phases of initial concept, appreciation, outline plan, and detailed planning was more specialized and involved far more conference and committee work than he was accustomed to. Their method was also far more thorough and secure than any he had known. A knowledge of British planning, organization, staff procedures, and tactical methods, and knowledge of British personalities, had been invaluable.

While serving in the cavalry, Truscott had been imbued with the value of speed in operations. As a teacher in army schools, he urged that the infantry should equal the endurance standards of Roman legions or Stonewall Jackson's foot cavalry in the Civil War, only to find that those charged with the development of infantry doctrines clung to the low standard of marching two and a half miles an hour and twelve miles a day. Experience with British Commando training in England had confirmed his opinions and had led him to believe that speed marching was practicable with modern American soldiers. Dieppe taught him about the fear and uncertainty of battle and how plans can go astray. He'd also seen that while Dieppe was rated as a costly failure, it proved the practicability and feasibility of the amphibious invasions.

In the Goalpost operation, plans were too optimistic with respect to the time required to accomplish the mission. Three days had been required to achieve what the plan anticipated would take one. Time and time again he'd observed a tendency on the part of commanders and comrades to display sympathy and pity in battles, when he saw that sentimentality deflected men from doing their duty. To give way to weariness gave the enemy the advantage. To allow able bodied men to stop to take care of wounded or sick comrades, rather than waiting until the battle was won, was a mistake. As staff officer for Eisenhower he'd learned the function of command. In his close association with the operations that brought American soldiers into collision with Germans for the first time, he saw Americans learn the art of fighting that the warriors of the Third Division would now bring to a gamble called Shingle.

★ THIRTEEN ★

ANZIO

ARRIVING IN ANZIO WITH MEMBERS of his staff at six in the morning on January 22, Truscott found its roads clogged with armor and other vehicles. The most serious threat to the landings had been an air raid against the beach that caused no damage. More than two hundred Germans had been captured while they were still in their beds. Information regarding what was happening with the Rangers, the First Division, and the British was slow in coming. After inspecting conditions on the beach, he went to the command post his staff had set up in some woods and was met by his orderly. A breakfast of bacon and four eggs out of three dozen that Private Hong had managed to purloin from the navy was prepared over a campfire to be served on a field mess tray, laid out on the hood of a jeep and eaten standing up. After Generals Clark and Lucas and several other officers eagerly accepted Truscott's invitation to partake of the same breakfast, Hong complained in a whisper, "General's fresh eggs gone to hell."

Informed that Major Robert Crandall's mobile cavalry detachments had seized crossings of the Mussolini Canal and advance detachments of the Thirtieth Division had taken other crossings, Truscott warned Crandall to be watchful against a German attack during the night. Truscott wouldn't see him again for more than a year.

That night, detachments from the Hermann Göring Panzer Division drove the cavalry detachment from a bridge west of Sessano and the advance detachments of the Thirtieth Division from the crossings they held. Arriving to inspect his bridge guard, Crandall ran into the German battalion and was captured. The Germans reached La Ferriere and destroyed the bridge just as the leading battalion of the Thirtieth reached the spot early the second morning. Later that day, they drove the Germans back across the canal with considerable losses. By nightfall they had established the beachhead line. On January 24 the First Division reached the Moletta River and the Third, with three Ranger battalions and the 509th Parachute Regiment, which had been held in reserve, extended the beachhead line from the mouth of the Mussolini Canal to the first of the overpasses on the Albano Road. This created a front of twenty miles. Brigade groups of the British First Division held a front of more than seven. Artillery, ammunition, and supplies were still pouring ashore.

Truscott recorded, "We knew that there had been a German division south of Rome and at least one other in easy reach behind the southern front. And we knew that the Corps attempt to cross the Rapido had ended in failure. Under such conditions, any reckless drive to seize the Colli Laziali with means available in the beachhead could only have ended in disaster and might have resulted in destruction of the force."

Anxious that road centers at Cisterna and Campoleone be held in preparation for a further advance from the beachhead, or for defense if an advance were impossible, Lucas ordered thrusts toward the towns. In Truscott's sector, an attack by two battalions on January 25 made little progress. The following day, two battalions with support by tanks and division artillery began two days of heavy fighting against fierce resistance and made some progress, but both were still three miles from Cisterna. Convinced that it could be taken if all of the Third Division were employed, Truscott and his staffers worked out plans for an attack. He proposed that the 179th Regimental Combat Team and elements of the First Division be used to release his division for an all-out assault, after which the Third Division could take over defense while the First Division seized the town of Campoleone. Lucas said that he was not yet ready. He preferred to await the arrival of the combat command of the First Armored Division, which was expected to land on the beachhead within the next day or so.

During an air raid on the afternoon of January 24, bomb fragments exploded close to Truscott's foot. If he had not been wearing the cavalry boots he invariably donned for battle, the wound would have been more serious. A surgeon had to cut out several fragments and wrap the leg in an adhesive cast. Added to a case of laryngitis that had been plaguing him since the rehearsal for the landings, reducing an already raspy voice to little more than a whisper, the wound left him feeling frustrated and impatient. The injury entitled him to a Purple Heart.

On January 27, General Lucas, motivated by Mark Clark's impatience to launch the postponed attack from the beachhead, called a conference to discuss the plan. The Third Division, with Colonel William O. Darby's Ranger battalions and the parachute regiment, would capture Cisterna, cut Highway 7, and be prepared to continue the advance toward Velletri. Elements of the Forty-fifth Infantry Division and the engineers were to relieve portions of the First and Third Divisions on the flanks of the beachhead so that both would have maximum strength for an attack on January 29. On that date, intelligence reports put the Hermann Göring Panzer Division, which faced the Third Infantry Division, in a position that extended over a wide front that it held with strong points supported by mobile armored detachments.

Truscott and Darby believed that the First and Third Ranger battalions could infiltrate between them under cover of darkness and enter
Cisterna. Trained and with a rich experience in such tactics, they were
also experts in street fighting and could be expected to create confusion
in the German lines. Meanwhile, the First Infantry and the Fourth Ranger
Battalion would attack an hour later to break through the defenses and
support the other Rangers.

On January 29, Lucas again chose to delay the action for a day to
permit two of the units to complete preparations. When it began on
January 30 with Rangers leading the way as planned, the Panzer Grenadier Division had arrived at Cisterna unnoticed by Allied intelligence to
relieve the Hermann Göring Division. This resulted in the attack facing
not one division extended over a broad front but two in positions to
present a formidable defense against unsuspecting Rangers. German
strength had reached seventy thousand.

The result was that as the Rangers' infiltration mission began they
faced roughly three to four times the forecast German strength and an
enemy that was not aligned in defense, but able to launch a massive
counterattack. To support it they had thirty-two 15-centimeter guns,
forty-two 10.5-centimeter guns, three 10-centimeter guns, and thirty-one
2-centimeter antiaircraft guns. Placed around the approaches to Cisterna
were rifle pits dug at ten-yard intervals and machine-gun nests every
hundred yards capable of interlocking fields of fire at a height of a foot.

Having gone less than half a mile along the Cisterna road, the leading company of the Fourth Ranger Battalion responded to German
machine-gun fire with an attack at close quarters with grenades and
bayonets. They knocked out two machine-gun nests, but others continued firing. After two ferocious assaults that failed to penetrate the line,
Lieutenant George Nunnelly and most of his company were killed,
while the remainder were forced to scramble into a shallow ditch.

When Colonel Roy Murray led an assault by two companies on the right flank, it was stopped by a system of direct and cross fire. Two more company commanders were killed and numerous men were badly wounded. About two miles from Cisterna, the battalions lost contact with one another. When a German infantry attack formed in the south near the Third Battalion's Company B and maneuvered against the Rangers on the north, the action blocked the Rangers from withdrawing and any chance of linking up with the Fourth Battalion. In an effort to assist the First and Third, Darby ordered two half-tracks and two tank destroyers to rush to the area. As the First and Third Battalions fought for their lives and the Fourth Battalion attempted to batter forward, contact between them became either intermittent or impossible.

The desperate nature of the battle was revealed in a telephone conversation that was picked up at Third Division headquarters: "The machine-gun fire is terrific from both flanks. The shells are landing all over the place. [They] look like 170s. Fourth Battalion is the boy that is in the jam."

Darby recorded, "When the sun came up, the two Ranger battalions at Cisterna were surrounded. Between sunrise and 0700, when radio silence was broken, we came to the realization that the battle was lost. All around Cisterna the Germans, who had shown no sign of strength twenty-four hours before, had moved in large numbers of soldiers. Their artillery sent its blistering fire into our attackers. The Germans had reinforced their lines on the exact day the Allies had selected for attack."

By field telephone, Darby informed General Michael O'Daniel at Third Division headquarters that the First and Third Ranger battalions had been destroyed. In two days of fighting at Cisterna, the Fourth Battalion had thirty killed and fifty-eight wounded. The First and Third had twelve killed and thirty-six wounded. The greatest toll was in the number of Rangers taken prisoner. Unable to fight on because they had run out of ammunition or found themselves outnumbered and overrun, some disassembled or buried their weapons. Many continued to fight as they fled, only to be caught while they attempted to find cover. Of 767

Rangers who infiltrated Cisterna, only 6 made their way back to friendly lines.

"It was a sad blow to all of us, and particularly to Colonel Darby and me," wrote Truscott in *Command Missions*. "He had organized the First Ranger Battalion under my direction in North Ireland, and had fought with them in North Africa, Tunisia, Sicily and southern Italy." Depicting relaying Darby's report on the annihilation of the two battalions of Rangers by phone to General Mark Clark as resulting in "quite a flap," he went on to describe a face-to-face confrontation the next morning in which he said that Clark implied that the Rangers should not have been sent on the mission because they were not suitable for it. Truscott wrote, "I reminded him that I had been responsible for organizing the original Ranger battalion and that Colonel Darby and I perhaps understood their capabilities better than other American officers. He said no more. However, General Clark feared unfavorable publicity, for he ordered an investigation to fix the responsibility. This was wholly unnecessary, for the responsibility was entirely my own, since both Colonel Darby and I considered the mission a proper one, which should have been well within the capabilities of these fine soldiers. That ended the matter."

Although Clark expressed distress in his diary that the attack began with the Ranger force going to Cisterna, calling the decision an error in judgment because the Rangers did not have support weapons to overcome the resistance indicated, he voiced no reservations when he approved Lucas's plan for the operation. How strongly Clark felt that Lucas had been at fault for the continuing disaster that Anzio had become was revealed two weeks after the obliteration of the Rangers as a fighting force. Shortly after midnight on February 16, Truscott was awakened by Colonel Don Carleton and shown a message from Clark that read:

ORDERS ISSUED THIS DATE AS FOLLOWS X MAJOR GENERAL TRUSCOTT RELIEVED FROM COMMAND OF

THIRD DIVISION AND ASSIGNED AS DEPUTY COM-
MANDER SIXTH CORPS X BRIGADIER GENERAL O'DANIELS
TO COMMAND THIRD DIVISION X COLONEL DARBY
TRANSFERRED FROM RANGER FORCE TO THIRD DIVI-
SION X ALL ASSIGNMENTS TO TAKE EFFECT SEVEN-
TEEN FEBRUARY X I DESIRE THAT COLONEL SHERMAN
BE DESIGNATED AS ACTING ASSISTANT DIVISION COM-
MANDER AND THAT DARBY BE PLACED IN COMMAND OF
SHERMAN'S REGIMENT X ACKNOWLEDGE

The message left Truscott stunned, not only because he was losing command of the Third Division but out of sympathy for Lucas. A friend who sought and received Truscott's advice and recommendations, he in turn treated Truscott with the utmost consideration. Keenly aware that their methods of command were different, Truscott also recognized that Lucas lacked qualities of leadership that engendered confidence, and that he leaned heavily upon his staff and trusted subordinates in diffi-cult decisions. It was no secret that he had little confidence in the British troops of his command, and that his British commanders had even less in him.

Suspecting that he was being used to pull someone else's chestnuts from the fire, Truscott had no desire to leave the division that for nearly a year had been under his command and forged an illustrious record. But he had no doubt that the order had been issued after all factors had been thoughtfully weighed. There was a job to be done, and he was a soldier.

At a meeting on the topic of Clark's desire for a breakout from the beachhead, Clark wanted to know how soon a counterattack could be organized. Truscott thought one could be launched the following morn-ing. According to Truscott, Clark pointed to a salient on a map created by the German push. In a tone of voice Truscott described as somewhat pontifical and reminiscent of an instructor at a service school, Clark said, "You should hold the shoulders [of the salient] firmly, and counter-attack the flanks."

Lucas had opposed a counterattack out of reluctance to commit reserves. Now that General Clark favored the movement, he reluctantly agreed. While preparations were under way, Clark asked Truscott to accompany him to another command post. On the way, he stated that Truscott would probably replace Lucas within the next four or five days. Truscott repeated that he had no desire whatever to leave the Third Infantry Division, but said that he recognized that the British had lost all confidence in Lucas. Clark then said he wanted to relieve the commanding officer of the 179th Infantry and needed someone to replace him. He declared that his choice was Colonel Darby.

During another conference on February 22, held at Clark's headquarters in the Villa Borghese's wine cellars, which served as an air raid shelter, Clark told Truscott that he was to relieve Lucas the following morning. Truscott again stated that he had no desire to do so and argued that no change should be made in command because it might have an unfortunate effect on morale and undermine confidence among other officers. He pointed out that Lucas had a host of friends and was popular among American officers. There was a grave danger that some might feel he was being sacrificed to British influence. Others might come to think that whenever they got into difficulty they, too, would be thrown to the wolves.

Clark said the decision had already been made. Johnny Lucas was also a friend of his, he said, and he would see to it that Lucas was not hurt. He intended to designate him as Deputy Fifth Army Commander for the time being. Although Clark did not say that the removal of Lucas had been approved by General Marshall, Truscott deduced that it had been. This meant that that there was nothing for Truscott to do but return to his quarters and break the news to his staff that he was leaving the Third Division.

Later, when General Lucas had returned from seeing Clark, Truscott went to express his regrets. "While Lucas was deeply hurt," he wrote, "he had no ill feeling toward me, and our friendship was unbroken up to the time of his death. But he was bitter toward General Clark and blamed his relief upon British influence. It was one of my saddest experiences of the war."

Returning to his quarters at Anzio, Truscott met with his staff for a review of the problems he had inherited. "The beachhead," he wrote, "had come close to disaster. Unnecessarily so, since we had demonstrated that we had sufficient means to stop the German offensive much earlier had we adequately organized, properly coordinated, and effectively employed our resources. Consequently our narrow escape caused a general lack of confidence, especially on the British side, but also within Corps Headquarters, and in numerous rear echelon service detachments and installations where discipline was never so firm as among combat troops, and where men were frequently exposed to exaggerated rumors."

With the shattered First, Third, and Fourth Ranger battalions officially removed from the order of battle, the few survivors were ordered to return to the United States for a period of recuperation before becoming instructors in Ranger training methods and battle tactics. On March 26, 1944, Truscott wrote to Darby's replacement, Lieutenant Colonel Roy Murray, "As you know, I have always taken a great personal interest in the Ranger Force, from the days when I was associated with organizing the First Ranger Battalion, and while it trained at Achnacarry, through the spectacular operations of the Tunisian and Sicilian campaigns, and finally to the magnificent part it played in this beachhead operation. I do feel, however, that the wisest step has been taken in returning these seasoned men to the United States, where the benefit of their great experience may be given to others and where they can form the fighting nucleus of a reborn Ranger Force."

Three weeks later, recognizing that Darby was a heroic figure and that his years of experience as the leader of the Rangers made him an asset that the army should not continue to put at risk in further combat,

Truscott urged Clark to direct that Darby be sent home. In a farewell meeting, both Truscott and Darby believed that they would not see one another again for the duration of the war. A confluence of events during the next year would prove them wrong and reunite them tragically in the mountains and lake country of northern Italy.

Comparing career army officers to old garments that become more comfortable with increased wear, Truscott chose to bring his Third Division staff to his new job. Discovering that Lucas had placed his headquarters safely within caves, he chose to make no attempt to remove the staff offices from their underground lairs. He set up his offices in a small wineshop over the entrance to the caverns. The space provided a war room, where the staff posted maps, orders, and other pertinent data. On the wall behind his desk, an enlargement of a Bill Mauldin cartoon was displayed. It showed Willie and Joe resting in water-filled foxholes at Anzio and looking at headlines in an issue of *Stars and Stripes* that heralded the impending cross-channel invasion as the major battle front in Europe. The caption was to the effect that Willie believed that to him the most important spot in the war on the continent was his own foxhole simply because he was in it.

The first conference of his new post, with all the chiefs of the general and special staff sections, was called late in the afternoon of his first day of command. Truscott asked each for a report on activities in their sectors. Finding only two or three of them fully informed, he told them that he would expect full and accurate reports at eight o'clock the following morning and every day thereafter. Many of the briefings were held with shells crashing in the square outside and the rumble of bombs bursting along the nearby waterfront, accompanied by busts of anti-aircraft fire. One shell from a huge German cannon, located miles away and called by the troops the Anzio Express, crashed through several adjoining buildings and buried itself almost directly under Carleton's desk. Fortunately it was a dud.

Not more than a hundred yards or so from the war room on a narrow street, a house with two small apartments, each with a living room, kitchen, and two or three bedrooms, was taken over and named the Villa. It became home to Truscott, Carleton, and two other aides. It also was the "Canton Restaurant" of the kitchen staff of Hong and Dare and chef Lee. Not long after they opened for business, Lee was standing in a small garden just outside the kitchen door. In his hands was a cloth doll dressed in women's clothes that he had bought as a souvenir in a shop in town. Talking with Hong, Lee was making the doll salute when a shell exploded in an adjoining lot. A jagged, razor-edged fragment whizzed through the air and severed the head from the doll. Untouched by the blast, Lee returned to his kitchen and never again ventured into the garden.

The mass of shipping offshore and the congestion of troops, vehicles, and supplies on the beachhead were ideal targets for the Anzio Express and less formidable German guns, with the Luftwaffe joining in the effort. Because Allied air bases were more than one hundred miles away, the beachhead had no fighter protection during the first and last hours of the day, nor in bad weather that kept Allied planes grounded. On the day of the landing, two attacks had sunk a cruiser and a Liberty cargo ship, damaged a few landing craft, and wreaked other damage. In a major German offensive that coincided with the week that Truscott served as deputy to Lucas, there were at least ninety separate attacks, including one that involved two hundred aircraft. These raids were the heaviest Truscott had known in the war. To add to these troubles, he noted, about the time he took over the corps, the Germans had established a ground station north of the beachhead with radar jammers that almost eliminated the early-warning system and reduced the effectiveness of antiaircraft artillery.

When the Germans began employing self-propelled 88mm guns that could reach any part of the beachhead from positions near the front lines, Truscott summoned his artillery chief and inquired, "How many guns do you actually control? How many in the beachhead?"

He was assured that including tanks and tank destroyers being used as artillery, the number was well over a thousand. Truscott replied, "It seems to me that a competent artillery staff, by studying the road nets and the terrain on maps, aerial photographs and the like, and by actual observation, should be able to select positions from which these self-propelled guns would be likely to fire."

When the artillery general and staff agreed that this should be practicable, Truscott asked why a gun should not be targeted against each location, loaded and ready to fire with a gunner standing by with lanyard in hand. At the first shot in any sector, every nearby gunner would pull lanyards, reload, and fire again. By that time the remainder of the gun crew should join him and the fire direction center should soon be able to assume control. "We would waste a few rounds," he said, "but it should discourage the German gunners if shells begin to land in their neighborhood before they get off their second round. Besides, we might hit something."

The artillery general said, "Well, General, that is not the way we do it in the Artillery. Now at the Artillery School—"

Truscott cut him off. "General, I heard that spiel the first time about twenty years ago. I don't give a damn what the Artillery School teaches. I want this problem solved and I want it solved right now. I have suggested a possible solution. You have until dark tonight to find a better one."

Within the next few nights, Truscott recorded, they had discouraged the German use of self-propelled guns. On February 27, he reported to Clark that he believed the attack would come from divergent directions to disperse the effect of artillery effort. Clark replied that he had personally informed General Alexander of the situation. They had alerted the British Fifth Division to prepare to be sent to the beachhead to take over the equipment of the Fifty-sixth Division. The first Brigade Group would depart Naples on the fourth of March and the Thirty-fourth

Infantry Division would also be sent. He suggested that Truscott thin out his eastern flank to strengthen the Fifty-sixth Division front. Truscott replied:

> I believe the next attack will develop from two principal directions in order to cause dispersion of our artillery effort. In addition, I expect relatively strong diversionary attacks against both the Fifteenth Infantry and Special Service Force sectors. I am holding two battalions Thirtieth Infantry in Corps reserve now. I believe that any further weakening of east part of Third Division and Special Service Force Sectors would be hazardous at this time.

As he was about to leave his command post around half past six that evening, he was told that radio intercepts showed the German command had set the morning of February 29 to begin the assault. Although this intelligence was not conclusive proof of German intentions, it warranted positive action. Truscott alerted the command to expect the German offensive to fall on the front of the Third Division west of Cisterna in an effort to break through the corps beachhead line near Campomorto. "We had, of course, studied the terrain on every part of the front," he wrote, "and we had selected the areas in which troops would assemble preparatory to attack, in which reserves might be expected to wait; and we had plotted location of gun positions, command posts, tank concentrations, supply dumps and the like."

Deciding to surprise the enemy before the assault began, he called in the artillery commander and directed him to prepare to have every gun in the beachhead pound German troop assembly areas, reserve positions, artillery locations, and tank concentrations for a full hour before they could begin their attack. It was possible, he thought, that this barrage might completely disrupt the German strategy. The countermeasure was to begin at 0430.

After a very late supper, he went to bed. Near dawn, he was awakened by the roar of guns battering German lines. After an hour, there was a lull. He wondered if the attack would come, or whether he had wasted a vast amount of artillery. Gradually, the guns began to fire again, almost sporadically, as first one battalion and then another responded to calls for fire, which gradually increased in intensity. When smoke shrouded the beachhead like a thick fog, he knew the German attack was on. During the usual staff conference at half past eight, enough information had sifted back that he could report to Clark that he anticipated an attack that morning and that the Germans probably hoped to draw their reserves eastward to facilitate a main attack down the Anzio Road.

Describing the unfolding battle in *Command Missions*, he wrote, "Our arrival on the Third Division front was timed beautifully with an Allied air mission over Cisterna as a hundred or more medium bombers soared over the town and released bombs which fell fair and square on the target and shrouded the whole place in a cloud of dust and smoke."

The thrill of watching the air power in action was marred by seeing one B-26 fall in flames from a direct hit by German antiaircraft. Seeing the loss of this aircraft and a half dozen men had a saddening effect upon all who witnessed it, Truscott observed, which was surprising, since everyone knew the Allies had already lost many hundreds in the ground fighting since the Anzio landings. The counterattack by the Third Division reestablished the front of the 509th Parachute Battalion the following morning. Heavy attacks by German tanks and infantry were beaten off on the front of the Seventh Infantry near Ponto Rotto and on the front south of Cisterna. Lighter thrusts were put down by the First Special Service Force and Fifty-sixth Division. Half the German tanks employed in the action were destroyed and more than a thousand prisoners reported numerous casualties had been inflicted on the Germans by the devastating effect of artillery. By nightfall of the second day, Truscott knew the battle was won. On March 2, Clark paid his first visit since Truscott had assumed command. He pledged that the British Fifth Division would soon arrive to relieve the Fifty-sixth Division, and that plans were afoot to renew the assault on the stubborn front at Cassino.

Before the U.S. Army landed at Salerno and became stuck about halfway between the toe of the Italian boot and Rome, requiring the Anzio invasion, only venturesome tourists who could afford to explore Italian byways, and Roman Catholics familiar with stories of saints who founded orders of monks, had ever heard of the small town called Cassino and of its mountain with a historic and venerated Benedictine monastery. Yet, in the autumn of 1943 and in the first months of 1944, the town was becoming as well known to Americans as Rome and Monte Cassino was as familiar as the active volcano Vesuvius. Founded by Saint Benedict of Nursia in AD 529 on the former site of the temple of Apollo, and looming above the town at seventeen hundred feet, the abbey had been destroyed by the Lombards in 580, rebuilt in 720, destroyed in 883 by Saracens, restored in mid-900, damaged by an earthquake in 1349, and rebuilt again in 1600, only to be sacked by French troops who invaded the Kingdom of Naples. Restored to the state in which it was taken over by the German army, it was a bastion to prevent the Allies from sweeping out of the mountains north of Salerno and up to Rome. Repeated attempts to break the roadblock had been stymied, not only because the Abbey of Monte Cassino proved to be as impregnable as a fortress, but because the Allies were reluctant to attack it and probably destroy an architectural and religious icon.

An attempt to scale the mountain by the New Zealand Corps and capture the heights above Cassino after four days of heavy fighting had recently failed. Plans for a renewed effort had been delayed by weather and the German offensive at Anzio. It was now decided, said Clark, to initiate a new assault. The exact date would depend on several consecutive days of clear weather to ensure proper ground conditions for the use of armor as well as for maximum air and artillery support. Clark wanted to know Truscott's views as to his force's capabilities for an attack from the beachhead in conjunction with the Cassino offensive.

Truscott reminded Clark they had just stopped the latest German assault with no loss of ground, and that he was confident they could hold the beachhead. Since the Germans had failed to destroy his command in two large assaults by five or six divisions, he thought they were unlikely to renew the effort with less. While he could not dismiss the possibility of another all-out attack if the Germans could find the necessary troops, he thought it more likely they would seek to contain the beachhead and take the opportunity to improve their own position. Asserting that Clark could expect German divisions to be withdrawn from the front for reorganization, he added that the Germans were likely to hold sufficient reserves within reach to foil any American breakout. By regrouping the beachhead forces, and with the arrival of the Fifth Division, he should be able to launch a limited-objective attack, if he were guaranteed adequate air support.

Clark agreed. Truscott was to plan such an operation for the earliest practicable date. If the move could precede the Cassino attack, it might force the Germans to keep its Anzio forces in place. Should the offensive follow a successful onslaught at Cassino, it might even achieve a breakout. The offensive was named Operation Panther.

The plan envisioned a converging attack in two phases. The First Division, assisted by the Fifth Division, would attack northward along the Albano Road while the Forty-fifth Infantry Division and First Armored Division would sweep northwest. The engagement would be supported by the Allied Air Forces and all the artillery that could be brought to bear. When Clark visited Truscott on March 9, he approved the plan and explained details of a Cassino attack to take place the following day. Bombers of the Allied Air Forces would blast the town of Cassino and hundreds of fighter bombers were to support the infantry. There would be the most impressive concentration of artillery yet employed on the southern front. Optimistic that the attack would succeed in opening a drive up the Liri Valley toward Rome, Clark thought Truscott's attempt to reduce the Carroceo salient might develop into a breakout.

Back at his headquarters that evening, Clark informed Truscott that the Cassino attack had to be postponed by one day because of poor weather. Truscott replied that his planning depended on continuous air support. He advised Clark that he was sending his assistant to present his views on the requirements.

Clark replied, "Weather permitting, all-out air effort will be given your front on March 14. However, it should be understood by you that Cassino attack has top priority and must take place as soon as weather permits. This means that if weather prediction indicates favorable weather for Cassino attack on following day air effort will support Cassino attack even though your attack still in progress. Moreover, bulk of air will probably be needed for Cassino attack for two days after Cassino D-day."

Truscott noted, "We had never entertained any thought of undertaking this venture without adequate air support. Under the conditions indicated in Clark's message, we might begin the attack and then find all the air support diverted to the Cassino front. The next morning I sent off a protest and late that afternoon I had a message from Butler saying the tentative date for the Cassino operation was now March 14 and that our attack in the beachhead was postponed to March 15 at the earliest."

On the night of March 14, Major General W. R. C. Penney began a limited-objective attack to seize a line of departure for the main attack later. The effort was unsuccessful and almost three full companies of infantry were lost. Penney was greatly depressed and doubted that his division would be able to carry out the mission assigned to it in the Panther plan. After examining the situation, Truscott realized that the original mission was not within the capabilities of the First Division. Accordingly, he modified the plan to place the main burden of the attack on the Forty-fifth Infantry Division and First Armored Division, less one combat command. He advised Clark of the changes. As the Cassino attack got under way on March 15, a radio message from Clark late that night said that progress was generally satisfactory, but it was slower than anticipated because tanks had been blocked by debris left from the bombing. He told Truscott that the earliest date for Truscott's attack would be March 19.

Confident his forces were ready and that the entire command looked forward to the attack, Truscott sent Clark a message saying it was essential that the troops be notified that close-in air missions would be flown during the following day. Soon after this message, he learned that instead of missions by fifty-six bombers, only nineteen had been authorized, and that they were not against targets he'd requested. Nor could he count on continued air support after D-day. Believing that without adequate air support losses would be heavy, he decided the attack was not worth the cost. A message to Clark recommending cancellation of the attack was answered with approval.

Truscott ruefully wrote of his keen disappointment that this meant the end of Operation Panther. He added optimistically, "While we had not reduced the salient, I think that our men in preparing Panther had been well spent. We had eliminated a defeatist attitude and had imbued the command with an offensive spirit which was never lost. Our labors had developed our planning methods and had created a spirit of mutual understanding and confidence within the command that was thenceforth to mark all command and staff relations."

Visiting Truscott again on March 19, Clark said that the Cassino attack had made very slow progress and had just about spent its force. General Alexander had decided to employ the bulk of the Eighth Army as well as the Fifth Army west of the Apennines. The Eighth Army was to take over the Cassino front while the Fifth Army was to be assigned the sector generally between the Liri River and the coast. A major assault was contemplated for about the middle of April. Meanwhile, the beachhead would regroup, reorganize, rest, and train in preparation for renewing the assault in connection with a major attack on the southern front.

Musing on the use of air power at Anzio in *Command Missions*, Truscott wrote, "One would think that after a year and a half of active operations, we should have solved the problem of air support for ground operations, but we had not. Air support was—and continued to be—the weak point in all beachhead operations. It was not until I joined the Corps and complained about the lack of liaison that an air officer was assigned to work with the beachhead staff—a month after the landing. Air support was the subject of many stormy conferences among representatives of Brigadier General Gordon Saville's Twelfth Tactical Air Command Staff, and ourselves. It is true that air attacks had inflicted heavy losses upon the enemy in both personnel and materiel during the trying days of the beachhead, but this air support had never been closely coordinated with the operations of the ground forces, and consequently had lost much of its effectiveness."

Explaining that ground and air commanders had different ideas as to what constituted air support for ground forces, he wrote, "The Air Force concept was that aside from aerial reconnaissance, aircraft should support ground forces by attacking objectives beyond the battle area—bridges, trains, convoys, troop concentrations, supply dumps, and the like. 'Isolation of the battlefield' they called it, and they had made valiant efforts to isolate the battlefield in preparation for Operation Shingle. They wished to designate a bomb support line (BSL) beyond the reach of beachhead weapons where the aircraft would be free to attack any target they might elect. They disliked attacking any objective close to our own front lines or within the bomb support line. Such missions the Air Force accepted only with great reluctance, insisting that pilots be carefully briefed upon each one which the Tactical Air Command would accept. Our concept did not deny that the effort expended in isolation of the battlefield was of value."

Exacerbating this clash of concepts was a disturbing pattern of the air force strafing and bombing Americans. Commanders irately announced that they preferred to attack with no air support rather than risk being shot by their own planes. When Saville told Truscott that he had received disagreeable messages from Clark concerning these incidents, including a sarcastic order to cease attacking our own troops, he informed Truscott that he intended to designate a BSL well in advance of U.S. ground troops and that no missions would be accepted within that line. This meant that no American planes would be over U.S. troops or attacking the enemy in contact with them. Worried that this would embolden the Germans, and recognizing that the air force's commander's anger was aimed primarily at Clark, Truscott pleaded with Saville that personal irritations not be permitted to jeopardize the fight against the Germans. A letter to Saville to be forwarded to pilots stated, "As you know, we have had a few cases where our ground troops have been bombed by our own aircraft. I believe that every officer and man realizes that such mistakes will occur. These incidents were reported in order to minimize such incidents. I sincerely trust that no member of your command will feel that because of such reports, the magnificent work you have done has not been fully and completely appreciated by the ground forces."

After the Anzio landing caught the Germans by surprise and the ensuing two months brought stalemate, German artillery and aircraft continued to strike the beachhead almost daily. While mass raids of fifty or more aircraft all but ceased during April, hit-and-run raids persisted and artillery continued to harass. In letters to Sarah, Truscott described the living accommodations as extremely primitive. Troops sought shelter in caves hollowed from canal banks, in tanks, trucks, and other vehicles. In forward areas, a few stone farmhouses of the Mussolini reclamation project remained standing to provide housing and command posts. Some became aid stations where men from the frontline companies could occasionally obtain a hot meal and dry out their clothing. Division commanders had the use of caravans or trailers as both homes and offices. Even under difficult conditions, troops found time to express humor in signs that designated "42nd and Broadway," the "Good Eats Cafe," "4794 miles to the Golden Gate," and "Beach Head Hotel, Special Rates to New Arrivals."

Luncheon conferences at Truscott's headquarters featured white tablecloths made from sheets pilfered from the navy or a hospital. China and crockery were found in bombed-out buildings. Silverware was army mess-kit issue. As spring came on, flowers were used to make centerpieces. Corporal Hong created arrangements in the form of the divisional crests or other insignia of the day's guest of honor. Climbing roses growing in the small garden of Truscott's "Villa" were cut and sent in large baskets to hospitals.

Springtime and the lull in fighting also meant relaxation with baseball. Truscott told Sarah that it was not unusual to see softball games in progress with German artillery shells landing within five or six hundred yards. There were devotees of volleyball and badminton. Bridge and poker were played. Swimming in the Tyrrhenian Sea was increasingly popular as weather became warmer and engineers cleared German mines from beaches. Warm weather encouraged fishing. Some GIs found that mines exploded beneath the water brought stunned quarry to the surface, where bare hands substituted for nets that the men did not have.

When the Panther attack was canceled and Truscott realized that his men were to be on the defensive for weeks, division commanders asked to have their bands brought up from Naples to give concerts. They played at decoration ceremonies in the square at Nettuno. Breaking up into smaller groups, they performed for every unit they could reach. It was during this period that the Third Infantry Division band made the beachhead familiar with "Dogface Soldier." Combined bagpipers of the Cameronians, the Royal Scots Fusiliers, Seaforth Highlanders, and Gordon Highlanders in kilts and tartans demonstrated perfect skills in drill and discipline in parades for hospitals and every U.S. division.

The only source of radio entertainment was German broadcasts, including "Axis Sally and George" with "Lili Marlene" as their theme song. Truscott wrote to Clark, "This program, naturally, is designed to appeal to Allied troops, and while it has a certain entertainment value, it is primarily used to disseminate enemy propaganda that on the whole is crude and ineffective. However, the psychiatrist with the Third Infantry Division contends that the program does have a positive morale effect on some men suffering from extreme exhaustion. He felt, as I do, that the program should be countered by one that would, first, offset the value of the propaganda by ridicule; and second, provide a high-class program which our troops would listen to in preference to the German broadcast. Such a program should feature the newest recordings from name orchestras, humorous broadcasts such as Jack Benny and Charlie McCarthy, as well as world news items and latest sports flashes. In addition to being extremely high-class entertainment, it is essential that the broadcast ensure clear reception on both Signal Corps and commercial receiving sets. Furthermore, broadcasts should be timed to coincide with Sally's programs."

When General Clark visited the beachhead on March 19, he had other problems in mind than German propaganda. General Alexander had announced plans for regrouping the Allied armies in Italy. He proposed a drive northward on Rome, with the British Eighth Army making the main effort in the Liri and Sacco valleys while the Fifth Army fought along the coast. Clark explained that Truscott's mission was to hold the beachhead and prepare for offensive action in conjunction with the main attack by the Fifth and Eighth armies about the middle of April. He promised to send the remaining combat command of the First Armored Division to the beachhead as soon as possible. He thought an additional infantry division might be available, but this was by no means certain.

Because Truscott's force was much better organized and stronger in reserves than when it stopped the major German offensives, Truscott had no doubt that he could counter any German assault. Regrouping had provided the minimum strength needed to hold the front. The offensive for his men would have one of two purposes. It would either improve their position by extending the beachhead or enable them to make a push in conjunction with the remainder of the Fifth and Eighth armies to destroy German forces. Analyzing what might be accomplished with the forces at hand, he found four possible alternatives: (1) reduce the Carroceto salient, recapture lost ground, improve positions, and facilitate deployment for future action toward Albano or Cisterna; (2) capture Cisterna, seize an important locality that would provide more depth within the beachhead, and divide the enemy forces in preparation for future operations toward Cori or Artena; (3) capture the east flank of Littoria and deny the Germans observation and reduce artillery fire on the port area; and (4) seize the Ardea area and accomplish on the western flank the same results as the attack on Littoria with the further advantage of threatening the German right.

It was obvious to him that the only operation that would produce worthy results would be one aimed at reducing the Carroceto salient or taking Cisterna. Because of the German defensive organization, heavy losses could be expected. Concluding that none of these attacks would be worth the cost, he felt that the offensive operations should be limited to patrol actions and small-scale attacks until his force was ready to make an all-out effort in conjunction with the main assault.

★ FOURTEEN ★

GREAT DAY

IN TRUSCOTT'S OFFICIAL DIARY ON WEDNESDAY, March 1, 1944, an aide recorded a visit by Ernie Pyle to headquarters. He brought a bottle of cognac, accepted an invitation to stay for dinner, and argued with Truscott far into the night. Topic or topics of the debate between the famous war correspondent and the major general were omitted from the entry. There was much they might have discussed. Since the start of Operation Shingle, the Rangers had been wiped out as a viable fighting force at Cisterna, the monastery on Monte Cassino had been bombed into rubble by the Ninety-sixth Bomb Squadron of the U.S. Fifth Army under the command of Air Corps Major Bradford A. Evans, and the Eighth Air Force had also begun a series of raids into Germany to pulverize Hitler's aircraft-building centers.

Pyle might also have mentioned to the heroic general who'd helped plan and carry out the invasion of French Morocco that in Hollywood the odds-on favorite to capture the Oscar for the best picture of 1943 was *Casablanca*. For the sixteenth Academy Awards ceremony to be held on March 2, the planners of the fete had decided that because of wartime rationing of food and shortages in grocery stores and meat markets in America, it seemed inappropriate to continue holding its lavish annual banquets. They'd moved the gala to Grauman's Chinese Theater. The Motion Picture Academy had also decided that the statuettes in the top categories would not be made of gold-plated bronze, but plaster. Winners for supporting roles and in other categories would get plaques. Hosted by Bob Hope, the awards were to be broadcast by shortwave to soldiers overseas.

In London, Eisenhower had assumed his new job as Supreme Commander. His top priority was launching history's greatest invasion across the English Channel to France to challenge the coastal defenses there. Erwin Rommel had ordered the defenses strengthened to back up Hitler's boast, made after the Allied failure in the Dieppe raid, that no one would breach the Atlantic Wall of his Fortress Europe. For evidence that his Wehrmacht could hold the British and Americans at bay, Hitler pointed out that his stalwart forces in the mountains of Italy and those arrayed at Anzio had prevented the Allies from breaking out and rolling to Rome for four months.

Assessing enemy dispositions, Truscott deemed them defensive. Intelligence showed that the Hermann Göring Division, two panzer grenadier divisions, and the 114th Light Division had been withdrawn from the beachhead front. He did not anticipate any renewed effort to destroy the Anzio forces unless there was a radical change. It seemed evident to him that the German high command considered six or seven divisions sufficient for containment of the Americans or to attack limited objectives to improve their positions. His own force was better organized and much stronger in reserves than when they had stopped the major German offensives. He had no doubt that he could counter any German assault.

During the last ten days of March, every headquarters in the beachhead worked to plan a breakout in conjunction with a British-American offensive in the Cassino region. When Clark returned to the beachhead on March 29, he said it appeared that the British Eighth Army could not be ready until after May 1.

The day Truscott and Clark conferred was Truscott's twenty-fifth wedding anniversary. After he saw Clark off late in the afternoon, the Germans provided what he called the noisiest serenade in his quarter century of wedded life in the form of an afternoon air raid involving more than forty German bombers. He noted, "It was quite a show."

At a meeting with all commanders during the first week in April, General Alexander outlined his intentions. On May 10, the Fifth and Eighth armies would attack simultaneously. The Eighth Army was to break through the Cassino defenses and drive up the Liri Valley as the Fifth Army broke through the mountainous areas west of the Garigliano River to turn the flank of German forces opposing the Eighth Army in the Liri Valley. Truscott's beachhead forces were to be prepared to attack on twenty-four hours' notice in the direction of Cisterna to cut Highway 6 in the rear of the German main forces. These operations were to destroy the German forces and drive the remnant far north of Rome, with the capture of the city the most important immediate objective.

Truscott recognized that the plan for employment of the beachhead forces could bring decisive results only if it were properly coordinated with the advance of the main forces, and launched at the proper time to cut the German line of communication. As he and Clark talked over the plan, they decided they should also be prepared to exploit their position on the flank and the rear of the German forces. If the Germans withdrew rapidly from the Eighth and Fifth Divisions front to defend a line south of Rome through the Alban Hills, an attack made in the Carroceto area passing to the west of the Colli Laziali might be the quickest way to turn the German position and to capture Rome. Moreover, if the offensive on the southern front were not successful, an attack from the beachhead might be desirable to unite it with the rest of the U.S. Fifth Army and reduce the logistical and naval burden of maintaining the beachhead.

During a visit by Alexander to Anzio on May 5, Truscott explained the details of his plans and preparations. "General Alexander, charming gentleman and magnificent soldier that he was," he recalled, "let me know very quietly and firmly that there was only one direction in which the attack should or would be launched, and that was from Cisterna to cut Highway 6 in the vicinity of Valmontone in the rear of the German main forces. He reserved to himself the decision as to when to initiate it."

Truscott dutifully reported the conversation to Clark.

Barging into headquarters the next morning, Clark exploded in anger about Alexander interfering in the American chain of command. He stated that the capture of Rome was the only important objective and that he suspected the British of laying devious plans to be first into the city. He was determined they not do so. Although Truscott left no record of how he received this admission that nothing was more important to Clark than getting to Rome ahead of the British general, it is not unreasonable to suppose that he recalled Patton's obsession with beating Montgomery to Messina, with each man acting only in the interest of garnering laudatory personal publicity that would translate into indelible glory on the pages of history books.

On May 18, Truscott received a message from Clark that he wished Truscott to be at the command post in Teano for a conference the following morning. Clark stated that he planned to discuss the feasibility of an alternative to Truscott's plan named Buffalo. It was now to include capturing Cisterna and Cori and regrouping to attack northwest from Cisterna. Truscott interpreted this change as evidence that Clark was still fearful that the British might beat him into Rome. At the conference, Clark declared his intention to establish his advanced command post at Anzio and relieve Truscott of responsibility for the two British divisions on the west flank of the beachhead. He later advised that Buffalo would be launched at 0630 hours on May 3 and that he would arrive to assume operational command the previous day.

On D-day, Truscott recorded, there was no sight or sound to indicate that more than 150,000 men were tensely alert and waiting. All was strangely quiet, and in the darkness that precedes the dawn, he wrote, the whole forward area seemed eerily empty. For better or worse, the die was cast.

Like a crash of thunder and with lightninglike flashes against the sky, more than a thousand guns, infantry cannon, mortars, tanks, and tank destroyers opened fire. As dawn broke, a pall of smoke and dust shrouded the battlefield. After forty minutes, the guns fell silent. From the east appeared three groups of fighters and light bombers with their wings glinting in the morning light. Towering clouds of smoke and dust rose in Cisterna as bombs crashed on the town and enemy positions. After five minutes the planes were gone, artillery signaled H hour, and Truscott's men moved ahead to avenge the slaughter of the Rangers.

During intense fighting all day, with smoke and dust haze obscuring the battlefield, an attack crossed the railroad west of Feminamorta Creek. First Special Service Force reached its objective on Highway 7 but was driven back half a mile by a counterattack of Mark VI (Tiger) tanks. The Third Infantry Division had severe losses, but it reached the first day's objectives as night fell. The Germans were dealt large losses and more than a thousand had been captured. Truscott felt that the attack was going well.

As the fighting continued into a second day, fighter-bombers were active over enemy areas. A German counterattack against the Forty-fifth Infantry Division was repulsed with innumerable losses. By nightfall, Truscott's men were advancing and an armor unit was probing toward Velletri. Remnants of the German garrison in Cisterna stubbornly resisted. With the Seventh Infantry preparing to storm the town in the morning, it was clear to Truscott that the main German defenses were crumbling.

In a meeting late in the afternoon, Clark wanted to know whether or not Truscott had considered changing the direction of the attack to the northwest toward Rome. Truscott replied that he feared continuing the attack might alarm the German high command to the danger to their line of communications and cause them to concentrate all reserves in the Valmontone Gap. He said that because the Hermann Göring Division was en route from northern Italy, it was possible that the German command might withdraw the Third Panzer Grenadier Division, or the formidable Fourth Parachute Division, or both, from the beachhead front to oppose the U.S. advance. Any such concentration, he warned, might delay his troops at Valmontone long enough to permit the German main forces to escape. If there was any withdrawal from the western part of the beachhead, he argued, an attack to the northwest might be the best way to cut off the enemy withdrawal north of the Alban Hills. His staff was already preparing plans to meet this contingency. Clark agreed with this analysis.

Confident on the following morning (May 25) that his men would be at the German line of withdrawal through Valmontone, Truscott arrived at his command post feeling good until he was told by the chief of intelligence that "the boss" (Clark) wanted Truscott to leave the Third Infantry Division and the Special Force to block Highway 6 and mount the assault Clark had discussed with Truscott to the northwest as soon as possible.

Dumbfounded, Truscott protested that the conditions were not right. There was not a shred of evidence of any withdrawal from the western part of the beach, he said, nor was there evidence of concentration in the Valmontone area except light reconnaissance elements of the Hermann Göring Division.

He told his intelligence chief it was no time to drive to the northwest, where the enemy was still strong. His force should pour its maximum power into the Valmontone Gap to ensure the destruction of the retreating German army.

Feeling that he could not comply with the order without first talking to Alexander in person, he was informed that Alexander was not in the beachhead and could not be reached even by radio. With Clark insisting on the attack to the northwest, he decided that there was nothing to do except begin preparations. He wrote ruefully in *Command Missions*, "Such was the order that turned the main effort of the beachhead east from the Valmontone Gap and prevented the destruction of the German army in Italy."

Truscott's diary and the official U.S. Army accounts of the offensive record that it began on May 11. An hour before midnight, a massive barrage by 1,660 artillery pieces opened fire along the entire front from Cassino to the sea. When the shelling lifted, twenty-five Allied divisions attacked. The British Thirteenth Corps immediately crossed the Rapido River at two points and established a small bridgehead, but a Polish Corps assault on Monte Cassino failed with more than 50 percent of the attacking force counted as casualties. In the II Corps area, the Eighty-eighth Infantry Division made slight progress against heavy resistance, while the Fourth Moroccan Mountain Division succeeded in taking Monte Majo on May 13 after bitter fighting, breaking the Gustav Line.

This penetration over rugged terrain succeeded in securing the high ground overlooking the Liri Valley and threatened not only the entire left wing of the XIV Panzer Corps, but also imperiled the Germans at Cassino. Sensing an opportunity to widen the breach in the Gustav Line in the Monte Majo area, the Eighty-fifth and Eighty-eighth smashed into the German positions and after savage fighting forced the defenders back. Having lost more than 40 percent of their combat strength in just three days, with pressure building along the entire Gustav Line, and faced with the encirclement of Cassino, the Germans began to withdraw to the north in rearguard actions. By the early morning hours of May 16, 1944, the II Corps and the Moroccans had breached the Gustav Line at several points at the cost of three thousand casualties. To the

east, the British Thirteenth Corps broke through the German de-
fenses, with the Canadians pouring across the Rapido and the British
Seventy-eighth Division cutting Highway 6. On May 17, the Polish
Corps, supported by the Seventy-eighth Division, again attacked Monte
Cassino. After a day of ferocious combat and heavy losses, they rendered
German positions untenable. During the night the remaining enemy
forces quietly retreated, allowing the Poles to take the summit unop-
posed the following morning.

Having dislodged the enemy from the Gustav Line, the Allies sought
to keep moving and to prevent the Germans from settling into new positions on the Hitler Line. By the time the British advanced up the Liri
Valley (May 18–19), the Germans had dug in, leaving the Eighth Army
facing a renewed round of costly frontal assaults. In the Fifth Army's
sector, things remained fluid. Because the Germans were withdrawing
northeast away from the coast to avoid being cut off, Clark made the
decision to thrust north to Fondi and Terracina to link up with the
Anzio beachhead and head toward Rome rather than relieving the pressure on the Eighth Army's left flank as he had been originally instructed.

At home, Americans who read *Time* magazine's issue of May 23,
1944, found an article that asked why the Allies had chosen to strike
now in Italy. To capture Rome? To wipe out the Cassino disgrace? It was
much more than that, the article stated. General Sir Harold R. L. G.
Alexander declared in his order of the day that the Allies were going to
destroy the German armies in Italy, *Time* noted, but speculated that
there were undoubtedly other factors that General Alexander did not
mention.

The item postulated that so long as Nazi Field Marshal Albert Kesselring found that his divisions were tied up in Italy, the Nazis would
have to divert supplies to them that might otherwise be used to resist the
impending invasion somewhere on the channel coast. Kesselring also
had to be prepared for amphibious landings in the north of Italy. Berlin
radio frantically forecast that Allied troops were poised in Corsica and

Sardinia for just such a purpose. The severest Italian winter in many years had melted into warm, hazy springtime. The Allies had complete naval supremacy, enabling them to bring in thousands of tons of supplies. They also enjoyed air supremacy. Major General John (Uncle Joe) Cannon, the tactical air commander in Italy, boasted that his planes had knocked out railroads, keeping trains from moving from the Po Valley to the Gustav Line and forcing the Germans to depend on truck transport, chiefly at night, over Highway 7 (the Via Appia) and Highway 6 (Via Casilina). Regardless of these advantages, troops confronted the stern necessity of climbing mountains strewn with land mines and entrenched machine-gun nests manned by tough and desperately determined troops.

On June 3, with the British II Corps advancing rapidly along the northern side of the Alban Hills, Truscott ordered tanks into the action for the final effort to break through to the Rome suburb of Campoleone. That night, he received a plan allocating sectors for the advance into the Italian capital, assuring the bridges over the Tiber, and continuing the pursuit of the retreating Germans beyond Rome. As he was studying the plan, he had an unexpected visitor.

The correspondent for William Randolph Hearst's International News Service, thirty-six-year-old Michael Chinigo, had been covering the Italian campaign since the landings in Sicily. An Albanian-born U.S. citizen, he had attended Yale University and had studied at the University of Rome. Slightly wounded in his left wrist and arm by shrapnel from a German shell, he was awarded the Silver Star. He had been with Truscott for the captures of Palermo and Messina, and now reported to him that he had just come from a press conference where the correspondents were told that II Corps would enter Rome the next morning. Truscott said that if Chinigo wanted to be the first correspondent in the city when it fell, he had better stay where he was. It would not be the British taking Rome, he said, but the U.S. VI Corps.

Although an assault in the morning encountered stubborn German rearguard action to protect the German flight north, the Thirty-fourth and Forty-fifth infantry divisions cleared out the last resistance around Lanuvio, Genzano, and Albano. The Thirty-sixth Infantry Division was pushing down the northern slopes of the Colli Laziali, and tanks were driving up Highway 7 and a parallel road to the south, all rushing for Rome.

Around noon, with Chinigo going along, Truscott traveled through all but abandoned villages and past ruins of a Roman aqueduct. At an intersection on the edge of the city, he saw General Fred Walker and other officers bustling about and trying to decide what to do next. Walker's force was supposed to have been on another road about a half mile to the east. Truscott set him straight and sent him on his way.

Turning to the colonel who commanded the stopped armored column, he asked if the officer knew what his orders were. The colonel replied that he was to secure the bridges over the Tiber. Truscott asked, "Well, Colonel, what are you waiting for?"

The colonel saluted, turned, signaled the column, and dashed to his own vehicle. With a grinding of gears, roaring of motors, and clouds of dust and smoke, the tanks rumbled toward the Tiber River. Addressing Chinigo, Truscott said, "If you want to be the first correspondent in Rome, you had better follow that leading tank."

Chinigo climbed into his jeep and sped away. When the tanks reached the center of Rome, he broke away from them and turned into a side street. There he encountered a German column moving in the direction of the American tanks. Using a walkie-talkie, he alerted the tankers and headed for the Excelsior Hotel. Finding it abandoned, he signed the register, "Chinigo was here." He visited several other principal hotels, repeating the procedure. Very early the next morning he made his way along the jammed Highway 6 until he located the press camp. When he sent his scoop on being the first correspondent into Rome, he triggered a stampede of newsmen.

Back at his command post, Truscott received reports of other tank columns rolling into Rome and finding most of the bridges over the Tiber intact. He also received notification that the Forty-fifth Division was at the river. Engineers were hard at work on a partially demolished bridge and others were building a pontoon bridge. The next morning as he was trying to get his scattered corps in hand again, he received orders to report to General Clark on Capitoline Hill. Neither his Italian-speaking aide nor he had ever been in Rome, and hadn't the slightest idea where the Capitoline Hill might be. Finding a sergeant who had visited the city as a tourist before the war, they set off along streets filled with people in a holiday mood. Italian and American flags hung from windows. Truscott's jeep, with siren wailing, was slowed to a snail's pace until an Italian boy jumped on the hood and shouted and gestured to clear the way. Threading through streets packed with crowds waving flowers and offering glasses and bottles of wine, fruit, and bread, they came to the historic square where Mussolini used to stand on the balcony and make bellicose boasts about a new Roman Empire. They found it empty and the buildings in the area seemingly deserted. Wondering if he was in the right place, Truscott was assured by the Italian boy that he was.

Informed by someone in the crowd that a large number of American vehicles were at the Excelsior Hotel and that the American commander was thought to be present, Truscott ordered his driver to take him there. On the way, they encountered General Clark's official party and a horde of reporters. Forcing its way through a boisterous and increasing throng of Romans, the column of jeeps led Truscott back to Capitoline Hill. From the balcony where Il Duce had held sway as dictator while Truscott was slowly rising in rank in a peacetime army, Clark basked in the pop and glare of flashbulbs and exclaimed to the swarm of war correspondents, "This is a great day for the Fifth Army."

Truscott recalled, "I reckon it was, but I was anxious to get out of this posturing and on with the business of war."

His only sightseeing venture was to the Colosseum. Gazing at the stately ruins of the most notorious amphitheater in the world, he saw it not as a relic of the fleshy excesses and brutal indulgences of a long-gone Roman Empire, but the place where hundreds of U.S. Army Rangers captured at Cisterna had been humiliated. Hauled to Rome by the Nazis, they'd been paraded past it like trophies and offered as living proof of German military invincibility.

On the night of June 4, 1944, the British Broadcasting Company reported on the fall of Rome and stated that Hitler's headquarters had announced that the Führer ordered the withdrawal of the German troops from Rome in order to prevent the destruction of the city. The statement said that the struggle in Italy would continue with unshakable determination with the aim of breaking the enemy attacks and forging final victory for Germany. From London, American military authorities broadcast a tribute to General Sir Harold Alexander. It described his leadership in the Italian campaign as "daring, unconventional and brilliant" and praised his methods of compelling the German army to evacuate Rome without destructive fighting.

At the Vatican, Pope Pius XII took to the papal balcony to tell thousands of Italians who gathered in St. Peter's Square, "Today we rejoice because, thanks to the joint goodwill of both sides, Rome has been saved from the horrors of war."

In a radio address, President Roosevelt reminded Americans that it would be unwise to inflate the military importance of the capture of Rome warning the country that its sons would have to push through a long period of greater effort and fiercer fighting before they vanquished Germany. As he spoke, he knew that thousands of troops were at that moment loading onto ships and boats on the coasts of Great Britain to cross the English Channel for landings on five beaches close to the important French seaports of Cherbourg and Havre.

In its military dimensions and historical magnitude the invasion of France would not only overshadow the capture of Rome but eclipse all the battles of the First and Second World Wars and every clash of arms in the chronicles of all peoples and all nations. But late in the morning of Tuesday, June 6, 1944, the staff aide to whom Truscott had assigned the task of keeping an official diary simply recorded the event in one line. He wrote, "Heard second front had begun with landings Cherbourg-Havre on wide front."

That day as Truscott established his command post north of the Tiber River, he did so with knowledge that he would soon have to leave Italy to assume command of assault forces in a second invasion on the southern coast of France. How he got the assignment was the result of a combination of strong personalities, ambition, decisions by men in the chain of command who were far removed from the Italian front, and severe pressures from the American public and newspaper editorial writers on Eisenhower to punish an old friend and comrade in arms.

FIFTEEN

DRAGOON

FOUR DAYS BEFORE THE CAPTURE of Rome, Americans all across the country found in their newspapers a story out of Italy and datelined "With Fifth Army Beachhead Forces." Written by Mike Chinigo, it began, "It is possible now to disclose that Major General Lucian K. Truscott, Jr., was supreme field commander of Allied troops on the Anzio beachhead from mid-February until Lieutenant General Mark W. Clark arrived to direct the present offensive which began May 23."

In the journalistic tradition of editors and headline writers looking for an angle to turn a national or international story into a local one, the item appeared in altered forms in scores of newspapers. In Ohio, the *Cleveland News* recalled that Truscott had been the polo coach of the Chagrin Valley and Kirtland teams and carried the headline:

GEN. TRUSCOTT, ONCE POLO CHIEF HERE, HAILED AS ANZIO BEACHHEAD SAVIOR

The *Amarillo Globe* in Texas ran the banner ANZIO COMMANDER KIN OF AMARILLOANS and built the story around Truscott being the brother of local resident Mrs. W. Cy King and a cousin of Mrs. Miles Bivins, also of Amarillo. The Fort Worth *Star Telegram* zeroed in on Truscott as a native of Chatfield in Navarro County. Running the Associated Press story with no changes, the *Houston Post* did note in the headline that Truscott was Texas-born.

With Lucian III at West Point and Mary married and living in New York, Sarah had moved back to Charlottesville, Virginia, with James. Surprised and thrilled by the explosion of publicity about her husband that friends sent her in clippings, she wrote atop the headline of the story in the *Houston Post*, "Gee whiz, this is something."

In Truscott's official diary, members of the staff were routinely cited as "the family." On Wednesday, June 14, 1944, the entry noted, "Family off for Papal audience at Vatican Palace 0845 all in best bib and tucker. Panoply of Swiss guards and major domos in scarlet palace rooms. General in for private audience in Pope's chambers. Very much impressed by Pope as a man. Pius then out with General to greet rest of family and staff members in throne room and bestow a blessing. Trip through St. Peter's and finally to Army CP, where General talks to Gens Gruenther and Clark."

The subject under discussion was a change in assignments that Truscott described as follows in *Command Missions*:

I had known for some time that I was to command the assault forces in the invasion of southern France which was to take place as soon as naval vessels and craft could be made available from the Normandy landings. The original plan was that General Clark was to command the Seventh Army for this invasion and that it was to consist of my VI Corps and a French Corps. Recently, it had been decided that General Clark was to remain with the Fifth Army in Italy. I had selected the Third Infantry Division, and the Forty-fifth and Thirty-sixth Infantry Divisions for this assault. The arrangement now was for the IV Corps to relieve the VI Corps as soon after the capture of Rome as possible. On June 7th, General Clark informed me that the relief would take place at noon on June 11th.

Clark told Truscott that in planning Overlord Eisenhower initially selected Clark to command the landing forces and that Ike also wanted Truscott to command the assault forces in a later landing in southern France. In the meanwhile, Clark would command the Seventh and Fifth armies until after the capture of Rome. George Patton would be moved to England to be in overall command of the Normandy landings, scheduled for May. But after the slapping incidents were revealed, Ike had been compelled to change the plan and give the execution of Overlord to Omar Bradley. At this point, the British general Sir Henry Maitland Wilson, Supreme Commander in the Mediterranean Theater, recommended to the Allied Combined Chiefs that Clark remain with the Fifth Army in Italy. When this was approved by the Combined Chiefs, they held to the part of the plan (code name Anvil) that put Truscott in charge of the troops for the landing in southern France.

Given the authority to choose the units to carry it out, Truscott selected the Third and Forty-fifth infantry divisions because they were the most experienced of the American divisions and both had training and expertise in landings. He wanted the Thirty-sixth Infantry Division as the third element because of its outstanding performance during the action following the breakout from the beachhead at Anzio. He also believed that the success of the breakout would erase in large measure the setbacks after Salerno. "Having tasted of the bitter cup and having more recently eaten of the fruits of victory," he said, "the division could be expected to equal and keep pace with its more experienced teammates."

Summoned to a briefing on Anvil at Algiers, Truscott met its overall commander. At age fifty-six, Lieutenant General Alexander McCarrel Patch, nicknamed "Sandy," was a native of Fort Huachuca, Arizona, where his father commanded a cavalry detachment. Graduating from West Point in 1913, he felt the cavalry was becoming obsolete and chose to be commissioned in the infantry. While commanding troops in France, he came to the attention of George C. Marshall, who was serving on General Pershing's staff. As one of the promising officers tapped for advancement by Chief of Staff Marshall prior to World War II, he was made brigadier general and sent to Fort Bragg, North Carolina, to train troops, then to the Pacific in 1942 to organize reinforcement and defenses of New Caledonia. The result was the formation of the Americal Division. They were sent to Guadalcanal to relieve the marines and clear the island of the Japanese. After a stint as IV Corps commander at Fort Lewis, Washington, in 1943, Marshall sent him to Sicily. Following Patton's removal from command after the slapping episode, he took over the Seventh Army.

Truscott wrote, "I was fully aware of his reputation and knew he was highly esteemed. He was thin and simple in dress and forthright in manner—obviously keenly intelligent with a dry Scottish humor. His quick and almost jerky speech and movement gave me the impression he was nervous and found some difficulty in expressing himself. Our conversation during the evening concerned our war experiences."

Also in Algiers for conferences at this time, General Marshall asked Truscott about his experiences at Anzio and elsewhere, particularly with reference to the performance of weapons and equipment, and the fighting quality of American soldiers. When he inquired if Clark had mentioned to Truscott that Eisenhower had asked for Truscott for the cross-channel assault, Truscott dissembled. Concerned about getting Clark in trouble, he replied that he had heard nothing of it. Marshall went on to say Truscott did not get the assignment because Marshall told Ike that he could not be spared from the Anzio beachhead command, but Marshall regretted the decision because the assignment would have given Truscott the command of an army.

He stated that he felt Truscott should know Eisenhower had asked for him and that his services in saving the situation at Anzio had been fully appreciated. Truscott answered that he was perfectly satisfied to do the best he could wherever Marshall thought his services were needed. He wrote of Marshall's explanation, "I was deeply touched, for there was no call upon General Marshall to tell me this. It was one of those generous and thoughtful things that always distinguished him in his dealings with his subordinates."

In a meeting with Patch, Truscott explained his views on assault landings. In particular, he emphasized the importance of undivided command responsibility during the initial phase, and the necessity of assembling army, navy, and air planners as soon as possible to allow them to work together in developing the detailed plans. He stressed the importance of rigorous training, and the need to move his headquarters to Naples without delay to coordinate the preparations. In a briefing by Patch's staff, officers described the landing areas, summarized the dispositions of the enemy in southern France, discussed outlying beaches and reasons for their selection, and indicated the beachhead objective for three simultaneous division assaults. The outline called for an assault by an American corps of two divisions, or three if shipping were available, and an airborne landing of one regimental combat team east of Toulon to establish a beachhead. Beginning on D-day plus three, two French corps of seven divisions would come ashore. The objective was the capture of Toulon and the major port of Marseilles.

Because the landings were to be in France, the question of French participation had been a thorny issue. General de Gaulle suggested the French be given command of the entire Anvil undertaking, but one of the planners predicted that if he were given authority over any part of the landing operation, the French would be insufferable. The unanimous feeling of the planners was that the French should not be entrusted with a controlling role in the assault. When this was made known, de Gaulle held out for a deputy commander, but Clark, who was then commanding the Anvil planners as well as the Fifth Army in Italy, refused. After Patch took over in March, he decided to integrate a French staff throughout all planning sections.

"The fact that the French had seven of the ten divisions involved," Truscott explained, "coupled with General de Gaulle's complete ascendancy, weighed heavily in all discussions of command during the rest of the planning period."

With Overlord having been postponed until June, Anvil planning continued on the assumption that its forces would still invade the south of France in conjunction with the landings at Normandy. With the channel-crossing date in flux and raising uncertainty that Anvil could ever occur, the British generals Alexander and Wilson, in keeping with Churchill's desire to stop the Red Army from taking over the Balkans, urged the Combined Chiefs of Staff to employ Anvil resources for a landing in the northern part of the Adriatic region and a drive to Hungary. Eisenhower insisted that to support the drive across France after the Normandy landings he would need Marseilles. The only way to get it was with Anvil. He won the debate.

Choice of a headquarters location for Truscott's family was left to the ever-reliable aide Don Carleton. He found a former Italian barracks not far from the waterfront in downtown Naples that had recently been used as a rest center for American troops. Called the Block House, it was a huge quadrangle with an interior courtyard surrounded by a high wall in which there were only two entrance gates. Two floors provided ample office space for the army, navy, and air staffs and living accommodations for some officers and all of the enlisted personnel. Corps headquarters, except for the planning staff, was established at Bagnoli, a suburb on the outskirts of the city.

Truscott received this farewell letter from Clark:

Dear Lucian:

It is with real and very deep regret that I see the VI Corps and its commanding general leave the fold of Fifth Army. After these many months and the momentous happenings which we have shared, an association has been formed between VI Corps and Fifth Army which nothing will be able to annul.

It seems superfluous to praise the accomplishments of VI Corps; its fortitude and stamina during the protracted siege at the beachhead, its brilliant and daring conduct during the breakthrough have already entered history.

Regardless of operations in other theaters and other operations to come, I am certain they will always be remembered among the outstanding feats of this war. I am deeply grateful to you for your loyal cooperation and I congratulate you for a task well performed. I wish you every success in your new assignment.

Both generals believed their soldierly paths would never cross again. They were wrong.

Truscott's plans for executing Anvil were based on a thorough knowledge of the terrain and beaches in southern France, particularly of the assault area, and on an unusually complete intelligence about enemy strength and dispositions that was deemed better than the advance information on Normandy. Basic intelligence provided by the British and similar studies by others was as complete and detailed as for any area in the entire world. Superior maps were available. Aerial reconnaissance was continuous and there were expert photo interpreters.

Truscott would also have the advantage of help from the French underground. Known as the Maquis, a name drawn from the scrub growth of southern France, its members were called maquisards and were primarily communists, anarchists, and right-wing nationalists. Some had fought the Fascists in the Spanish civil war. They used guerrilla tactics to harass the Germans and Vichy supporters, assisted downed Allied airmen and Jews to escape France, and provided a continuous flow of communication with the Allied high command in Algiers that kept Truscott up to date about every German movement and change in disposition.

Truscott noted that about twenty miles west of Cannes lay the town of Frejus, where Napoléon had landed from Elba to begin his last one hundred days as emperor. The Anvil area ran from Theoule sur Mer, about midway between Cannes and Fréjus, southwest to Cap Benat, sixteen miles east of Toulon. The Argens River, which emptied into the Mediterranean Sea a few miles south of Fréjus, and the Golfe de St. Tropez, a dozen miles to the southwest, divided the assault area into three sectors. The German Nineteenth Army, with headquarters in Avignon, was responsible for the enemy's defense of southern France. Deployed along the coast and at strategic points in the interior, it had twelve divisions that varied in strength and efficiency. The 157th Reserve Division and the 148th Infantry Division were rated first-class. The 242nd and 244th Infantry Divisions were known to be about 15 percent understrength in personnel and equipment. West of the Rhone River were two veteran divisions that were also reduced in strength. German defenses included coastal defense guns, railway artillery, French and Italian naval guns, medium and light field artillery, and self-propelled guns and tanks. All beaches were mined, and obstructions were protected by machine guns, self-propelled guns, and tanks. Intelligence showed undersea obstacles on three of the assault beaches and indicated that the Germans were expanding these measures as rapidly as possible.

In reviewing these defenses and judging them to be not well organized in depth, Truscott believed that the enemy would most likely follow tactics that Kesselring had found effective against the landing at Anzio. Their purpose would be to delay the landing forces and gain time in order to assemble reserves for a counterattack once the Allies' main effort could be determined. In the invasion area, Truscott expected to find opposition by infantry battalions, tanks, fixed coast defense guns, and self-propelled guns. He anticipated confrontation with at least a division and a half on D-day, more than two divisions by the morning of D-day plus one, more than three divisions on D-day plus three, including half of a panzer division with eighty or more tanks, and more than five divisions on D-day plus four, including an entire panzer division.

On June 19, the Third Infantry Division moved for training to Pozzuoli, where it had rehearsed for Anzio. Three days later, the Forty-fifth Infantry Division reached Salerno to go through its paces at the Invasion Training Center. On July 4, the Thirty-sixth Infantry Division returned to its first battlefield on the Paestum beaches at Salerno. With the land and naval elements assembled in areas of easy communication, and close to the Seventh Army headquarters in Naples, Truscott took another look at the forces and found that the troop lists contained some units he did not need and omitted others he required. He submitted a revised list to Patch with specific requests for additional units he considered essential.

During the planning period, visitors included King George VI, who reviewed the fleet in the Bay of Naples and for whom Sir Henry Maitland Wilson entertained at a luncheon in the Palace at Caserta attended by all the senior British, French, and American commanders in the Italian theater. Secretary of War Henry Stimson also visited. After Patch and Truscott briefed him on Anvil, he said he was greatly reassured over the prospects of success.

On August 1, the code name Anvil was dropped. Because the Combined Chiefs of Staff feared that the name had been compromised, they renamed the operation Dragoon. Truscott viewed the adoption of a term for a troop of mounted soldiers dating back to the reign of Britain's King James II to be a good omen.

Final orders were packaged for distribution on board ships with instructions that they were not to be opened until the invasion force was well out to sea. Truscott wrote, "This may seem surprising, but no one outside commanders and their staffs knew where we were going. Most men understood we were to make an assault landing somewhere, but few had any inkling it was to be southern France."

On August 12, the entire command was finally loaded. At nine o'clock that night, Truscott boarded the headquarter ship *Catoctin* and was greeted by Admiral Hewitt, General Patch, and a few members of the Seventh Army staff.

For the fourth time in a little more than two years, Truscott found himself in command of an invasion force, but none had been larger. In the assault wave were more battalions than those that landed in Normandy. Nine days earlier, he'd given the officers who would lead them in combat a portrait of the men and their commanding general. "Our American soldiers are, by nature, hunters," he said. "The vast proportion of these lads are farm-raised or have a farm background. They are all hunters by instinct. Encourage that hunting instinct. Make every soldier go into every fight feeling like a hunter. Finally, I say to you, get forward. No battle was ever won by any commander sitting in a dugout with a telephone in one hand and a radio in the other. You have to know from your own personal observation what the score is. I say to you, from Division Commander down to squad leader, get forward."

★ SIXTEEN ★

CHAMPAGNE CAMPAIGN

ALTHOUGH PRIME MINISTER WINSTON CHURCHILL had been thwarted in his desire to scrap the invasion of the south of France and send the Allied forces in Italy into the Balkans to keep Josef Stalin's Soviet Union from grabbing and keeping Eastern Europe, on Sunday morning, August 13, 1944, in the port of Naples, he put on the naval uniform he'd worn as First Lord of the Admiralty and stepped into a speedboat to salute the Dragoon invasion fleet. As it set sail for the French Riviera, where he'd often gone on holidays before the war, among the ships in a flotilla that was bigger than the D-day armada was the U.S. cruiser *Augusta*. On her deck in 1941, Churchill and President Franklin D. Roosevelt had agreed on the strategy to defeat the Axis Powers and sealed the alliance that Churchill would hail as a special relationship. The conference had ended with them, aides, and crews of the *Augusta* and the British destroyer that brought Churchill to waters off Newfoundland singing "Onward Christian Soldiers."

Aboard the invasion fleet flagship *Catoctin*, Truscott's diarist recorded, "Ship finally under way after lunch, and Gen. spends afternoon reading. Heat most oppressive, ventilating system broken."

On Monday, August 14:

> **Another bad night in ovenlike cabin.** Day quiet and almost uneventful, with flagship passing through Sardinia-Corsica strait at noon and skirting western coast of Corsica all afternoon. Gen. Saville in during morning to straighten out question of bombing enemy.
>
> CPs. Destroyer alongside. Gen. Somerville, Secretary of War Robert Patterson request permission to come aboard tomorrow.
>
> Msgs from Gen. H. M. Wilson and Adm. Cunningham wishing all good luck. In late evening begin to pass through LCIs. Some 1001 ships making this invasion. Largest in history. Jitters cooling off a little, and General writes letter to wife before starting to bed.

For days, the Bay of Naples had been filled with ships and boats of every description, but when the *Catoctin* weighed anchor and headed out to sea, most of the shipping had already departed. Slower-moving LCTs, LCIs, and LSTs with naval escorts had sailed the previous afternoon. Most of the French II Corps had loaded in the ports of Taranto and Brindisi in the heel of Italy, and other elements of the French Corps were en route from Oran. Truscott wrote, "Organizing this vast armada, planning and directing its routes, coordinating and protecting its movements so that each of a thousand pieces fell into place at the exact time, fully prepared for its manifold duties, was something of a gigantic jigsaw puzzle or a chess game of the gods with the broad Mediterranean as a board. Our admiration for the professional ability of our naval comrades was boundless, and our respect for their achievement in this complicated operation was profound. Routes for all convoys converged off the west coast of Corsica, and then flowed northward during the night, like a mighty river, toward the transport areas where the troops would disembark and head ashore."

With the first glimmer of light on the morning of August 15, formations of transport and fighter aircraft passed over the coast and released clouds of parachutes, followed by hundreds of heavy, medium, and fighter bombers blasting the beaches and coast defenses along a twenty-five-mile strip of shoreline east of Toulon. While the debris and smoke thickened the soft morning haze, dozens of warships opened a bombardment. Three veteran U.S. infantry divisions in landing craft waited to go in. Feeling that time seemed to drag while the guns of battleships, destroyers, cruisers, and a host of lesser craft poured a hail of steel on the landing beaches, Truscott could only imagine the landing boats heading ashore with wave after wave loaded with grave, intent, and anxious soldiers. Other boats led the way, towing devices to blast through the underwater and beach obstacles. Then came blunt-nosed tank carriers with long ramps that dropped to disgorge them. Since being present for the first clumsy attempt to land men and machines upon the coast of France at Dieppe in 1942, he had observed and taken part in the evolution of invasions from the sea into the choreographic display two years later that was at the same time terrible and beautiful. Now came the first action reports.

Landings on time.

Opposition light.

Scattered artillery. Mortars and small arms.

Operation going well.

The airborne landing near Le Muy successful.

Although First Special Service Force landed on offshore islands as planned, it was in a bit of trouble. A later message said the problem was solved.

About the middle of the morning as the *Catoctin* stood in near the beaches of the Third Infantry Division in Cavalaire Bay, Truscott noted that all seemed to be going well with less confusion on the beaches and in the waters offshore than was to be expected. There were air alerts, but no enemy bombers. Looking eastward off Tropez peninsula and into Golfe de St. Tropez, toward the beaches of the Forty-fifth Infantry Division, he saw steady progress of craft toward shore without disorder or disarray. At noon, the ship was near Frejus to watch part of the Thirty-sixth Infantry Division land. Truscott noted delightedly, "We had a grandstand seat."

The only disappointment was a report that while Major General John E. Dahlquist's landings had gone off satisfactorily and the opposition had not been heavy, the French naval party to the east of Dahlquist that was to help take Beach 264A had been unsuccessful. This required Dahlquist's troops to take over the mission. Born in Minneapolis, Minnesota, and a year younger than Truscott, Dahlquist had also started his army career in 1917 as a reserve second lieutenant, but served with the occupation forces in Germany. He'd been an instructor in the Infantry School (1924–28), a student at the Command and General Staff School (1930–31) and Army War College (1935–36), and had served in the Philippines (1931–34). Promoted to brigadier general, he was Eisenhower's assistant chief of staff when Truscott joined the Mountbatten organization in 1942. After serving as the assistant commander of the Seventy-sixth Infantry Division (1942–43), he was shifted into the same post with the Thirty-sixth Infantry Division and had been an integral part of Anvil/Dragoon planning. On August 15, 1944, he told Truscott he was confident he would have Beach 264A cleared by morning.

Truscott lamented that the French failure to carry out the landing as arranged was to hold up the clearing of that beach by more than a day. The result was to delay the seizure and occupation of airfields near Fréjus and in the Argens valley. This foreclosed air support east of the Rhone in a drive to the north a few days later.

After returning to the *Catoctin* to report to Patch and Admiral

Hewitt, Truscott and several of his command group set off for the St. Maxime beaches to join a forward echelon of his command post staff. He was also accompanied by Colonel Jean Petit. The French liaison officer for Dragoon, Petit had been in the opposition at the 1942 Port Lyautey landing in Morocco. When they stepped onto the beach at St. Maxime in mid-August 1944, Truscott scooped up a handful of sand, turned to Petit, and asked, "Well, Jean, how does the soil of France feel to an exile?"

Eyes brimming with tears, Petit was unable to speak.

Back at the command post, Truscott reviewed complete reports from both the Third and Thirty-sixth Infantry Divisions. Except for Frejus and Beach 264A, which Dahlquist said he expected to take during the night, all initial objectives for the assault were achieved and both divisions were pushing on. In recording these successes, Truscott noted they occurred on the twenty-fifth anniversary of the day he received his original commission.

Believing that the power of two enemy divisions had been broken, Truscott found the evidence in 12,129 German prisoners. Allied casualties were much lighter than anticipated, with 183 killed. Attributing the success to speed, power, thorough planning, training, and meticulous preparations, he viewed the situation through the prism of his experiences at Salerno and Anzio. The aim of attacking the enemy in flank and where he was most vulnerable had not been achieved primarily because the forces placed in the enemy's rear had not been strong enough, allowing the mobile Germans to escape. If they were to be snared in southern France, the trap would have to be sprung in the region between the Italian and Swiss borders, marked by Maritime and High Alps on the east, and the Rhone River on the west. Broad and deep with an unusually swift current, it began amid the glaciers and lakes of the Swiss Alps, passed through Geneva, tumbled on southwest to Lyon, and turned southward toward the Mediterranean. If its bridges were destroyed, which was well within the capabilities of air forces, German armies to the east and the west of the Rhone would be effectively isolated from each other. Those beyond the river could only escape northward by roads. The vital point on this route was the narrow Curas Gorge several miles to the north of Montelimar.

From Truscott's accounts at the time and in the retrospective records of U.S. Army historians and military analysts, Operation Dragoon benefited from the failure of the Germans to launch an immediate counterattack in Normandy on and after D-day. With many of their divisions surrounded and in danger of annihilation in the Falaise region, the German commanders chose to order a total withdrawal from France. Instructions were sent from Berlin ordering the Atlantic coast forces to pull out of western France and those in the south of France to withdraw north via the Rhone Valley. The only exceptions were the 148th Division in the Cannes-Nice area and a mountain division held in reserve at Grenoble, both of which were to withdraw into Italy. In accordance with long-standing plans, strong garrisons were to remain at Toulon, Marseilles, and several key Atlantic ports. At Hitler's personal order, these vital coastal enclaves were to be defended to the last man.

As the Germans scrambled to deal with forces on two fronts in France, the Allies had the benefit of knowing exactly what they were planning. Having obtained one of Germany's intricate cyphering machines, the code breakers in Britain in a program code-named Ultra figured out how it worked. They passed on orders for German field commanders to the Allied generals in France. Consequently, on August 17, General Patch was learning of the withdrawal plan at the same time as German generals. A second factor in Truscott's favor was the action of a small mobile striking task force that he formed in July. Under assistant corps commander Brigadier General Frederick B. Butler, and drawn primarily from the Thirty-sixth Division, it consisted of a motorized battalion from the 141st Infantry, two medium tank companies, a tank destroyer company, a light cavalry squadron, and one self-propelled artillery battalion. Assembling the force on the night of August 17–18,

Butler headed west and then to the north into the mountains heading in the general direction of Grenoble. By August 19, Task Force Butler had reached the Digne-Sisteron region about fifty miles north of the Forty-fifth Division and a third of the way to Grenoble. Although the mechanized unit met no organized German resistance, it was still without a specific mission except for carrying out a general reconnaissance in force.

A result of the Ultra information about the German retreat was a splitting of Truscott's campaign into three parts. First was the conquest of Toulon and Marseilles. Second was a drive west to secure the northern flank of French forces along the coast. The third was Butler's foray to the north. In Truscott's plan, if Butler could get behind the German line of withdrawal and be adequately reinforced, Germany's Nineteenth Army might be destroyed and all of the kind of grueling fighting that had typified the Italian campaign would be avoided.

In the Toulon-Marseilles sector between August 21 and 23, the French slowly squeezed the Germans back into Toulon in a series of almost continuous street battles. As the German defense lost coherence, isolated groups began to surrender, with the last organized resistance ending on August 26 and the formal German surrender occurring two days later. The battle cost the French about twenty-seven hundred casualties, but they claimed seventeen thousand prisoners, indicating that few Germans had followed Hitler's stand-and-die order. Meanwhile French troops drove within five to eight miles of the center of Marseilles, while within the city the Maqui and other Resistance groups launched an uprising.

While the French forces besieged the ports, Truscott ordered Task Force Butler west toward Montelimar to establish blocking positions and await the arrival of Dahlquist's Thirty-sixth Division. This plan was complicated on the afternoon of August 21 by Truscott's receipt of an Ultra intercept informing him that elements of the Eleventh Panzer Division had crossed the Rhone and were headed directly for Aix-en-

Provence. This caused him to hesitate to send specific instructions to Dahlquist and to temporarily cancel the northward movement of one of the Forty-fifth Division's battalions. In addition, limited distribution of the Ultra information, as a security precaution, meant that neither Butler nor Dahlquist had any clear idea of German withdrawal plans up the Rhone Valley or east from Grenoble into Italy. The result was that the American units arrived at Montelimar in piecemeal fashion.

With air reconnaissance reports showing that German columns were moving north on both sides of the Rhone, despite the establishment of a blockade north of Montelimar, Truscott hurried to Dahlquist's command post a few miles north of the town. When he pointed out that Dahlquist's essential task was to occupy a long ridge overlooking Highway 7 to the north of Montelimar, Dahlquist replied that he had launched an attack to capture the ridge that morning and his troops were now on the northern end. He expressed confidence in his ability to block any enemy withdrawal up the Rhone. The following morning, Truscott was "most unhappy" about the situation at Montelimar. Air reconnaissance made the previous day had reported that Germans were continuing to withdraw to the north. In spite of assurances, the roadblock on Highway 7 was not effective.

Returning to Dahlquist's CP, Truscott said, "John, I have come here with the full intention of relieving you from your command. You have reported to me that you held the high ground north of Montelimar and that you had blocked Highway 7. You have not done so. You have failed to carry out my orders. You have just five minutes in which to convince me that you are not at fault."

Dahlquist explained that he had believed from reports sent to him that his troops were on the hill along Highway 7 north of Montelimar. He said he had not discovered the error until the day after. When he visited the regiment, he found it on the hill to the east of the ridge. During the preceding day, he continued, he made every effort to make the block effective but the enemy had been too strong. He also had been threatened by an attack east from Loriol in the direction of Crest, which virtually cut his supply road south of Crest, and by an armored attack north from Puy St. Martin toward Crest. Nevertheless, he now had a block at Coucourde and had four battalions of artillery where they could interrupt the road. Except for his initial mistake, he said, he thought he had done as well as could be expected.

Truscott did not fully concur, but he decided against relieving him.

By the evening of August 27, the Third Infantry Division had driven from the south hard on the heels of the retreating Germans, reaching a point within five miles of Montelimar. As heavy fighting raged for two days, Truscott shuttled in a Piper Cub between the VI Corps command post at Aspres, the Third Division front, and Dahlquist. Looking down on a field of battle that his traveling companion, Captain James M. Wilson, called "carnage compounded," he observed division artillery using direct and tank fire on Highway 7 that delivered a punishing stream of fire on a disorganized, bumper-to-bumper column of German vehicles, armor, and horse-drawn guns and equipment. While Thirty-sixth Division artillery hammered the stuck vehicles, fighter-bombers strafed the desperate retreat. In one instance, a double column of 350 German guns and vehicles that stretched along the highway for two kilometers were trapped and destroyed.

Despite this assault, Truscott was chagrined that most of the Eleventh Panzer Division and much of the 198th Reserve Division had broken through the roadblock. "I was disappointed that any Germans on the east bank of the Rhone had escaped our trap," he wrote. "However, when I later flew over the entire area at low elevation and at slow speed to examine the battlefield, I found that we had done better than I had thought while the battle continued."

From Montelimar north to Loriol, roads were lined with tanks, trucks, guns, and vehicles of every description. Hundreds of railway cars were loaded with weapons and equipment, including seven of the long-range railway guns like those of the Anzio Express that tormented the beachhead at Anzio. Hundreds of dead soldiers and horses littered the plain south of Loriol. "I know of no place where more damage was inflicted upon troops in the field," Truscott wrote, "and it is rather interesting to note that it was done almost entirely by ground weapons, artillery, tanks, tank destroyers and demolitions. Our air support, because of the lack of forward ground control, was employed only on missions for which they had been briefed or for armed reconnaissance north of the Drome River and east of the Rhone."

The battle of Montelimar netted 5,000 prisoners, destroyed hundreds of vehicles, and eliminated two German Divisions. In fourteen days, at a cost of 1,331 killed and wounded, the VI Corps had encircled Toulon and Marseilles, nearly destroyed the German XIX Army east of the Rhone, captured 23,000 prisoners, and was more than a hundred miles north of the beaches with elements still hundreds of miles farther on. "Even if Montelimar had not been a perfect battle," Truscott said, "we could still view the record with some degree of satisfaction."

While the battle at Montelimar was still in progress, General Patch issued orders that outlined plans for continuing the advance to the north with the object of joining up with the recently activated Third Army. Speeding east from the Normandy beachhead as part of an operation named Cobra to break out of difficult hedgerow country, it was commanded by George Patton. In a ruse to lead the Germans into believing that the invasion would take place at Calais, he had been assigned by Eisenhower to command a fictitious army based in northern England. Arriving in France in a shroud of secrecy, he launched the Third Army breakout drive on August 1. In Patch's plan to link up with him, VI Corps would continue to Grenoble and Valence to Lyon. Elements of the French Army B were to cross the Rhone at Avignon, take up the pursuit west of the Rhone, and assist VI Corps. After the capture of Lyon, VI Corps was to cross to the west bank of the Saone and drive northward on the axis Autun-Beaune-Langres. After capturing Marseilles, French Army B was to advance north on the line of

Sisteron-Grenoble-Bourg-Besançon and relieve all elements of VI Corps in the mountain passes north of Briangon.

As the drive north began on August 29, the primary difficulty for Truscott was keeping up the momentum in the face of an increasingly serious problem with his fuel supply. In one instance, he had to issue an order to a French unit to stop its advance so he could shift its gasoline to an American outfit with a higher-priority objective. He learned later that at a meeting with General Marshall on a visit to the French sector, the commander bitterly denounced Truscott for favoring VI Corps and putting the French at a disadvantage by stealing gasoline allotted to the French. In a letter to General Patch, Truscott said, "Our supply situation problem has been difficult and, of course, will become more so when heavy fighting incident to the reduction of the Belfort Gap [the gateway into Germany] requires enormous ammunition expenditures. I have no doubt that, by strenuous effort, solutions can be found and adequate supplies for the operations can be provided."

Resistance by the Germans was largely from relatively small units protecting retreating forces with delaying actions. GIs also found their advances into and through towns slowed by French citizens thronging narrow streets to welcome them. Hailed as liberators, they were deluged with cheers, embraces, kisses, baskets of fruit, long loaves of bread, and so many bottles of wine that someone named the invasion the champagne campaign.

A portrait of Truscott at this time was provided to Americans at home by a reporter who could not by any stretch of the imagination be mistaken for an Ernie Pyle. The son of the controversial pioneering tycoon of American journalism, William Randolph Hearst, who'd been the inspiration for the 1940 Orson Welles film *Citizen Kane*, William (Bill) Randolph Hearst, Jr., provided a three-part series for the Hearst chain of newspapers. Datelined "At the Front Somewhere in France with the 7th Army," it started with Hearst declaring that Truscott was his favorite general. Noting that Truscott commanded the VI Corps in the

Seventh Army, but that by right his rank entitled him to command an army made up of several corps, Hearst provided this physical description:

> He is a big, strongly built, 49-year-old Texan with large piercing eyes. His graying black hair is now handsomely whitening about his temples, and when he flashes those big, cold gray eyes on you, you feel as if you were looking at an eagle. He habitually dresses in a green air corps shirt with a parachute silk map scarf around his neck, riding breeches, cavalry boots and a worn leather jacket. He varies this sometimes by wearing officers' pinks, so called, stuffed into parachutists' boots. The scarf, incidentally, is something neat. Printed on both sides are detailed maps, in pastel shades, of the terrain for several hundred miles in which the parachutist will find himself when he gets down to earth.

In the second article depicting a venture to the front with Truscott, Hearst recorded a general with a bad cold and "one of those irritating coughs that catch in the chest." By the time Truscott was through coughing, he was almost purple in the face and his usually raspy voice sounded like "a beaten-up foghorn." On a rainy and cold Tuesday afternoon, Hearst and Truscott headed for what Hearst called "the to-hell-and-gone up front." Passing through divisional and regimental headquarters and medical battalion aid sections, the general was in the front seat of a jeep wearing his lacquered helmet and a .45-caliber pistol strapped to his right side. Flying from the jeep's radiator cap was the VI Corps flag. Bolted to the left fender was a siren. On the right was a red light. Hearst found it funny to see GIs slopping along in the rain and mud, or talking to French girls, then suddenly looking up and seeing a general bearing down on them. Most were too surprised to salute.

Providing a picture of both a war reporter and Truscott in action, Hearst wrote:

> On we went through ever thinning traffic, a sure sign you are near the lines, finally driving up a side of a hill right out in the open, facing the enemy, and then coming to a stop. In the valley below flowed the swollen Volagne River. Out ahead to our left ran a wooden bridge, then came a single high, wooded knoll, and then another ridge running off down to our right. At the foot of the knoll lay the town of Bruyères, which our troops had just taken after three or four days of bitter fighting. A lieutenant and a private hastily scrambled to their feet as we walked up to them. They had a phone back to some artillery battery and were directing fire into the town as well as on such other targets as they thought promising. We stayed a good twenty minutes, the general leaning against a tree, peering through the field glasses he carried and occasionally consulting his map. I do not suppose he spoke more than fifty words either querying the lieutenant or issuing orders.

Truscott recorded that at this time almost incessant rain vastly increased the hardships of moving and fighting. Cold caused extreme discomfort, and the losses and exertions of the preceding weeks were having their effect. All units were under strength, and officers and men were in dire need of rest.

On September 2, 1944, Hearst's speculation that Truscott would soon receive the boost in rank that he thought the general deserved appeared about to come true. Word came that the U.S. Senate had been asked to approve President Roosevelt's nomination of Truscott to the rank of lieutenant general. But putting the three stars on his shirt and helmet came at a cost. Called to a meeting with Patch and Eisenhower at Épinal, he expected a discussion of what would be VI Corps' next mission. Instead, Ike stated, "Lucian, I am going to relieve you from the Sixth Corps. Now that you've been made a lieutenant general, you have become an embarrassment to me because all of my corps commanders want to be lieutenant generals. I'm going to assign you to organize the new Fifteenth Army. You won't like it. It is not going to be operational. It will be an administrative and training command, and you won't get into the fighting."

Truscott replied that he preferred to remain with the VI Corps and was perfectly willing to remain a major general. He added that he hadn't asked to be promoted. Patch said he would like to have him remain. But Eisenhower replied that it was not practicable to leave him with VI Corps and that he needed him for organizing the new army. Besides, Major General E. H. (Ted) Brooks, who was to replace Truscott at VI Corps, was already on his way. In the meantime, Truscott would remain in command until Brooks had affairs well in hand. Truscott would then go to SHAEF headquarters, stopping off on the way to discuss organization of the new army with General Omar Bradley, under whose command Truscott would serve. After that, Ike would send his new lieutenant general home for a short leave. When he returned, he would take command of the Seventh Army.

For a reporter assigned to cover the invasion of the south of France, Truscott's new rank and imminent change of jobs required a little revising of a cover story he was writing for the October 2, 1944, issue of *Life*. A buddy of Ernie Pyle and Bill Mauldin, and therefore well acquainted with Truscott's Chinese kitchen crew and late-at-night drinking sessions, Will Lang had come to *Time* and *Life* in 1936 from a stint with the *Chicago Daily News*. A veteran of covering the Battle of Kasserine Pass, he had been the first reporter to enter Tunis and was nearly killed in the fight to take Naples. With the help of Sarah Truscott, who sent him a lengthy letter with details of her husband's childhood in Oklahoma and a chronology of his army career, Lang produced a profile of Truscott that ran eight long pages in *Life*, with a cover photo by *Life* cameraman George Silk of the general in full battle array from knee-high boots to gleaming helmet. With large hands hooked into the pockets of his riding breeches, the general identified in the caption as "Truscott of the 7th" was pictured with jutting iron jaw and steely eyes gazing into the distance, as if he were staring down the enemy. Inside in a full-page photo, he squints in bright sunlight and wears the shoulder patch of VI Corps and the twin stars of a major general on the shoulders of a leather jacket and on the front of his shiny helmet.

"By now it is clear," wrote Lang, "that the invasion of southern France was one of the most amazing exploits yet seen in amphibious warfare. It was an operation that generals dream about, although its spectacular success was dimmed by the breakthrough in Normandy and the fall of Paris. Originally the attack was designed to coincide with the Normandy landings. It was delayed but then set up again to draw off German troops pinning down Allied forces in Normandy's tall hedgerows. When Patton's armor broke loose unaided, Truscott's southern invaders gained the psychological and military advantage of having the enemy off balance."

Illuminating Truscott's lack of a need for self-aggrandizing publicity, Lang cited a case of a high-ranking German general who was proudly marched into Truscott's headquarters by the paratrooper who captured him. It was a chance for a picture that Patton or Clark would have relished. When the proud soldier announced, "Here's a general, sir, all served up on toast," Truscott stayed at his desk and grumbled, "Send him back to the Seventh Army. I've got other things to do."

Depicting Truscott's forces often running ahead of his maps, Lang portrayed the general keeping up with his men and sharing the taste of victory made doubly sweet by contrast with the frustrations of Cassino and the Anzio beachhead. It was a victory such as all victories should be, said Lang. Swift and complete.

In an analysis of Operation Dragoon and subsequent action for the

U.S. Army Center of Military History, Jeffrey L. Clarke wrote that the southern France campaign showed what experienced, well-led Allied troops could do against their German foes. Neither Truscott nor Patch wanted a repeat of the protracted agony Truscott endured in the Italian campaign, the lengthy slugging match Patch had experienced at Guadalcanal, or the two-month stalemate that frustrated Eisenhower following Normandy. Observing that Truscott and Patch were willing to take risks to shorten the campaign, Clarke found that each was confident that his troops and commanders could carry out even the most difficult maneuvers. The result of the campaign in the south of France was the presence on Eisenhower's southern flank of a strong Allied army group rather than a concentrated powerful resistance to a sweep toward Germany.

On October 24, Truscott, Don Carleton, and other aides visited the divisions for farewells with commanders and staffs with whom they had been comrades in arms for so long. The following morning, he said good-bye to Patch and the Seventh Army staff and departed for a visit with Lieutenant General Jacob Devers and the Army Group staff. Next came a reunion with Patton at Third Army headquarters in Nancy, a call on Bradley at his headquarters in Luxembourg, a visit to First Army headquarters in Spa, and on October 30 a meeting with Walter Bedell Smith at SHAEF on organizing the Fifteenth Army.

On November 4, Truscott left France for his first visit home in more than two years.

★ SEVENTEEN ★

FORGOTTEN FRONT

WHEN COLONEL LUCIAN K. TRUSCOTT, JR., left Washington, D.C., in the spring of 1942, the mood in the nation's capital had been anxious. Although President Roosevelt had promised Americans that triumph in the war that had been foisted on them was inevitable, anybody familiar with the true state of the country's readiness understood that victory was far from certain.

As Lieutenant General Truscott returned to the United States on November 5, 1944, North Africa had been swept clean of the Germans, Vichy collaborators, and Italians. Sicily was liberated. The Allies had driven the Germans in Italy to the northern mountains. The past year brought the smashing of the Atlantic Wall at Normandy, liberations of Rome and Paris, and a string of victories in the Pacific. Despite Hitler's unleashing of flying bombs against London that he named V (for victory) weapons and the British called doodlebugs, Londoners went about their daily affairs with the fortitude, patience, and faith in the victorious outcome of the war that they'd demonstrated during the Blitz and after the failure at Dieppe.

In the United States in November 1944, gasoline and almost all of the basics of living were still scarce. Investigators on behalf of the Senate reported that the only way to end the shortages was by winning the war. The government announced an increase in the draft rate for January and February of 1945 from sixty thousand to eighty thousand and raised war production goals on the basis of the belief that the fighting in Europe would continue for a year or more.

While war weariness was widespread, it hadn't kept the country from going agog over a sexy first novel titled *Forever Amber*. By some accounts, its young author, Kathleen Winsor, was getting more publicity than Roosevelt and Frank Sinatra combined. For a book one literary critic summed up as "a tale of a trollop left to unshift for herself," the publisher had spent in the neighborhood of $40,000 in advertising, but the success of the bawdy 972-page saga that was set in Restoration England was assisted by a bonanza of publicity for being banned in Boston. Also on the proscribed reading list in the city that called itself the cradle of liberty was another first novel, *Strange Fruit*. A lurid story about whites and blacks in the South by Lillian Smith, it zoomed up the best-seller lists. So did movie and radio comedian Bob Hope's book *I Never Left Home*, about his shows for GIs at the front. It sold nearly 1.5 million copies, putting it far ahead of the sales of any other title on the fiction and nonfiction shelves in bookstores.

Virtually every form of entertainment was also benefiting from a desire to escape the grim reality of war. A play that endeared itself to thousands of Americans was *Harvey*. By Mary Chase, it was a comedy about a lovable inebriate's friendship with an imaginary giant rabbit. Also deemed by drama critics as praiseworthy were *I Remember Mama*, John Van Druten's dramatization of Kathryn Forbes's book, *Mamma's Bank Account*; *The Late George Apley*, John P. Marquand's novel made into a play by himself and George S. Kaufman; Paul Osborn's dramatization of John Hersey's novel *A Bell for Adano*, about a town in Italy where the people pestered the U.S. Army to restore its church's carillon; and Philip Yordan's melodrama about a black prostitute, *Anna Lucasta*. Another Broadway hit was *Jacobowsky and the Colonel*, a Franz Werfel comedy that was adapted by S. N. Behrman. Of the new musical shows only two were conceded by most New York reviewers to possess superior merit. They found that *Song of Norway* made skillful use of the music of Edvard Grieg and *The Seven Lively Arts*, a revue by the flamboyant impresario Billy Rose, provided Cole Porter songs performed by Beatrice Lillie, Bert Lahr, and Benny Goodman. Also enjoying sellout runs were *Follow the Girls* and *Bloomer Girl*.

Motion-picture critics in a nationwide poll opined that the best performances of 1944 were given by Bing Crosby in *Going My Way* and Jennifer Jones in *The Song of Bernadette*. New York film critics named *Going My Way* as the foremost picture of the year, but awarded top honors for best male performance to the Irish character actor Barry Fitzgerald as an elderly priest in the picture. Tallulah Bankhead was chosen as the best female performer of the year for her performance in *Lifeboat*. The *Motion Picture Herald*'s yearly popularity poll found that the ten leaders at the box office were Crosby, Hope, Gary Cooper, Betty Grable, Spencer Tracy, Greer Garson, Humphrey Bogart, Abbott and Costello, Cary Grant, and Bette Davis.

Although the tunesmiths of Tin Pan Alley had made 1944 a considerably better than average year for new popular music, high on the public's list of favorite pop songs were the revivals "I'll Get By," "It Had to Be You," "Together," and "Paper Doll." The fresh tunes to sell briskly on record were melancholy reminders that there was a war going on, including "I'll Be Seeing You," Jerome Kern's "Long Ago and Far Away," and "I'll Walk Alone." Cole Porter had smash hits in "I Love You" and "Don't Fence Me In," a cowboy song that was surprisingly out of character for the sophisticated and urbane composer of "Night and Day."

Romance-minded Americans were dancing to Big Band renditions of "Amor," "My Heart Tells Me," "Dance with a Dolly (with a Hole in Her Stocking)," and "Besame Mucho." To satisfy the persistent American penchant for the zany and the nonsensical there were the delightfully dizzy "Mairzy Doats," "Is You Is or Is You Ain't My Baby?" and a plea from someone who worked the late-night shift in a war-industry plant, "Milkman, Keep Those Bottles Quiet." With December 25 looming just around the corner, Bing Crosby's previous rendering of Irving Berlin's "I'm Dreaming of a White Christmas" was back on the radio and in soda fountain jukeboxes.

That the country was in a holiday mood would be observed by sales staffs, who found that Americans bought more Christmas gifts than ever before, allowing happy merchants to finish off a year in which total retail sales reached record-breaking proportions. Consumer spending in 1944 would amount to $67 billion, bettering the previous year's tally by almost 4 billion bucks. The U.S. Department of Commerce would point out that they might have spent much more if there had not been shortages of some classifications of durable goods. A large part of the record-smashing sales was made up of luxury and semi-luxury items, such as lingerie, furs, jewelry, fancy apparel, and accessories. Writers on the subject of women's fashions noted that in the fall of 1944 American ladies discarded the tiny hats they'd been wearing for years in favor of a new creation in the form of tall, mostly brimless chapeaux inspired by Parisian styles that were widely publicized after the liberation of the City of Light.

Two days after Truscott stepped into this revitalized nation from an army transport plane and into Sarah's embrace, Americans elected Franklin D. Roosevelt to a fourth term. Scheduled to return to Europe on November 21, Truscott spent most of his leave time with Sarah and Jamie in Virginia. After taking a day to visit Lucian III at West Point, he was back in Washington to confer with General Marshall. During a briefing by the chief of the Operations Division, Lieutenant General John E. Hull, on the deployment of U.S. forces in all parts of the world, the meeting turned to the recent death of Sir John Dill, the chief of Britain's military mission in Washington. Hull reported that Prime Minister Churchill planned to bring General Sir Henry Maitland Wilson from the Mediterranean theater to replace Dill and have General Alexander replace General Wilson as Supreme Allied Commander Mediterranean. Hull said that he supposed that General Mark Clark would then replace General Alexander as Allied Commanding General in Italy. This would leave the Fifth Army command vacant.

Following his custom of addressing everyone by last name, Marshall turned to Truscott and asked, "Truscott, how do you feel about going back to Italy?"

Surprised, he answered, "Sir, I will do the best I can wherever you send me."

"I know that," said Marshall impatiently. "That is not what I asked you. How do you *feel* about going back to Italy?"

"Well, sir, if the choice were left with me I would prefer to remain in France. I have looked forward to serving with General Eisenhower again."

"I suppose you prefer France because you think France is the decisive theater," General Marshall said. "You think that is where the war will be won."

"Yes, sir. Something like that. Of course you know that both corps commanders in the Fifth Army have always been senior to me."

Turning to Hull, Marshall ordered, "Query General Eisenhower on this subject."

The conference ended.

Because Truscott was to leave from LaGuardia Field in New York for Paris late that afternoon, he reasoned that if he could see Eisenhower before he replied to Hull's cable, Ike might make it possible for him to remain in France. After delays in departure and en route kept him from arriving in Paris earlier than November 24, he rushed to see Walter Bedell Smith at Versailles. Eisenhower's deputy looked up at him and said,

"Well, you are a nice one. No sooner do we get you back under our command than off you go and find yourself a new assignment."

Truscott replied that he hoped Eisenhower would reply to Hull's cable by saying he had need of Truscott's services.

"Not a chance," said Smith. "The PM [Churchill] personally asked for you."

He handed Truscott a cable in which Eisenhower said that Truscott's experiences in Italy, his familiarity with conditions there, and his record of good relations with the British made him the logical choice for the Italian assignment.

Departing from Orly Field near Paris on the afternoon of December 8, Truscott arrived in Caserta, Italy, later the same day. For the previous week, he had visited various American headquarters in France to collect staffers he'd had brought from VI Corps to serve with him in the Fifteenth Army. Arriving in Florence, Italy, they proceeded to the Fifth Army command post at Futa Pass and found Generals Clark and Gruenther, and other old friends. They were told that General Alexander had fixed December 16 as the date for the changes in command.

Army records show that while Truscott took VI Corps to the south of France to execute Dragoon, Clark's Fifth Army had been left with only five divisions and the Eighth Army with sixteen. Both had pressed the pursuit of the retreating Germans and by mid-August had reached a line from Ancona, Perugia, and Arezzo to the Arno River. After necessary resting, regrouping, and reorganizing supply lines, they were ready to launch General Alexander's plan for a major offensive to break through the German "Gothic Line." By the first week in September, they had smashed through it south of Rimini. The Fifth Army then crossed the Arno, and by September 22, after bitter fighting in some of the most difficult terrain yet encountered, General Keyes's II Corps had reached Il Giogio and Futa passes. Meanwhile, the Eighth Army, impeded by torrential rains, lagged behind. Clark then changed the direction of his main effort toward Faenza in an effort to get into the plain of the Po River and assist the Eighth's advance.

Shifting toward Bologna, Clark moved in unfavorable weather and against increasing opposition, making slow progress. After halting in mid-October with II Corps south of the town of Pianoro, ten miles away from Bologna, he turned to the northwest in a maneuver in which the Eighth Infantry Division captured Mount Grande near the edge of the Po Valley in the vicinity of Castel San Pietro. With success almost within their grasp, torrential rains, physical exhaustion, and supply troubles brought the advance to a stop.

In command of the German forces since the invasion of Italy, Field Marshal Albert Kesselring had at his disposal in Army Group Southwest thirty-three divisions, including twenty-seven German and six Italian. They opposed twenty-seven British and American divisions. The actual infantry strength of the forces was not disproportionate, but the Allies had the advantage because of the larger size of their divisions. The Allied trump card in the impending confrontation was overwhelming air power.

When General Alexander renewed the offensive at the end of November, his plan was to have the Eighth Army begin the attack in the Adriatic plain and drive the Germans west of the Santerno River. When the Eighth reached there around December 7, it was to turn north to outflank Bologna from the east, while the Fifth Army joined the attack, making its main effort with II Corps. The attack was named Pianoro.

Stretching from the Mediterranean coast near Genoa toward Rimini on the Adriatic, the mountainous region was called the Northern Apennines. Truscott recalled, "This was the most heavily fortified area along the entire front, held by German forces not materially inferior in strength to those which we would be attacking. Under unfavorable conditions of weather and terrain, it seemed to me an appalling undertaking. Even with overwhelming support of our air forces, I thought it would be a difficult and costly venture even if it could succeed. When Clark asked my opinion, I mentioned these reservations and suggested a maneuver west of Highway 64 might be much easier going and perhaps accomplish the same purpose more quickly at less cost. Clark disagreed, and he was always thereafter sensitive to any criticism of Pianoro."

Beginning the day after his arrival, Truscott spent several days visiting various parts of the front, familiarizing himself with conditions among the troops, renewing acquaintances with many commanders and staffs, and becoming acquainted with others. Keyes and Major General Willis D. Crittenberger were cavalrymen. Keyes had been Truscott's instructor at the training camp in Arkansas in 1917 and had been his superior as General Patton's deputy in Africa, in Sicily, and for a brief period prior to Anzio. Crittenberger had been on the faculty of the Cavalry School when Truscott was a student. Both had always been senior to him.

On Truscott's second night as an army commander, Bill Mauldin showed up with a copy of his new book, *Up Front*, and a copy of *Time* magazine for November 6, 1944, with an article about Mauldin. Referring to Joe in the Willie and Joe cartoons as the most famous fictional GI in America, it said that Joe kept pace with his creator in the process of becoming a soldier. "From an average, homely rookie, surprised at being jolted out of his civilian rights," said the profile, "[Mauldin] has slowly hardened into the seemingly resigned, latently hopeful man he is. In battle his hatred for MPs has softened, because MPs also die. His enthusiasm for undermining the officer system has waned. He studiously avoids talk of fear and death. He knows that his only reward for pushing the enemy back over one cold, rocky mountain is a chance to push him over the next one."

The cartoonist and the general chatted over cocktails and had dinner in Truscott's van next to the command post that someone had named the Hut.

The change in Fifth Army command took place on December 16, following a farewell ceremony for Clark. The next day, Truscott found himself host to members of the Military Affairs Committee of the House of Representatives. Its chairman was the California Democrat John M.

Costello. The ranking minority member was J. Parnell Thomas of New Jersey. Both found themselves overshadowed in the attention of a flock of war correspondents by a member of Congress who was arguably the most notable woman in America, next to Eleanor Roosevelt. A glamorous and witty novelist and playwright, Clare Booth Luce was the wife of the most powerful magazine baron in the country.

Having met the founder of *Time*, *Life*, and *Fortune* at a New York cocktail party in 1935, Clare Booth married Henry Robinson (Harry) Luce one month after his divorce from his wife of twelve years. Her original ambition was to be an actress, and she'd understudied Mary Pickford before enrolling in the Clare Tree Majors School of the Theater. Losing interest in the stage, she dropped out to go on a European tour with her parents. Through this she met Mrs. O. H. P. Belmont, a New York society matron, who introduced her to George Tuttle Brokaw, a New York clothing manufacturer. When their marriage ended in divorce in 1929, she joined the staff of *Vogue* as an editorial assistant. Two years later as associate editor of *Vanity Fair*, she began writing short sketches satirizing New York high society. These were published under the title *Stuffed Shirts* in 1933. In pursuit of a career as a playwright, she resigned from the magazine in 1934. In the same month in which she wed Luce, her first play, *Abide With Me*, opened on Broadway and was panned by the critics. Her second effort, *The Women*, in 1936, was a satire on the idleness of wealthy wives and divorcees that overcame a very cool reception by reviewers to run for 657 performances, tour the United States, and be a hit in eighteen countries. It was later made into a successful movie. In 1938, *Kiss the Boys Goodbye* was a political allegory about American Fascism, but was viewed as a comedy about the highly publicized search for an actress to portray Scarlett O'Hara in *Gone With the Wind*. In *Margin for Error* in 1939 and two later plays, Clare Booth Luce solidified her standing as a leading American playwright.

Traveling to Europe in 1940 as a journalist for *Life*, she offered observations of Italy, France, Belgium, the Netherlands, and England in the midst of the German offensive that defeated all but England. In 1941, she and Luce toured China (where Luce had been born to American missionaries) and reported the odyssey in *Life*. After the United States entered the war, she toured Africa, India, China, and Burma for *Life* and interviewed General Harold R. L. G. Alexander, commander of British troops in the Middle East; Jawaharlal Nehru; Chiang Kai-shek; and General "Vinegar Joe" Stilwell, commander of American troops in the China-Burma-India theater. Claiming her travels as firsthand experience with international affairs, she agreed to pleas from Republicans to run for Congress in the Fourth Congressional District of Connecticut and won. In her maiden speech, she assailed Vice President Henry A. Wallace's ideas on ways to ensure international peace as "globaloney." Because of this and other fiery assertions, a journalist cited her as "Hell on high heels." The darling of the ultraconservative isolationists in Congress, she landed appointment to the Military Affairs Committee.

Clearly as smitten by Mrs. Luce as the war correspondents, possibly because he saw in her the qualities of independent thinking, resolute purpose, charm, sophistication, and polish he found in Sarah, Truscott invited Luce to share his Christmas dinner. Although Truscott chose not to mention in *Command Missions* that Mrs. Luce visited him as a member of the Military Affairs Committee delegation and had been his dinner guest, the war correspondent Jack Foisie provided a lengthy account of what the general and the congresswoman did the day before Christmas. Describing her in the story's second paragraph as a "glamorous blonde" and in the third as being "indefatigable," he wrote that she was "up early this morning" (December 24) and with Truscott as her guide had set off to venture even farther up front.

Foisie wrote:

> She wangled permission from the pleasantly gruff general. In a conversation that began with Mrs. Luce asking: "What security restrictions are there on you and me

in regard to going up to exposed positions?" the general smilingly answered there were none on him and only those that he imposed on her. Mrs. Luce made known her desire to go where there is no Christmas.

The general countered by asking her how she was at walking.

"I walk very fine," Mrs. Luce replied, her eyes twinkling.

The Fifth Army commander, smilingly admitting defeat, said that he would take her up front himself. At Co. A of an armored infantry battalion she was shown about by Master Sergeant Harry Naveley of Lebanon, Pennsylvania. Once the men had shaken off their awe at the sight of a beautiful woman they began to answer her questions in language overflowing with well-known Army complaints.

The article depicted Luce bundled in GI winter clothing, "Ernie Pyle style" knit cap, and a sleeping bag in the rear of Truscott's jeep. Foisie wrote that she was "a cute Christmas Eve package" and was often recognized by GIs along the road.

A result of Luce's visit was a turning of the spotlight on war coverage from the action in France to the Italian front. Perhaps because Luce was the wife of *Life*'s owner, the magazine sent its most prestigious photographer to Truscott's Fifth Army front. In a multiple-page photo essay by Margaret Bourke-White titled "Forgotten Front," with the subtitle "U.S. Fifth Army Fights a Plodding War in Italy," the text noted that Truscott was in command of troops from several nations in "the greatest military experiment in history of the welding of fighting men of many countries in the common cause of freedom." Side by side in Italy's mountains with GIs were soldiers from England, Canada, New Zealand, India, Poland, Brazil, Italy, and a newly activated Jewish brigade flying the flag of Palestine. The

Leading troops in invasions and combat in North Africa, Sicily, Italy, and southern France in World War II, Lucian K. Truscott, Jr., earned a reputation for toughness and victories without seeking the fame and glory craved by other generals.

Courtesy of George C. Marshall Library and Museum

As deputy to General George S. Patton in the Operation Torch invasion of French Morocco, Brigadier General Truscott confers with aides after leading troops in capturing the vital port of Lyautey.　*Courtesy of the National Archives*

In September 1942, Truscott (in cavalry boots) inspects the first members of the new U.S. Army Rangers Battalion in training at the British Commando school in Scotland with Ranger organizer and commander Major William Orlando Darby. Darby led them in four invasions and combat in North Africa, Sicily, and Italy. *Courtesy of the National Archives*

With Truscott serving as General Eisenhower's field deputy after a humiliating defeat at the Kasserine Pass, Tunisia, U.S. artillery, armor, and infantry rallied to defeat the Germans at El Guettar. *Courtesy of the National Archives*

Racing past a captured German antitank gun, this GI totes a submachine gun in pursuit of retreating Germans at El Guettar. Capture of Tunisia cleared the way for an invasion of Sicily. *Courtesy of the National Archives*

The crew of a 105-mm antitank gun mounted on a half track swings into action in Tunisia on March 3, 1943. *Courtesy of the National Archives*

During a brief lull in the fighting at El Guettar, officers study a map while the crew of a tank-destroyer outfit takes a break.

Courtesy of the National Archives

Through a gap in a wall, a 105-mm howitzer team reloads in the final stage of the advance in Tunisia. Two months later, with Truscott in command of the Third Infantry Division, the Allies landed in Sicily.

Courtesy of the National Archives

Following a rapid attack by Patton's Seventh Army and Truscott's Third Division, U.S. tanks roll into the key city of Palermo.

Courtesy of the National Archives

Touring Palermo, Patton observes captured Italian troops. The fall of the city opened the way for a race between Americans and the British to take Messina and conquer Sicily.

Patton discusses the situation at Palermo with Brigadier General Ted Roosevelt. Eldest son of President Theodore Roosevelt, he was deputy commander of the First Division and later earned the Congressional Medal of Honor for heroic leadership on Utah Beach on D-day.

Following the invasion of Italy, a 168th Infantry patrol looks out for snipers as it enters the town of Calazzo.   *Courtesy of the National Archives*

Troops of Truscott's Third Division march past a dead German in Italy. An article in *Time* magazine in 1943 praised Truscott for turning the Third Division into one of the greatest combat divisions of the war.   *Courtesy of the National Archives*

As the U.S. Fifth Army drove north in Italy, a squad of Rangers laid down a barrage of rifle fire to cover the advance of an assault against stubborn German resistance.

Courtesy of the National Archives

When a drive toward Rome was blocked by Germans in an ancient Benedictine monastery on top of a mountain at Cassino, the Allies were forced to bomb the monastery. But the Germans fought on in the rubble, and several infantry assaults were needed to break the resistance.

Courtesy of the National Archives

In an effort to bypass the
Germans in the mountains,
American troops land on
the beach at Anzio.

Courtesy of the National Archives

Major General Truscott
in his VI Corps headquar-
ters in the Anzio area,
March 7, 1944.

Courtesy of the National Archives

World War II cartoonist Bill Mauldin
drew this sketch of a humble GI in
Truscott's autograph book. Flanked by
two generals in Truscott's command
post, known as "the Hut," he says,
"Geez, wotta joint!"

Courtesy of George C. Marshall Library and Museum

When Truscott and other famous officers from the Lone Star State were honored with a parade and reception by the city of San Antonio, they were overshadowed by the most-decorated enlisted man of World War II, Medal of Honor recipient Audie Murphy.

Courtesy of the National Archives

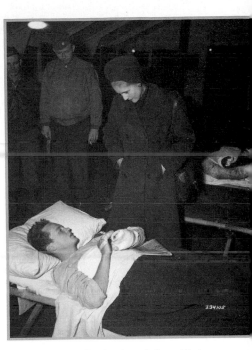

During an official visit to Italy at Christmas 1944, Congresswoman Clare Booth Luce was accompanied by Truscott on a tour of the Fifth Army's Italian front. Here, Luce chats with Walter McKinney of Washington, D.C., at the Eighth Evacuation Hospital.

Courtesy of the National Archives

Friend and frequent visitor to Truscott's headquarters, war correspondent Ernie Pyle never failed to show up with a bottle of cognac. This photo was taken at Truscott's command post at Anzio.

Courtesy of the National Archives

The breakout from
Anzio meant taking the
town of Cisterna street by
street and house by house.

Courtesy of the National Archives

Men of Company D, 338th
Infantry, direct machine-
gun fire at a German patrol
in the Fondi area of Italy in
the Fifth Army's push to-
ward Rome, May 23, 1944.

Courtesy of the National Archives

When the Fifth Army liberated Rome on June 5, 1944, its commander, Lieutenant General Mark Clark, held a triumphal ceremony and told reporters, "This is a great day for the Fifth Army." Truscott said later, "I reckon it was, but I was anxious to get out of this posturing and on with the business of war." *Courtesy of the National Archives*

With Rome taken, U.S. forces led by tanks pursued the Germans into the northern mountains and began a lengthy battle. Following the D-day landings in France, the Italian campaign became known as the "forgotten front." *Courtesy of the National Archives*

Shifted from Italy for an invasion of southern France in August 1944, Truscott commanded the 45th Division. In this photo, troops land near St. Maxime.

Courtesy of the National Archives

A squad of the First Airborne Task Force in action near La Motte.

Courtesy of the National Archives

American tanks rolling past destroyed German vehicles on Highway 7 leading to Montelimar, France. *Courtesy of the National Archives*

Sent back to Italy to replace Mark Clark as Fifth Army commander, Truscott (center) is shown here at a forward observation post with VI Corps commander, Major General Willis D. Crittenberger (right), and Truscott's chief of staff, Brigadier General Don E. Carlton. *Courtesy of the National Archives*

Truscott and Mark Clark pose for photographers as Truscott replaces Clark as commanding officer of the Fifth Army in December 1944. *Courtesy of the National Archives*

Near Mount Della Vedetta, Italy, on March 3, 1945, three members of Company K, 87th Mountain Infantry, Tenth Mountain Division, cover a house while German prisoners remove wounded Germans. The Germans had refused to surrender until an assault team with heavy machine guns surrounded them. *Courtesy of the National Archives*

Truscott with Deputy Supreme Allied Commander of the Mediterranean Theater, General Joseph T. McNarney (center), and Allied Air Forces commander in chief, Lieutenant General John K. Cannon, at Fifth Army HQ, April 23, 1945. The German forces in Italy capitulated twelve days later, and Germany surrendered on May 8 (V-E Day). *Courtesy of the National Archives*

When Eisenhower fired Patton after public protests against Patton for comparing the Nazi Party to the Democratic and Republican parties, Ike appointed Truscott to take over command of the Third Army.

Courtesy of the National Archives

A commander of the Arlington National Cemetery honor guard in 1931, Truscott wrote in his memoir of World War II, "A military funeral is a beautiful and impressive ceremony. One learns that there is beauty in death and the respect accorded the dead by the nation and those who live on after them." Three days after his death on September 12, 1965, at the age of seventy, with the rank of four-star general, he was interred at Arlington. *Courtesy of George C. Marshall Library and Museum*

Fifth Army also had an infantry division of black Americans. For these disparate soldiers, said the print accompanying White's pictures, the war meant creeping forward from rock to rock and crag to crag, without help from tanks, in weather that often conspired with ragged peaks to make tactical support from planes either impossible or ineffective.

Truscott attributed the lack of public knowledge and interest in the Italian front to many correspondents—with little liking for spending uncomfortable days in the mountains—seeking stories of small action that would have limited news value. "Rome not only offered far more in the way of physical comforts," he mused, "but the chance for an important news story in a capital city of that size." In an effort to stimulate press attention, the Fifth Army's public relations branch and historical sections sent out press releases that described actions of various units and gallant exploits of individuals. These were mailed to newspapers in hometowns, counties, and states of units and individuals in the hope that the stories would elicit mail from home that would make the troops feel less forgotten. It was a valiant effort, but with rare exceptions, such as the flurry of press interest in Clare Booth Luce's visit and Bourke-White's photo spread in *Life*, the rain-drenched dogfaces slogging in mud and up and down mountains in Italy remained eclipsed by the dashing of George Patton's tankers across France, which was favored by correspondents who preferred to cover the war from the comforts of Paris.

With Mrs. Luce gone and the publicity spotlight off him, Truscott began each day as usual with a staff meeting in which each of his field commanders reviewed their problems and activities. Once a week, he assembled special staff officers from the rear headquarters for a conference with his staff at the Hut.

On December 22, he'd visited the Sixth South African Division in rugged terrain between Setta Creek and the Reno River. Late in the afternoon, he went to Florence in response to a message from Mark Clark requesting a meeting there. Clark said he had received solid aerial and other intelligence that indicated a strong buildup of the enemy forces in the Serchio Valley. A relatively inactive area of the front, it was held in part by the Ninety-second Infantry Division. The outfit consisted of "colored" troops under the command of white senior officers. (Author's note: because the unit was called "colored" or "Negro" in the U.S. Army records, in Truscott's accounts, and by the press and the public, both white and black, the terms are used in this book to provide in the language of the time a depiction of the racial, ethnic, and multinational makeup of Truscott's command. It was an army that would also include Japanese Americans, then and herein called Nisei, and the mixture of troops from the countries cited by *Life* in the Bourke-White story.)

While a German counteroffensive in the Ardennes Forest of Belgium that had started on December 16 and became known as the Battle of the Bulge was still rolling unchecked, Clark expressed concern that the German command might be preparing a similar unpleasant surprise in Italy, using the 148th Grenadier Division and an Italian division in the area. There were also signs that the 157th Mountain Division, and possibly the Sixteenth SS Panzer Grenadier Division, were moving up. Clark's intelligence chief thought the Germans might be able to free at least two other divisions for a mighty push.

The day after Christmas, the Germans launched several limited-objective attacks in the area of the Second Battalion, 366th Infantry, Ninety-second Division, under the command of Major General Edward M. Almond. Born at Luray, Virginia, in 1892, he'd graduated from the Virginia Military Institute in 1915. As a first lieutenant in the infantry in 1917, he served with the Fourth Division and ended the war a temporary major. From 1919 to 1923, he taught military science at Marion Institute, Alabama. After attending Infantry School at Fort Benning, Georgia, he graduated from the Command and General Staff School in 1930. Following a tour of duty in the Philippines, he attended the Army War College, and from 1934 to 1938 was attached to the General Staff. Made lieutenant colonel in September 1938, he completed a course at the U.S. Navy War College in 1940, and in January 1941 was assigned to staff duty at VI Corps in Providence, Rhode Island. Promoted to the temporary rank of colonel (October 1941) and brigadier general (March 1942), he was named assistant commander of the Ninety-third Infantry Division in Arizona. In July 1942 he took command of the new outfit listed in the army roster as the Ninety-second Division (Negro). With its activation, he was given the rank of temporary major general.

Known as the Buffalo Division because of a black shoulder patch they wore in the shape of a bison, the Ninety-second traced its roots to the Ninth and Tenth Cavalries. Established in 1866, they were tasked with protecting westbound settlers from outlaws and Indians. According to one account, the men of the Tenth Cavalry first acquired the name Buffalo Soldiers during the 1871 campaign against the Comanche in the Indian Territory because the Comanche had respected the soldiers' tireless marching and dogged trail skills. Other stories suggested the nickname referred to buffalo hides used by black soldiers to supplement inadequate uniforms during the harsh western winters, or to the fact that Indians thought the black soldiers, with their dark skin and curly hair, resembled the buffalo. As a boy in Oklahoma, Truscott listened to tales told by old-timers of what they called "blackies going after redskins." He'd also known and liked black settlers who'd taken up the offer of the U.S. government to settle in Oklahoma with the goal of bringing the territory into the Union.

In Almond's Ninety-second Division, all the senior commanders and staff were white, except in the all-black 597th and 600th field artillery battalions. Enlisted men were almost entirely from the rural South. Most had been sent as children to work in the fields and never had a chance to learn to read or write. After training at Fort Huachuca and participating in corps maneuvers in Louisiana in early 1944, the division was committed in piecemeal manner to combat in Italy and assigned to the IV Corps of the Fifth Army in the Serchio Valley and the coastal sector along the Ligurian Sea at the westernmost end of the Allied front.

During the German assault on December 29, 1944, some failed to stand and fight. The term used in reports to Truscott was "melted away." To stem the tide of the German attack, Crittenberger was forced to move British Indian brigades forward. With air support by the Twenty-second Tactical Air Command, they retook two towns that the Germans had overrun. Truscott wrote, "It was fortunate the Germans did not make any greater effort than they did. Elements of four German divisions had been identified in these actions, but none of them involved more than combat groups with limited objectives. It seems likely the Germans were making a reconnaissance in force that they might have exploited if additional troops had not been encountered there. We were relieved that this was so, for a major attack could have been embarrassing, or even gravely dangerous."

In a report on an investigation ordered by Truscott regarding the performance of the Ninety-second Division since its arrival in Italy in August 1944, Crittenberger told Truscott that he'd found that the division had not demonstrated effectiveness in combat equal to that of the seven other American divisions in IV Corps. Describing Almond as a commander of proven superiority with an efficient staff, Truscott wrote, "Frequently, in various offensive operations which have been carefully planned and initiated under circumstances more than warranting every expectation of success, these troops have subsequently failed in the accomplishment of their assigned mission, when this mission involved standing fast under enemy counterattack or mortar or artillery fire. The demonstrated unreliability of these troops has thus not only caused the failure of the immediate operations, but on one occasion, has also jeopardized the success of the entire Corps mission. The infantry elements of the division have more than once demonstrated an unwillingness to close for hand-to-hand combat with the enemy. When such combat has been imminent, individuals have withdrawn from combat in disorder."

Crittenberger closed his report by stating that he was forced to conclude that the division be used in a relatively quiet and unimportant defensive position rather than in vital offensive operations in which dependability and staunch resolution were essential. Deeply troubled, Truscott decided that he had to forward the report to Mark Clark and the commander of the Mediterranean theater, Lieutenant General Joseph T. McNarney. In a tone of regret, he stated that he concurred with Crittenberger's assessment and recommendation. He wrote that while he realized fully, as did Almond, that there were "good colored" enlisted men and officers, "I think we must face the fact that we will never develop a combat unit capable of offensive power under our present system. What the answer is, I do not know."

Reflecting on the history of racial mixing in the U.S. Army in *Command Missions*, Truscott recalled:

> Most officers who served during World War I and who remained in the Army afterwards came to know in one way or another of the unsatisfactory combat record of the colored troops, although the story was never publicized so far as I know. During my twelve years as student and instructor in service schools, we examined many failures of troops in combat but I do not recall that any of these dealt with colored troops. The problem was not new, for there had been colored troops in the Army since the Civil War. But it was not serious, however, until total mobilization brought a pinch in manpower. When I was ordered back to Italy to command the Fifth Army, I was aware that the Ninety-second Infantry Division had joined the Fifth Army. Just before leaving France for Italy, I saw General Devers, who had been Deputy Supreme Allied Commander Mediterranean and Commanding General Mediterranean Theater of Operation (US), before organizing VI Army Group in September. He told me General Clark had already reported that the division was wholly unreliable in combat. But Devers remarked that he was convinced colored troops had not yet had a fair chance. He was confident the division would fight. I agreed with General Devers. I had never been assigned to either of the two colored cavalry regiments during my

service, but I had been connected with both of them for considerable periods. I knew many fine soldiers among them, men whom I was proud to number among my friends.

Truscott's first visit to the Ninety-second Division front had been on December 19–20. The occasion was a presentation of forty bronze stars and combat infantry badges to members of the division. With a platoon from each company assembled for the ceremony, he had been impressed with all that he saw. Personnel presented a smart appearance. The units were well equipped, worked in a professional manner, and gave every indication of being highly trained. A spirit of optimism pervaded. He knew that there were many black service units in the theater rendering satisfactory service as drivers and in engineer units, bridge companies, ordnance, and quartermaster units. He recorded, "There were many brave and competent colored officers and men in this infantry division. By no means were all prone to terror and fright; not all 'melted away' in the face of danger and the unknown. I decorated some and commissioned or promoted others who were worthy members of the fraternity of gallant soldiers and who would have been a credit to any organization. It was a matter of deep regret to all the officers who were concerned with the employment of this division that the proportion of those who failed to measure up was so large. But it was to the credit of colored Americans that many did."

Although he understood that these soldiers were the product of the environmental, educational, economic, and social ills of a race-conscious country beyond their control, and beyond the sphere of military leaders, he faced the challenge of using them to best advantage and decided that a further test was desirable. All blacks who had been decorated, all who had earned the combat infantry badge, all who'd been given battlefield promotions, and all of the best personnel of the three infantry regiments of the division would be put into one regiment. The others of the Ninety-second would be withdrawn to inactive areas and replaced by the 442nd Infantry Regiment (Nisei), who would be brought back from

France, and the 473rd Infantry Regiment, which had just been formed from converted antiaircraft artillery battalions.

On the overall issue of racial segregation at that time, Truscott found agreement among commanders that complete integration was impracticable and would lower the standards of combat divisions. "Some recommended including colored regiments in divisions," he recalled. "Others advised including colored battalions in infantry battalions, or even colored platoons in infantry companies." He personally felt that the association of blacks with other soldiers would result in no undue friction, and would do much toward developing individual pride, loyalty, a sense of responsibility, and a spirit of cooperation.

Despite these doubts about the fighting ability of black soldiers, by the day the war ended in Italy the Ninety-second had lost almost one-fourth of its strength, with about three thousand killed in action, captured, wounded, or missing, while capturing nearly twenty-four thousand prisoners and garnering more than twenty-one thousand decorations and citations for gallantry in combat.

The year 1945 began with expectations of a spring offensive. On January 19, Clark told Truscott that he had talked strategy with Mc-Creery. Because the British had three times the number of divisions in Italy as did the Americans, McCreery wanted Clark to concentrate the Eighth Army front in the Adriatic plain. Clark disagreed. He contended that the Fifth Army should make a strong effort south of Bologna because the German defenses were much less fortified there. As the planning proceeded, it became likely that three more British infantry divisions would be available in time for the offensive. There would also be a new American force coming to Italy from the United States that would be ready for combat by mid-February.

The story of how a general raised on the plains of Oklahoma found himself in command of a mountain division began when a Greenwich, Connecticut, insurance broker took a spill in Vermont and snapped an ankle.

While Charles Minot (Minnie) Dole lay helpless, his friend Frank

Edson stayed with him as their wives went down the mountain for help. The first person they met was a local farmer who said anyone foolish enough to ski got what he deserved and went on his way. The women located two people who helped them build a rescue toboggan improvised from a piece of corrugated roofing. The break was so severe that Dole was told he might never walk again. He not only recovered and resumed skiing, but organized a local ski rescue patrol that was soon expanded nationally.

When the United States entered the war, Dole recalled the success of Finnish ski troops fighting invading Soviet troops in 1939. By now he was the chairman of the U.S. National Ski Patrol Association, and believed that the army should have troops capable of fighting the same way. He wrote to General Marshall and President Roosevelt urging creation of a unit of experienced skiers. The War Department had been exploring adding ski patrols within several existing divisions, and in 1941 had created a Mountain Winter Warfare Board to design and test winter equipment and transportation, but it was only after Dole's pleading that the First Battalion of the Eighty-seventh Mountain Infantry Regiment was formed at Fort Lewis. This was followed by the Mountain Training Center (MTC) at Camp Carson, Colorado. After a search for a more suitable location for winter and mountain training, the facility was moved to Camp Hale in the Rocky Mountains close to Leadville, Colorado. During May and June 1942, the Second and Third battalions of the Eighty-seventh Regiment were activated and Camp Hale became the home of the MTC. Drawing its initial members from men already in the army who had previous ski and mountaineering experience, it had the National Ski Patrol's assistance in recruiting volunteers under a contract with the War Department. In 1942 and 1943 additional regiments that became part of the division were activated. The Eighty-seventh participated in an assault landing on the Alaskan island of Kiska in the Aleutians (August 15–17, 1943). It found that the Japanese had abandoned it, but the outfit suffered casualties from friendly fire and booby traps.

Welcoming the assignment of the Tenth Mountain Division to the

Fifth Army, Truscott was delighted to learn that among its generals was an old friend. Brigadier General David L. Ruffner had commanded a battalion of pack artillery when Truscott was at Fort Lewis as a member of the IX Army Corps staff. He was also pleased that the division commander would be Major General George P. Hays, brought to Italy from the Second Division Artillery in France. His assistant was another veteran, Brigadier General Robinson E. Duff.

With the Tenth Mountain Division and the additional British divisions in the mix, the Eighth Army was to strike first, supported by the whole weight of Allied Air Forces in Italy. When it reached the line of the Sillaro River, the Fifth Army was to join in, making its major onslaught west of Highway 65 to capture Bologna. Both armies would then regroup in the vicinity of Bologna to press the drive, unless the Germans quit and withdrew from Italy. If not, the offensive would continue until they were destroyed.

When the high command confirmed that one German division had pulled out of Italy in November and another had departed in December, it learned that the Sixteenth SS Panzer Grenadier Division was being withdrawn, indicating that a general abandonment of Italy was a possibility. Accordingly, the Allied Army Group put their forces on alert to strike on short notice. At that point, weather took control of the war. Steep mountain slopes became sheathed in ice, preventing movement of the supporting weapons. "An attack through the most heavily defended portion of the German lines under such oppressive conditions," Truscott recorded, "would have been an appalling undertaking which would have had little prospect of success."

On February 4, 1945, he was called to Florence for a conference. Clark and McCreery informed him that the Combined Chiefs of Staff had decided to send five divisions from the Eighth Army and the Canadian Corps to reinforce Montgomery's forces in France. Most of the American fighter-bombers would also go.

"It was," wrote Truscott, "a sad blow to our hopes."

EIGHTEEN

Italian Spring

Most American soldiers who'd stormed ashore at Normandy and then crashed through Hitler's Atlantic Wall, and those who hit the beaches at Salerno and Anzio, probably did not know or had forgotten having been taught in their high school English classes that they were in William Shakespeare territory.

In *Henry V*, he gave the king of England a speech that defined soldiering. Before the Battle of Agincourt in France on Saint Crispin's day in 1415, Henry told outnumbered troops:

> *We few, we happy few, we band of brothers;*
> *For he today that sheds his blood with me*
> *Shall be my brother; be he ne'er so vile,*
> *This day shall gentle his condition;*
> *And gentlemen in England now-a-bed*

Shall think themselves accurs'd they were not here,
And hold their manhoods cheap whiles any speaks
That fought with us upon Saint Crispin's day.

Among the dogfaces in Lieutenant General Truscott's Fifth Army in the mountains of northern Italy in January 1945, and those he'd led from Salerno to Rome, few probably knew that Italy was not only the setting for *Julius Caesar* and *Antony and Cleopatra* but also *All's Well That Ends Well*, *Coriolanus*, *Cymbeline*, *Much Ado About Nothing*, *Othello*, and *The Winter's Tale*. Driving north from Rome, they drew closer to the settings for *The Taming of the Shrew*, *The Two Gentlemen of Verona*, and *Romeo and Juliet*.

Ahead of Truscott's force lay an organized and determined foe made up of twenty-four German and five Italian Fascist divisions. The units were divided among the Tenth, Fourteenth, and Ligurian armies, all under Army Group General Heinrich von Vietinghoff. Lieutenant General Joachim von Lemelson commanded the Fourteenth Army. Opposite the British Eighth Army to the east was the German Tenth Army, commanded by Lieutenant General Traugott Herr. The Allied objective, the city of Bologna, still in Axis hands, formed a boundary line for both sides. The majority of enemy troops, noted a U.S. Army estimate, were seasoned veterans in relatively intact units. Although they'd been fairly well led and supplied in 1944, they now lacked vehicles, firepower, and air support and were experiencing increasingly troublesome shortages in nearly every kind of equipment. The winter had allowed them an opportunity to rest and construct a defensive system in three lines that maximized the tactical potential of the rugged Italian terrain.

Army records show that their first defensive line along the northern Apennines was to protect the city of Bologna and block Allied entry into the east-west Po River Valley, fifty miles farther north. The German generals planned to anchor their second defensive line along the river. From its source in northwestern Italy, it meandered east to the Adriatic

Sea, varying in width from 130 to 500 yards and frequently bordered by high levees that served as natural fortifications made stronger by field-works on both banks. Towns and villages along the river provided other obstacles. Although the top Axis commanders had repeatedly begged Berlin for permission to withdraw from the Apennines to stronger positions along the Po River before the expected Allied spring offensive, permission was denied. Hitler's directives told the local commanders to hold to their positions until enemy action forced their retreat.

As the Germans and their Italian allies feverishly dug in, the U.S. Fifth and British Eighth armies prepared for the coming battle with troops that were exhausted from months of fierce fighting. Truscott's Fifth Army had about 270,000 soldiers (with over 30,000 more awaiting assignments in replacement depots), more than two thousand artillery pieces and mortars, and thousands of vehicles, all positioned along a 120-mile front extending east from the Ligurian coast, across the crest of the Apennines, to a point southeast of Bologna. The major combat units included five infantry divisions, the fresh Tenth Mountain Division and First Armored Division, the Nisei 442nd Regiment, the First Brazilian Infantry Division, the free Italian Legnano Combat Group, and the Sixth South African Armored Division. The Fourth Corps in the west, under Major General Willis D. Crittenberger, and II Corps in the east, under Major General Geoffrey Keyes, shared control of these ten division equivalents.

On Truscott's right flank was the British Eighth Army under General Sir Richard L. McCreery. Containing the Polish Second Corps and the British Fifth, Tenth, and the Thirteenth corps, the Eighth Army controlled eight divisions from four different nations, as well as four free Italian battle groups and the Jewish brigade. By April 1945 their line extended from the Bologna area east to the Adriatic, ten miles north of Ravenna. General Clark had scheduled a new general offensive to begin in early April. Unlike previous campaigns in Italy, he'd assigned the major role to American forces. Prior to the main offensive, D-day minus five, the Ninety-second Infantry Division was to launch a diversionary attack, Operation Second Wind, to capture Massa along the Ligurian coast. The Eighth Army was to hit defenses east of Bologna.

Dogfaces for whom Bologna was a fancy way of spelling a sandwich meat that they called baloney learned in briefings that they were attacking not only a major rail and highway hub but an ancient city that was significant in the history of European civilization, Western culture, and Christianity. Crowded with venerated cathedrals, it was the birthplace of several popes, the inventor of radio, Guglielmo Marconi, the composer Ottorino Respighi, and famous painters. It was also where stylish, expensive, and speedy Lamborghini and Maserati cars were built and the site of the world's oldest university. West lay Genoa. North were Padua, Venice, Verona, Parma, Milan, and Turin.

Truscott intended to attack with forces from two corps advancing side by side along two major avenues, staggering the assaults to allow the maximum concentration of air and artillery support for each. Crittenberger's IV Corps would attack first, west of Highways 64 and 65, which led north to Bologna. One day later, Keyes's II Corps would attack northward along Highway 65 and take Bologna. During Phase Two, both Allied armies would continue north to the Bondeno-Ferrara area, thirty miles north of Bologna, trapping Axis forces south of the Po River. Phase Three would see combined Allied armies cross the Po and advance to Verona, fifty miles farther north, before fanning out into northern Italy, Austria, and Yugoslavia, completing the destruction of the Axis forces in southern Europe.

On April 9, with the initial phases of the offensive under way, Truscott met with war correspondents who saw themselves as patriots first and newsmen second. Even if they did not wear army uniforms and their stories were not under the scrutiny of the military censors, they would not publish what they were told until after the battle or, if they were able, rush to the enemy to solicit their viewpoint, as some U.S. news organizations would feel compelled to do in the Vietnam War and Iraq conflicts. Throughout the Second World War there is no record of any journalist deliberately breaking the censorship code that war correspondents voluntarily observed. Reporters knew that if they wanted to interview Truscott, he was available simply by showing up at his headquarters or a command post at the front. This openness policy was stated at the start of the April 9 press conference. "I believe the future of our country depends upon informed public opinion," he said. "Consequently, I have followed an invariable policy with correspondents since my first battle. I have told them they are at liberty to go any place in my area and write anything they want, provided they follow two points. First, that they stick to the facts, and, second, that, under no circumstances, will they disclose anything that we are going to have to pay for in the blood of Allied soldiers later. Beyond these two points, I have no restrictions whatever. You are perfectly welcome to go where you will."

He went on to detail for the correspondents the objective, strategy, and tactics for the offensive. On April 9, the attack was in its fourth day. It had begun with the 442nd Infantry (Nisei) and other elements passing through the front line and advancing toward the mountain town of Massa.

The history of the 442nd records that prior to the attack on Pearl Harbor, the only all-Japanese-American (Nisei) military unit was the 100th Battalion. It was formed with Japanese Americans in the Hawaiian National Guard. Sent to Camp McCoy, Wisconsin, for combat training and later moved to Camp Shelby, Mississippi, for additional training, they adopted the phrase "Remember Pearl Harbor" as their motto. In one of the bitter ironies in American history, families of these men had been rounded up on orders from President Roosevelt and placed in detention camps because of suspicions that they were spies and a security threat. When the War Department needed manpower, it sent recruiters to the relocation camps asking for volunteers to form a new Japanese-American combat unit to be designated the 442nd Regimental Combat Team. Volunteers were also accepted from Hawaii, where 12,500 men signed up. The Nisei volunteers were combined with Japanese Americans still in the military and sent to Camp Shelby, Mississippi, for combat training.

At Camp Shelby, they were formed into the 442nd Infantry Regiment, consisting of three battalions plus support companies. Designated the 442nd Regimental Combat Team, with most of its officers Caucasian, the men of the 442nd chose the motto "Go for Broke." A Hawaiian slang term from the dice game craps, it meant to risk everything. While the 442nd was being formed and trained, 1,432 men of the 100th Battalion entered combat in Italy. Suffering heavy casualties, they earned the nickname "Purple Heart Battalion." Replacements came from men who had finished training with the 442nd at Camp Shelby.

On June 2, 1944, the 442nd landed at Naples and pushed to the Anzio beaches. On June 15 the 100th Battalion and the 442nd were merged into a single unit and attached to the 133rd Regiment in the Thirty-fourth Division. After fighting at Belvedere, Luciana, and Livorno, the 442nd was pulled back for a rest and was presented with a Presidential Unit Citation. After the fighting at the Arno River in August 1944, the 442nd moved to France for an attack in the area of the Vosges Mountains. Assigned to capture the town of Bruyeres, the 442nd fought a bitter house-to-house battle and captured more than two hundred Germans. Their bloodiest battle occurred in a rescue of the First Battalion of the Thirty-sixth Division, which had been cut off by the Germans, earning the name Lost Battalion. In five days and nights of continuous combat, the 100th/442nd RCT suffered more than eight hundred casualties.

Sent to Italy in the spring of 1945, the 442nd was made part of the Ninety-second Infantry Division and came under Truscott's command. By the end of the war, the Nisei suffered an unprecedented casualty rate of 314 percent and received over 18,000 individual decorations. Many were awarded after their deaths for bravery and courage in the field of battle. Among the decorations received by the 100th/442nd soldiers were 1 Medal of Honor, 52 Distinguished Service Crosses, 560 Silver Stars, 28 Oak Leaf Clusters to the Silver Star, 4,000 Bronze Stars, and 1,200 Oak Leaf Clusters to the Bronze Star, and, perhaps most telling of the sacrifices made by these gallant soldiers, 9,486 Purple Hearts. The 442nd Combat Infantry group was the most decorated combat unit of its size in the history of the U.S. Army. For its service in eight major campaigns in Italy and France, the 100th Battalion and 442nd earned eight Presidential Unit Citations.

Among the wounded was the future U.S. senator from Hawaii Daniel K. Inouye, then a second lieutenant after a battlefield commission in November 1944. On April 21, 1945, while he led his platoon in an attack on enemy positions on Mount Musatello, he was wounded in the right arm by an enemy grenade and in the right leg by another bullet. For his bravery in leading the attack while wounded, he received the Distinguished Service Cross. His arm proved to be more seriously injured than was first realized and required amputation. Inouye was promoted to captain but not released from the hospital until February 1947.

By dark on April 5, 1945, the 442nd had taken Mount Fragolito and was well on the way to taking the high ground at Massa. Truscott recalled, "When I visited the division on April 6, the 442nd Infantry was still making progress in the difficult mountain terrain, but the lag of the other regiment on their left was causing concern. I visited Lieutenant Colonel Virgil L. Miller at his command post near Azzano, with General Almond, and then we conferred with Lieutenant Colonel Harry B. Sherman. An attack ordered for the morning had not come off because the battalions could not be reorganized in time. Another scheduled for the afternoon was canceled, since straggling had reduced the infantry battalion to overall strength of less than one hundred men. Accordingly, I authorized General Almond to employ the 473rd Infantry in the coastal sector, replacing it in the Serchio Valley with the 365th and 370th Infantry Regiments. The following day, the 442nd Infantry captured the heights overlooking Massa, and was then confronted with the hazards of mountainous terrain, unfavorable weather conditions, and delay in the attack on its left flank."

Reinforced by the 473rd Infantry on April 8, the 442nd fought its way through minefields and pillboxes to the outskirts of the town. Truscott's diary recorded that when they entered, there was "much flag waving and excitement on the part of the citizens of Massa."

As the advance continued against stiffening enemy resistance, Carrara was taken on April 11, but there was a delay while the Massa-Carrara road was repaired sufficiently to permit the maintenance and supply of the 442nd in the mountains. On April 14, as the major offensive of the Fifth Army started to roll to Bologna, the Ninety-second Infantry Division was confronting a strong defensive position defended by all available German troops in the coastal sector. With the Fifth Army surging across the Po plain, the Ninety-second, with the 442nd and 473rd Infantry Regiments sparking the advance, captured La Spezia and occupied Genoa.

"As a diversionary measure it was wholly successful," Truscott wrote, "the success being due to the courage, endurance and heroism of these two regiments."

Coinciding with these successes in Italy, word that the drive through France toward Germany was at full speed, and news that the Russians had entered Vienna, Austria, and were turning toward Berlin, a bulletin flashed from Washington, D.C., that President Roosevelt had suffered a fatal stroke while sitting for a portrait at his cottage at Warm Springs, Georgia. On that morning, Truscott was frustrated to learn that every Allied air base in the coastal sector was socked in by fog, forcing him to delay an attack. With the weather improved on April 15, he attended a memorial service for Roosevelt in a natural amphitheater, then took off from the Florence airport in a P-51 fighter with Brigadier General Thomas R. Darcy at the controls to survey the front.

He wrote:

> We climbed up over the Alps to an elevation of nearly 20,000 feet to watch the strategic bombers "clobber" the area south of Bologna on the front of the II Corps. At that elevation the sky seemed

strangely bright and empty. The earth below, where thousands of men and guns were waiting, looked like a miniature relief map, a patchwork quilt in dull, neutral colors. Darcy jiggled his wings and pointed. Below us was a black line, and as I watched the regular flashes and black puffs I realized I was looking at the Bomb Release Line marked by bursting antiaircraft shells. Then off to the south, with the sun glinting on silvery sides and wings, came the bombers. Flight after flight, more than 800 heavy and 250 medium bombers, in a steady formation gliding on below us to the north. Another jiggle of wings, and Darcy was calling my attention to the bombs dropping below. Then the whole earth was carpeted in flashes and towering columns of smoke. Among the bombers as they made their way steadily to the north, there were flashes and puffs that marked the effort of the German antiaircraft artillery. It was the first bombardment I had ever watched from above. It was a breathtaking sight and an unforgettable experience.

In the air again the next morning, but in a Piper Cub, he had as his traveling companion General McNarney. Their destination was the IV Corps front. Met at the corps' air strip and taken to the command post, Truscott and McNarney went over the situation with Crittenberger and his staff. The Tenth Mountaineers were still advancing, as was the Eighty-fifth. The First Armored was beginning its movement across the rear of the Tenth Mountain to the west flank, an enormously difficult movement because of the restricted net of second-class roads, which had been rendered even more precarious by enemy demolitions. Deciding to visit the Tenth Mountain command post of General George Hays, they found several roads blocked by demolitions, but finally made their way through traffic jams to Tole and found Hays well up toward Mount Moscoso, with his troops still advancing. On the way back they encountered the commander of the First Armored Division, whose leading combat team was now fighting in the Samoggia valley. A little later,

General Crittenberger informed them that air force reports said the Germans were beginning to withdraw on the front of II Corps.

Before McNarney left the command post that afternoon to depart for Caserta, he asked Truscott when he expected to reach Highway 9 in the Po Valley. Truscott replied that they would be across it by one o'clock on April 20.

McNarney said, "I'll bet you a quart of Scotch that you are not."

Truscott accepted the wager, but lost by about an hour. He wrote this to McNarney and sent on the prize. A few days later, the bottle was returned with a request that it be presented to the first soldier of the Tenth Mountain Division who actually crossed the highway. Truscott sent the liquor to General Hays, but doubted that the soldier would ever be found. Hays later sent him a photo showing him presenting the Scotch to Private First Class B. L. Lessmeister of Montrose, Missouri, the lead scout of Company A of the Eighty-sixth Mountain Infantry.

By the afternoon of April 19, the Tenth Mountain was on the spurs overlooking the Po Valley, with the Eighty-fifth Infantry Division moving up on its right. On the front of II Corps, the enemy had begun to withdraw. For most of April 20, Truscott was in the IV Corps sector traveling by jeep. Finally, he commandeered a Cub of the Tenth Mountain Division artillery for a reconnaissance over the battle lines.

Early in the morning of April 21, tanks and infantry of the Thirty-fourth Infantry Division rolled up Highway 65 and into Bologna. Elements of the Polish Corps of the Eighth Army entered from Route 9 almost simultaneously. Bologna was taken.

Truscott wrote exultantly, "We were now out of the mountains at last!"

On April 19, when the advance of the IV Corps had caused a German withdrawal on the II Corps front, Truscott had issued orders for continuing the pursuit to the Po River as soon as Bologna was isolated or in American hands. Two units, each with one armored and two infantry divisions, were to press on boldly and rapidly seize the line of the

Panaro River. They were then to continue on to the Po to secure crossing sites and cut off German forces still south of the river.

At this point, a new element entered the picture. As in France, the Allies had organized an extensive partisan underground movement in northern Italy. These anti-Fascist partisans were organized into guerrilla bands, armed and equipped by air drop, and directed by Allied officers who parachuted in to join them. Although they had been active in some sectors during the winter, they reserved their principal effort to coincide with the spring offensive. Truscott explained, "They were of invaluable assistance, not only for their knowledge of the country and enemy dispositions, but also for important assistance in clearing out snipers and enemy opposition in some of the towns and cities. Bologna was the first place where they distinguished themselves during the campaign."

In fact, Truscott noted, partisans took over some of the cities before the Americans arrived on the heels of the departing Germans.

While Crittenberger continued the advance of IV Corps with the divisions in the same order as they had entered into the Po plain, with the Eighth on the right, the Tenth Mountain in the center, and the First Armored Division on the left, the Brazilians followed to protect the left flank and rear. Keyes started with the Sixth South African Armored Division leading the corps' advance with the First and Eighty-eighth infantry divisions following abreast. Hays organized a task force with armor, infantry, engineers, and artillery under his assistant division commander, General Robinson E. Duff. They seized a crossing over the Panaro twenty miles northwest of Bologna, then pressed on to the Po River at San Benedetto on the morning of April 22. By midnight, Hays had most of his mountain division assembled in that area. The Eighty-fifth Infantry Division and the Sixth South Africans in the II Corps zone were still engaged along the Panaro River north of Bologna.

That same afternoon, Truscott, Keyes, and Crittenberger, with the division commanders of II Corps and a group of Polish generals, were ordered to join General Mark Clark for the triumphal entry into Bologna.

Truscott's description of the occasion read, "We assembled at Brigadier General Charles L. Bolte's command post in the Zoological Gardens on the southern outskirts, stood around while photographers recorded the event for posterity, and then Clark led a procession of jeeps, escorted by military police with wailing sirens, on a tour of downtown streets. What we were supposed to accomplish, I do not know. There were few Bolognese about and these did not seem overly enthusiastic. It was a far cry from the tumultuous reception in Rome the previous year."

At Truscott's morning staff conference on April 23, reports indicated that Hays was making preparations to cross the Po at San Benedetto, and that other elements of the IV Corps were now approaching the river. The II Corps seemed to be moving more slowly. Prisoners were flowing into detention cages by the thousands, and Truscott was hopeful of cutting off most of the German forces south of the river. After the conference, he and General Darcy flew by Cub to Florence, transferred to Darcy's P-51, and took off for another survey of the battle area. They found some fighting in progress on the II Corps front and on the left flank of the IV Corps. Occasionally greeted by bursts of flak, they saw that the German forces were now in a state of confusion and disorder. Columns were moving in opposite directions on adjacent roads. Hundreds of vehicles were streaming toward the river in a desperate effort to escape.

A short distance west of San Benedetto where the Tenth Mountain Division was making preparations to cross, Darcy circled, pointed downward toward a column of troops moving eastward, and shouted, "Boche!"

Truscott nodded agreement.

"The next I knew," he recalled, "we were plunging in a steep dive and Darcy was strafing the Germans. In several attacks, he set a number of vehicles on fire and dispersed the German column; then we turned eastward. Below Ostiglia, we found several other German columns approaching the river with none of our own troops in the vicinity. We circled over these, making one or two strafing passes to keep them halted and dispersed, while Darcy called other fighter bombers to the area and directed them onto the target. While some of the German forces had escaped to the north bank, vast quantities of weapons and equipment had been abandoned on the south bank, for there was no means of conveying it across."

Following this unprecedented case of a commander of an army riding along in a strafing attack, Truscott found himself in another breathtaking aerial drama. After returning the P-51 to Florence, Darcy and he climbed into a Cub and went to San Benedetto to confer with Hays. While setting the plane down in a wheat field that had been converted to a landing strip, Darcy, in Truscott's phrase, "cracked up." Neither was hurt, but the U.S. Army had come perilously close to losing two generals.

For Truscott, this doubly memorable day brought one more surprise. When he and Darcy entered General Hays's command post, they found him talking with Colonel William Darby. The architect and leader of the Rangers had been sent home following the destruction of the Rangers at Cisterna and given a desk job in the War Department's Operations Division. Now he was back in Italy with a group of dignitaries and Air Force General Harold "Hap" Arnold on a tour of the European and Mediterranean theaters. Darby had hated being stuck in Washington. Trying to get back in the war, he'd written to Mark Clark for assistance. Clark replied that there was nothing he could do to help. This may have been true, but it is likely that Clark had no interest in bringing back to his theater of operations a dashing, handsome, certified war hero. Darby then seized on the ninety-day tour of the fronts with the intention of finding another way to wrangle a combat command. Before leaving on March 29, 1945, he'd explained to his former deputy, Herman Dammer, that he planned to meet with General Hays and ask to be attached to Hays's Tenth Mountain Division. This hope rested on Darby's association with Hays in the Ninety-ninth Field Artillery before the war. Darby was so confident he would succeed with his old friend that he promised to also arrange to have Dammer transferred to Italy.

Arriving at Hays's headquarters, Darby was told that hours earlier Hays's assistant commander, General Duff, had been seriously wounded by a mine. Darby proposed that Hays give him the post. When Truscott showed up at Hays's command post a few hours later, Hays asked if Truscott could arrange the appointment. Truscott said he thought he could. He told Darby to consider himself assigned. Back at his own headquarters, Truscott sent a message to Clark and McNarney asking them to arrange with the War Department for Darby's transfer. The order quickly followed.

The task for Truscott was to seize Verona, seal off the Brenner Pass, turn east, and assist the Eighth Army in capturing Padova. At the same time, it was desirable to prevent the escape of the German forces to the northwest as well as those still south of the Po River. Accordingly, the next week the Fifth Army fanned out in all directions in what Truscott termed "controlled dispersion." As soon as Hays's Tenth Mountain Division and the Eighty-fifth and Eighty-eighth infantry divisions were across the Po, all three pressed on at top speed toward Verona. It fell on April 25. Hays then continued north along the eastern edge of Lake Garda.

South of the Po River, there were considerable German forces still trying to escape from mountains west of Modena. On April 24, Truscott left the Legnano Group to garrison Bologna. The Thirty-fourth Division drove westward to Piacenza, covering seventy-five miles in three days against scattered but stubborn opposition and destroying two German divisions. Others moved to the north of Milan for operations against the last intact German forces in north Italy, the German LXXV Corps, leaving the Brazilians to clear up the area south of the Po and block the escape route. Action ended on April 29 when the 148th Panzer Grenadiers and the Italian Bersaglieri Division surrendered. The Brazilians took fifteen thousand prisoners and captured immense quantities of supplies and equipment.

At this time, Truscott believed that the Tenth Mountain Division was within reach of capturing Mussolini at his headquarters on the western shores of Lake Garda, but when the Tenth staged an amphibious operation in the swimming tanks designated DUKWs and called "ducks" across the lake, they found that Il Duce and other Fascist officials were in a dash toward Switzerland. Intercepted by partisans, he and his mistress were shot and their bodies hanged by their heels in a square in Milan on April 29.

On the same day, Truscott had another close call with death. Flying with an aide as pilot over the II Corps and leading elements of the Eighty-eighth Division near Bassano and the First Infantry Division toward Treviso, they turned southward to look for the Sixth South African Armored Division. At the place where they thought it should be, they were greeted by several batteries of German flak. The pilot twisted and turned the plane earthward through a hail of bullets to treetop level. Truscott noted with relief, "We made our escape with no more damage than a few holes through wings and fuselage."

Called to Florence to confer with Clark on April 30, he was told that arrangements had been made for the surrender of the German forces, effective at noon, May 2, 1945. Until then, the troops were to keep up the advance. At noon, hostilities would cease and the forces would halt in place.

While Truscott was meeting with Clark in Florence, Colonel Darby was in his eighth day with the Tenth Mountain Division and in hot pursuit of Germans. On that morning, he and division officers crossed the lake to inspect Mussolini's mansion and estate on the outskirts of Gargnano. At about 1400 hours, he arrived by DUKW at Torbole. Germans on high ground to the north had almost perfect observation of the movements on the opposite shore. After landing, he walked immediately to the Eighty-sixth regimental command post in a small hotel close to the waterfront. For about half an hour, he conferred with the regimental commander and his staff concerning pushing the attack northward. A few minutes before he concluded the conference, a single 88mm round was heard exploding in the town.

When the meeting was over, Darby stepped outside, intending to take a jeep along the eastern shore to examine a road and a series of tunnels that had been blocked by German demolition teams. Because his engineers were supposed to have cleared the first tunnel, he wanted to be sure everything was open for a movement forward by tanks and heavy artillery to provide proper support to a projected infantry attack into the mountains to the north. As he paused to talk with Lieutenant Colonel Robert L. Cook and Brigadier General David Ruffner, they knew that the end of the war was close at hand.

When a jeep driven by Regimental Sergeant Major John T. Evans swung around the corner and stopped, an incoming artillery shell hit. Half of the dozen men surrounding Darby were wounded by shrapnel. General Ruffner was unhurt. A large chunk of hot metal nearly decapitated Evans. He died instantly. Another officer was struck in a thigh and ankle and one took shrapnel in the left hip. Darby was slammed to the ground with a piece of shrapnel about the size of a dime in his heart. As he was taken inside the hotel and put on a cot, two medics were called from a nearby building. Two minutes later, he was declared dead.

The press release disclosing Darby's death issued on May 1, by the War Department's Bureau of Public Relations' Press Branch, stated:

Colonel William Orlando Darby, organizer of the First American Ranger Battalion, was killed by German artillery fire while commanding a combat team of the 10th Mountain Division in the closing but still hard-fought phases of the battle for Italy.

Lieutenant General Lucian K. Truscott, Commanding General of the Fifth Army, in notifying the War Department this afternoon of Colonel Darby's death, stated that "Never in this war have I known a more gallant, heroic officer."

Colonel Darby died with the kind of men he knew well. Since the 10th Mountain Division entered the line on February 2 on one of the most fiercely contested fronts of this global war, it has spearheaded the Fifth Army's offensive to drive the German Wehrmacht out of Italy.

On May 2, Truscott waited for confirmation of the surrender in his command post and reviewed court-martial records, went over other papers, and wrote letters to Sarah and the three children. After lunch, he talked by phone to Clark about the wording of a press release to be sent out by Clark's headquarters announcing the surrender. He also reviewed the draft of an Army Order of the Day on the same topic. Mike Chinigo arrived, up from Rome. Truscott and an aide then left by Piper Cub in heavy rain and flew to the II Corps command post at Bassano. When the poor weather kept them from landing, they went on to Vicenza Airport, where he made phone calls. With the weather improved, he flew back to II Corps and landed at two o'clock. Half an hour later, General Keyes arrived to inform him the surrender had taken place. He returned to his command post in an olive grove south of Verona at six forty-five p.m. There he got congratulations on the surrender from Chinigo, followed by members of the staff. The journal keeper noted, "Few magnums of champagne are cracked open to celebrate the victory. News is broadcast to troops in the area and there is a great deal of noise, fireworks, and so on from all Army and civil personnel in the Verona area. Very late dinner and bed."

On May 3, representatives of General von Vietinghoff arrived at U.S. lines north of Lake Garda. They were met by General Hays and a party from the Tenth Mountain Division and escorted to Truscott's command post. In a gesture that would be repeated by Eisenhower on May 8 at the surrender of Germany, Truscott refused to see them. He wrote, "I had never had any wish to exchange civilities with any of the numerous enemy generals who passed through my headquarters during the war."

On May 4, Truscott and members of his staff were ordered to Florence to be present with General McCreery of the Eighth Army and his chief of staff, and members of the Fifth Army Group, as Clark staged what Truscott called a "surrender" meeting with another German general, Ernest Schlemmer. Clark's remarks and the German's reply, Truscott decided, had obviously been prepared in advance. "The meeting struck me as pointless," he wrote, "for which the only purpose was a photographic record in the Hollywood tradition."

In a "Dear Lucian" letter on May 25, Clark wrote, "With the closing of the campaign in Italy I express to you my deep feeling of appreciation for the magnificent performance of the Fifth Army in the long battle to smash the German forces here. The Army excelled in the spring offensive which ended in the German capitulation on May 2. The courage, tenacity, initiative and aggressiveness of your troops never were displayed to better advantage. No Army ever deserved a great victory more than the Fifth, and I am happy and proud that it was a part of the 15th Army Group which was the first Allied unit to which the Germans surrendered. I therefore desire to commend the troops of your command for their outstanding achievements and you personally for your superior leadership."

Five days later, Truscott returned to Anzio for a Memorial Day ceremony at the American cemetery. In graves beneath white crosses and the Stars of David reposed 6,614 men and women. They included 5,843 enlisted men, 468 officers, 7 nurses, 42 naval officers, 5 merchant mariners, 1 Coast Guardsman, 2 Red Cross workers, 1 civilian army employee, and 245 unknown. The correspondent Bob Fleisher called the gathering of survivors of Anzio "a heartfelt tribute to the guys who didn't quite make it."

Of Truscott, he wrote, "The Fifth Army leader with the rasping voice and the piercing blue eyes spoke briefly, but with an honesty and sincerity which the men under him have come to recognize as something special."

Turning from the living to speak to the fallen in a gesture that Bill Mauldin would cite as the most moving he'd ever witnessed because it came from a hard-boiled old man who was incapable of planned dramatics, Truscott spoke of the ending of the war in Europe and the unfinished fight with Japan, then said, "We pray that when the job is done, the statesmen of the world will make sure the lasting peace for which these men made the supreme sacrifice. It is a challenge to us, all the Allied nations, to ensure that they do not and have not died in vain."

★ NINETEEN ★

Just the Man I Need

With customary modesty, Truscott wrote in *Command Missions* that in June 1945 he visited several key cities in the United States especially chosen to honor and fete representative groups of senior officers and enlisted men of all ranks and grades from the various theaters of the war. By American citizens and journalists who wrote about the coast-to-coast flurry of receptions, parades, and ceremonies orchestrated by the War Department, these homecoming warriors were called heroes.

In the biggest of the demonstrations, General Dwight Eisenhower was greeted at New York City's LaGuardia airport by a sixteen-cannon salute. The next day on the steps of City Hall, after the largest ticker-tape parade in the city's history, the man for whom the airport was named, Mayor Fiorello H. La Guardia, presented him a hand-carved gold medal. Ike responded, "New York simply cannot do this to a Kansas farmer boy and keep its reputation for sophistication."

Along the way to New York, Eisenhower had been made a freeman of London and had shown the skills that he had used to hold together contentious Allies to win a war. He told an assemblage of Englishmen that was larger than the crowd that came out for the coronation of King George VI that he was merely a man from Kansas who found himself "temporarily amongst a people of ancient lineage, whose heritage of political and artistic magnificence was one of the glories of the human race." When he arrived in Washington on June 18, half the population of the capital turned out to cheer in a reception the Associated Press called "a vast affectionate homecoming which only warriors such as Grant and Sherman and Pershing had known before him."

Although in terms of length of residence, Lieutenant General Lucian King Truscott, Jr., was more Sooner and vagabond army man than Texan, having been born in Chatfield was sufficient reason for the city officials and people of San Antonio to put him on a roster of heroes for a celebration of Lone Star State valor on Wednesday, June 13. The list included thirteen generals and forty-five other officers and enlisted men from the battlefields of Europe. Besides Truscott, those with three silver stars on their collars were Truscott's boss in Operation Dragoon, Alexander Patch; J. K. "Uncle Joe" Cannon, commander of the Twelfth Air Force in Italy; and J. Lawton Collins, of the Seventh Corps. The major generals were Robert C. Macon, the Eighty-third Infantry Division; Norman D. Cote, the Twenty-eighth Infantry Division; I. D. White of the Second Armored Division, H. M. Turner, the First Air Division, Eighth Air Force; and Ira Eaker, commander in chief of the Mediterranean Allied Air Forces and chief of the air staff in Washington, D.C.

Of the festivities in the city best known for its icon of American heroics, the Alamo, Barry Bishop of the *Dallas Morning News* wrote, "Trails once followed by the Conquistadores and the padres of early Texas resounded with the throbbing of Army vehicles which wound through historic San Antonio streets. Tears came to the eyes of many of the officers and men as they saw the welcome and responded to the greetings. As the heroes went to the St. Anthony Hotel, they found baskets of fruit awaiting them as gifts from the City of San Antonio."

Writing that stars fell on the city on June 13, Bishop noted that the 300,000 Texans who formed the biggest turnout in the city's history cheered loudest and longest for a shy, slight, freckle-faced lieutenant whom Bishop described as a "typical Texas lad" who was a week short of his twenty-first birthday.

Born on June 24, 1924, Audie Leon Murphy of Farmersville had tried to enlist after Pearl Harbor, but was rejected because he was underage. Turning eighteen six months later, he attempted to join the marines and paratroopers and was turned down because he was underweight and of slight build. Accepted by the army, he was sent to Camp Wolters, Texas, for basic training. When he passed out during close order drill, his company commander tried to have him transferred to a cook and bakers' school, but Murphy insisted on being a combat soldier. He was sent to Fort Meade, Maryland, for advanced infantry training. Shipped out to Casablanca, Morocco, as a replacement in Company B, First Battalion, Fifteenth Infantry Regiment, Third Infantry Division, he saw no action in Africa, but had participated in training maneuvers with the Third Division and took part in the Sicily invasion. Shortly after the landing, he killed two Italian officers as they tried to escape on horseback.

When the Third Division landed at Salerno, Murphy distinguished himself in combat, then fought at the Volturno River, Anzio, and in the mountain campaigns. During Operation Dragoon, his best buddy, Lattie Tipton, was killed by German troops feigning surrender. Enraged, Murphy single-handedly wiped out the German machine-gun crew, then used their weapons to destroy several other nearby enemy positions. For this, he received the Distinguished Service Cross. Weeks later, he received Silver Stars for two more heroic actions. Given a battlefield commission to second lieutenant, he was wounded in the hip by a sniper's ricocheting bullet twelve days after the promotion and spent ten weeks recuperating. Within days of returning to his unit, he became commander of his company while still wearing bandages and was wounded by a mortar round. The next day, in a battle at Holtzwihr, France, with his unit cut to an effective strength of 19 out of 128, he sent all his men to the rear while he sniped at the Germans until he ran out of ammunition. Using a burning, disabled tank destroyer's .50-caliber machine gun, he fired into German infantry at a distance, including a full squad that crawled in a ditch to within one hundred feet of him. This nearly single-handed battle continued for slightly more than an hour. He ceased fire only when his telephone line to the artillery fire direction center was cut. As his men came forward, he quickly organized them to conduct a counterattack. His action that day earned him the Medal of Honor and the Legion of Merit. Presented by Patch on June 3, 1945, they made Murphy the most decorated GI of the war.

With his tour of celebrations completed, Truscott had a brief visit with Sarah in Virginia, then made a stop on the way back to Italy to inform the War Department that he wanted to serve in the war against Japan, if there should be an opportunity. Back in Italy on July 29, he received a message from General Marshall reminding him of the conversation and suggesting that he take a few key members of his staff and visit China to confer with General Wedemeyer and Generalissimo Chiang Kai-shek concerning a combat assignment in China. Leaving on August 8 with members of the team that had been with him throughout the war, he heard during a fueling stop in Cairo that the atom bombings of Hiroshima and Nagasaki had resulted in signals of a Japanese willingness to surrender. Calling Washington, he was told to proceed with the trip to Asia.

Arriving in China, he found many old friends. Wedemeyer and he were classmates at Leavenworth. His chief of staff, Ray Maddocks, had been an instructor with Truscott at Fort Riley. There were others from his Leavenworth days and old cavalry friends who were now in the Chinese Combat Command. Under Major General B. Robert McClure at Kunming, it was not a large command, with only a few American officers. Their task had been to assist in the organization, training, and direction of Chinese armies that were little more than divisions with American arms and equipment.

The War Department plan had been for Truscott to command a group of Chinese armies in northern China to take part in the fight against Japanese forces on the mainland of China while the Allied forces were making an assault on the Japanese home islands that the A-bomb made unnecessary. Noting in *Command Missions* that he and Don Carleton were present when Japanese envoys arrived to negotiate surrender with the Chinese command, Truscott recalled, "Having seen what we could of China, there was nothing further to hold us. We packed up and returned, detouring to spend one day in Ceylon visiting Admiral Mountbatten, who was now Supreme Allied Commander in Southeast Asia."

Back in Italy on August 30, they discovered that Fifth Army headquarters would become inoperative in Italy on September 9. Truscott pointed out that the date would be the second anniversary of its first battle at Salerno. Announcement of the disbanding was headline news at home, in large measure because the Fifth's Eighty-fifth (Custer) Division was the first all-draft division in the army to be deactivated. An Associated Press story recorded, "The veteran Fifth Army, which battled up the Italian boot from the Salerno shinbone to the Tyrolean kneecap is about to be broken up." Most of the personnel had already been transferred elsewhere. Those remaining packed records and prepared to close the headquarters. A month later, Truscott was on the dock to say farewell as the last of his staff boarded the *Hagertown Victory*. He pledged to meet them in Boston for the official deactivation. He was so sure of this that except for clothing for a week of paying farewell visits to comrades remaining in Europe, his baggage was put on the ship.

First on his good-bye odyssey was George Patton on September 22 at

Bad Tolz, Germany. A few miles north of the Austrian border, the city beside Lake Tegernsee had become the Third Army's base and Patton's headquarters as military governor of Eastern Bavaria. On that Saturday after a routine morning briefing by his staff, Patton held a press conference at which the main interest of the eleven reporters was the progress in his area of Eisenhower's "de-Nazification" policy of purging every level of government in Germany of officials who had been Nazis. Patton told the reporters that he knew of none still in office in Bavaria. Instead of leaving it at that, he went on to state that if the United States had lost the war and the Germans removed all political officials in America, they would exclude all Republicans and Democrats. "The Nazi thing," he continued, "is just like a Democrat-Republican election fight back home."

What Truscott and Patton talked about on that afternoon and for how long isn't known. Hopes of both for transfers to the Pacific theater had been dashed by the Japanese surrender, leaving their futures in question. Truscott knew he was going home, but not to what post. A former cavalryman who'd gotten his first taste of combat in the Punitive Expedition and risen to command armies in the greatest battles of the Second World War, Patton chafed at being saddled with an administrative job in an occupation army. The only sounds of guns he heard were when he went on deer hunting trips on a vast estate in Czechoslovakia or while shooting chamois in the mountains of the French occupation zone of Germany. Describing his mood as "hysteria" about the future, the Patton biographer Martin Blumenson wrote, "Everyone except him had found a new place for himself." Omar Bradley was heading the Veterans Administration. Mark Clark was the American High Commissioner in Austria. Eisenhower was in line to succeed Marshall as the army chief of staff. In a letter to his wife, Patton complained that it was hell to be old and passé and know it. "Now all that is left to do," he had said, "is to sit around and await the undertaker and posthumous immortality."

From Patton's headquarters, Truscott traveled on September 23 to

Heidelberg, Germany, to see General Keyes, now in command of the Seventh Army. Then it was on to Frankfurt and an overnight visit with his good friend Walter Bedell Smith before a meeting with Eisenhower that Truscott expected to be their last for a long time. With twenty-eight years of service behind him and the world at peace, retirement had suddenly become an inviting possibility. Ike greeted him in what Truscott described as his usual warm manner, but this time there were no questions about wife and children, no query as to what Lucian III would do after graduation from West Point, and no banter about the old days or gossip concerning comrades.

"Lucian, you're just the man I need," said Ike. "Unless you have some objection, I think I will send you down to relieve George Patton."

In the few days since Truscott had met with Patton, Eisenhower had been swept into a firestorm of outrage at home from the press, the public, and politicians over Patton's comparison of Nazis to Republicans and Democrats. On orders from Eisenhower to "clarify" his statement, Patton had held a second press conference and explained that his remark had been an unfortunate analogy. With the storm unabated, Ike had summoned Patton to Frankfurt. In a two-hour meeting, Eisenhower told him that he was being removed from Third Army command and put in charge of Fifteenth Army headquarters. Considered "a paper" outfit, its work consisted of compiling and writing the lessons of the war, preserving archives, and disseminating to the army successful methods of combat. Fed up with governing Bavaria, and fascinated by the notion of shaping the official memory of the war, Patton accepted the decision.

Truscott wrote of Eisenhower offering him the Third Army, "Since ill-considered words and actions could only embarrass the administration and jeopardize the occupation, he thought that General Patton should be replaced by someone not as inclined to intemperate outbursts. General Eisenhower knew, of course, that Patton was my close personal friend. I explained that I had no desire to supersede him, but that I wished to be of service. If General Patton had to depart, I thought he would probably prefer being replaced by me than by someone who might be less sympathetic. General Eisenhower said he would consult with General Marshall. Meanwhile, I was to go on to Berlin and Paris, but I was not to leave for the United States until he authorized me to do so."

For two days in Berlin, another in Frankfurt and two in Paris, Truscott scrambled to make arrangements to remain in Europe, retrieve his personal possessions, and inform Sarah of the change in plans. During this period, Patton's dismissal made banner headlines in newspapers at home. Under one that blared PATTON AND HIS PISTOLS SENT PACKING in the sensation-seeking New York *PM Daily*, which had yelled for Patton to be fired, Richard A. Yaffe crowed, "Gen. George S. Patton, the brilliant military commander who can't keep his mouth shut or his hands to himself and who can't tell the difference between Nazis and Republicans and Democrats, will finish his career behind a desk in command of a phantom army."

A story below said of Truscott, "For an ex-schoolteacher, he is a tough guy, and his men cuss him but respect him."

The paper in Corsicana, Texas, noted Truscott's Lone Star State birth and called him a "strict, hard-driving disciplinarian, rated by fellow soldiers as brilliant both in planning and execution" who had "commanded such personal loyalty from subordinates that many refused promotions to continue serving under him."

Washington, D.C.'s, *Evening Star* provided details of Truscott's career and ended by noting that he'd served in the cavalry at Fort Myer from 1931 to 1934 and played on the army polo team at that time. The *Philadelphia Record* headlined FORMER SCHOOL TEACHER WILL MAKE THE NAZIS STEP. The correspondent Pat Frank recalled covering Truscott in Italy and said in his story, "The Nazis will get no comfort from Truscott. He can be relied upon to go about the task of de-Nazification of his area of Germany with gusto. If I were a Nazi, I'd be more afraid of Truscott than any other American leader. He hates them. He was set on wiping them out in battle and I believe he feels the same way about them today."

At Frankfurt, Truscott reviewed background material and files and discussed occupational problems with members of Eisenhower's United States Forces European Theater (USFET) staff and their civilian political advisors. Besides matters of Allied military government, and prisoners of war, which had concerned him in Italy, there were the problems of displaced persons, the repatriation of Soviet nationals, and the prosecution of war criminals.

On October 4, he had a final conference with Eisenhower before leaving for Bavaria and the new assignment. Ike repeated that the most acute and important problems everyone faced in Germany at that time were those of de-Nazification and handling the victims of Nazi persecution. Eisenhower stressed that unfavorable publicity in either case would embarrass the administration and would have extremely ill effects on occupation policies. Truscott was to adopt stern measures toward the Nazis. He was to be ruthless in eliminating them from all positions in government and industry and in the seizure of Nazi properties. Ike said he had prescribed preferential treatment for Jewish displaced persons in allowances of food, clothing, housing, and supplies, and that he had directed that no restrictions whatever were to be placed upon them.

That night, Truscott went to Bad Tolz to meet Patton. They spent most of two days in a review of occupation procedures. Patton told Truscott, "Lucian, if you have no objection, I want to have a big formal ceremony and turn over the command to you with considerable fanfare and publicity. I don't want Ike or anyone else to get the idea that I am leaving here with my tail between my legs."

Truscott assured him he was willing to participate in any ceremony Patton arranged. The handover was scheduled for October 7, 1945. Because of rain, it was held in a gymnasium of a former SS base where the Third Army headquarters was located. Truscott, Patton, four corps commanders, and principal members of the Third Army staff took positions on a stage that had been appropriately decorated. They faced the rest of Third Army headquarters and all Third Army troops that were available in the Bad Tolz sector (about four hundred). Honors were rendered. When Patton rose to speak, tears glistened on his cheeks. He took a deep breath and said to the men of the Third Army in an emotion-choked tone, "All good things must come to an end. The best thing that has ever come to me is the honor and privilege of having commanded the Third Army. The great successes we have achieved together have been due primarily to the fighting heart of America. Please accept my heartfelt congratulations on your valor and devotion to your duty, and my fervent gratitude for your unwavering loyalty."

Of his successor, Patton declared, "A man of General Truscott's achievements needs no introduction. His deeds speak for themselves."

After Patton handed over the Third Army flag, Truscott said to the officers and men of his new command, "You of the Third Army have written one of the most glorious pages in all military history. Your deeds will forever thrill and inspire our country." Turning to Patton, he said, "It is only in a sense that you take leave of this army, for so long as any man who has served under you shall live your place will remain secure in his heart. I am sure I speak for them, as well as for myself, when I say that wherever you go the best wishes of this army go with you."

Taking over from Patton meant not only big shoes to fill and the challenge of being in command of an occupation army, but inheriting Patton's house. On the Tegernsee a few miles east of Bad Tolz in a resort spot where top Nazis had built villas, it was a swank, modern, and rather luxurious mansion with a fine view of the lake and mountains, game rooms, a bowling alley, an indoor target range, squash courts, and every possible convenience. Because it had belonged to the publisher of *Mein Kampf*, quotations from Hitler's book were molded in relief in the plaster on the ceiling of the drawing room. "The place had escaped damage during the war, although some fighting had flared up nearby," Truscott observed. "Luckily, unlike other buildings it had not suffered from looting. Carleton, the aides, and I lived here during our stay at Bad Tolz, and it was a rare week when we did not have guests from among the many persons who visited the Army Headquarters for one reason or another."

Third Army headquarters was divided between Munich and Bad Tolz. The rear echelon and most of the administrative services were located in Munich. Patton had put the command post at Bad Tolz in the former SS facility, which consisted of a quadrangle that housed the offices and most of the enlisted personnel, houses, a riding hall, stables, and various shops. Most of Truscott's staff were billeted in hotels and requisitioned houses in the town of Bad Tolz, which had been a health and pleasure resort.

Truscott recalled, "Just a few miles from the Austrian border and almost in the shadow of the Alps, this part of Bavaria is of surpassing beauty. It was not, however, a convenient location for an army headquarters. And it was just about as far from the theater headquarters in Frankfurt as it was possible to be and remain in Bavaria. I considered moving it to Munich. However, we finally established the Office of Military Government for Bavaria there, and assembled the rest of the army headquarters in Bad Tolz, where it remained until we moved to Heidelberg the following spring."

An agreement between Roosevelt, Churchill, and Stalin at the Yalta Conference in February 1945 listed in detail the political and economic principles and policies that were to govern the treatment of Germany after the war. As a result of the destruction of the German government, the Allied commanders in chief assumed supreme authority over all powers possessed by the German government, its military high command, and the state, municipal, or local authorities on June 5. Allied policy was directed toward decentralization of the political structure and the development of local autonomy. While self-government and responsibility would be restored, no central government was to be established.

Truscott wrote, "We had already found that occupation problems were far more numerous and perplexing than we had known in Italy. This was due, in part, to the different status accorded the two countries by the Allies, and in part to their divergent economic and political orders. The Allies had accorded Italy the status of co-belligerent. The aim of Allied Military Government had been to return control of government to the Italians as soon as possible, to sustain the established government pending postwar elections, and to restore the economic system. Allied Military Government in Italy was well organized, and staffed with qualified British and American officers and men. Huge funds and enormous quantities of supplies had been poured into Italy. Except for the more important party members, no great effort was made to eliminate Fascists from positions in government and industry."

In Germany, where the entire structure of government had been destroyed, the country was divided among the four powers (U.S., British, Soviet, and French), with an Allied Control Commission as the sole governing authority. While the economic structure of Germany had greater potential assets than the Italian, greater demands were placed upon it, and almost no assistance was extended to it. In a reorganization of government and industry, great emphasis was laid on the elimination of Nazi party members from the government and industry. Truscott felt that Patton's mistake had not been in believing that removing Nazis eliminated the best-trained individuals from the government, but in failing to appreciate that the fundamental objective of the occupation had to be the training of democratic-minded officials.

At a press conference just five days after taking over the Third Army, Truscott made clear in his opening statement that nothing he said about his intentions as the new military governor should be interpreted as criticism of Patton. He told the newsmen, "He and I are friends of many years. We played polo together and I served under him in peacetime. I commanded a division under him throughout the Sicilian campaign. I do not believe there is a finer soldier alive or dead. He is undoubtedly the outstanding battle leader of the war, and I am confident that he always carried out every order that he had received to the best of his understanding. So, anything that I say is in no way a criticism of General Patton. I don't think I have ever been placed in a position that I hated worse."

Complicating the challenges of command was a crisis of morale among Truscott's soldiers. Ruminating on this difficulty in *Command Missions*, he wrote:

Officers and men were transferred wholesale and without regard to individual preference to units designated for return to the United States as shipping space became available. This procedure completely destroyed the close and intimate relationship which existed normally between officers, non-commissioned officers and men which is the fundamental basis for discipline and control in any military organization. Since availability of shipping was never known accurately, plans were continually changing. It was not unusual for men to be transferred several times in the course of a week or ten days. Soldiers are habitually loyal to the division with which they trained and served in combat; consequently these mass transfers had an adverse effect upon morale and were even worse upon discipline. There has probably never been in all history a comparable destruction of a fighting force by the people to whom the force belonged. The hysterical demand of the American people to "bring the boys home" wrought greater demoralization in a few weeks than a major defeat in battle would have done. What had been a magnificent fighting force became little more than a rabble and undisciplined mob. The damage to American prestige was incalculable. Had our high military authorities taken a strong and positive stand in opposition to such hasty dissolution of the forces, it is likely the American people could have been made to understand the logic of their position and would have supported them. There is no doubt that the soldiers would have done so.

Suddenly, the former schoolteacher who had abandoned the classroom to become a soldier stood at the head of an army of occupation like none before. When the U.S. Army went into Germany in 1918, it found a nation that was defeated, but not a ruined country. After years of incessant Allied bombing, the cities and towns of 1945 Germany had been reduced to rubble and their inhabitants left homeless and adrift. The term for one of these refugees was "displaced person," which brutal headlines and a postwar vocal shorthand reduced to "DP." Truscott recorded, "Hundreds of thousands of people were involved, and most of them had their origin in lands now dominated by the U.S.S.R. However, most of them hated and feared the Russians even more than they hated the Germans. This was to make repatriation impossible in a vast number of cases, and was to complicate the displaced persons problem enormously. When American troops entered Germany, they found more than a million of these unfortunate persons in the American Zone, a major portion of them in Bavaria. They represented almost every European and Asiatic nationality with whom the Germans had come in contact during the war. Some had come to Germany of their own accord to work on farms and in factories. Others had been imported as forced labor. Still others had been Russian or Polish prisoners of war. Some of these had changed sides and fought with the Germans, and many thousands had been in concentration camps."

Hundreds of thousands of refugees, liberated by the advance of the Allied troops, became a serious hazard to military movements, to health, and to the maintenance of order. Immediately after the cessation of hostilities, they were collected, sorted out by nationality as far as practicable, and placed in camps where they could be fed, clothed, and cared for until disposition could be made of them. Camps varying in size from those housing a hundred to thousands were scattered all over Bavaria. While Eisenhower had accepted an offer by the United Nations Repatriation and Rehabilitation Administration (UNRRA) to assist the armed forces in caring for these displaced persons in the U.S. Zone, when

Truscott took over the Third Army, UNRRA Headquarters had been established in Frankfurt and UNRRA teams had already taken responsibility for administration in a number of camps. Others were being taken over as rapidly as personnel became available and arrangements could be completed. But extensive support, both logistical and administrative, continued to be required from the U.S. military.

In this mass of tormented humanity, Jews presented Truscott a unique challenge.

"Many factors contributed to making the problem of dealing with Jewish displaced persons a thorny one," he wrote. "In the first place, worldwide sympathy for these luckless people, and the deep and almost universal desire to make some recompense for the trials which this pitiful remnant had survived, created an emotional atmosphere that influenced every decision and action with respect to them. The Jewish displaced persons were quick to realize this fact, which they did not fail to exploit to their own not always unselfish ends."

As Jews carried on a program of clandestine emigration to Palestine by smuggling groups from Bavaria to Italy or southern France, where they boarded chartered ships bound for Palestine, Truscott saw that this traffic only served to complicate matters. "The problem had political implications both national and international," he recalled. "Jewish leaders were determined to exploit the worldwide sympathy for the Jews to obtain the refuge in Palestine which had long been their aim. Britain, mindful of the Arabs, and sensitive to the oil of the Middle East, was reluctant to admit further Jewish immigration even though it was financed by American money. Jewish leaders were also aware of the Jewish influence in American political life, and this movement was largely directed by American Jews. In fact, nearly all of the Jewish displaced persons were concentrated in the American Zone, with the vast majority of them in Bavaria. Munich became the center of Jewish activities."

Another hindering factor was the number of agencies and individuals who were active in the cause of Jewish relief. Besides the military authorities, military government officials, and UNRRA personnel, there were others of nonofficial or quasi-official in nature, including the American Joint Distribution Committee. Representing various Jewish congregations and welfare groups, it maintained an extensive network of activities that were not limited to welfare and to charitable work. "The Committee had political objectives," Truscott wrote, "It sought to control and direct the Jewish displaced persons movement and to influence government policy with respect to it. To complicate matters further, the Committee was torn by internal strife. Orthodox Jews did not get on with their Reformed brethren, and there was no general agreement among the liberals."

Truscott's first visits to Jewish camps were at Landsberg, Feldafing, and Wolfratshausen, in the Munich area. Former German army camps, each was governed by a citizens committee, elected by popular vote. They made the camp rules, appointed the guards, and made other camp details. Men and women were housed in separate barracks, usually three or four to a squad room that was intended for six or eight soldiers. Families were kept together, and those cared for in requisitioned dwellings were allowed to run their own messes, but most of the camp population were fed in central dining rooms. The accommodations were equal to those provided for U.S. soldiers in Bavaria, though they were not as clean, sanitary, and well ordered as the military installations.

Reports in American newspapers on complaints about the conditions in the camp had contributed to the downfall of Patton. Asked about the reports in the same press conference in which he said that the Nazi Party was equivalent to Republicans and Democrats, he replied, "There is a very apparent Semitic influence in the press."

Truscott noted in *Command Missions*:

This camp life was no more than a temporary measure, and any permanent solution required governmental action by more than one country, which was far beyond the scope of responsibility of the military authorities in Germany. Since members of the American-Jewish Joint Distribution Committee, the UNRRA teams, the Camp Committees, and many others were fully cognizant of this fact, one would have thought that these unfortunate individuals would have displayed a more cooperative spirit toward the military authorities than was ever actually the case.

It was soon evident to Truscott that there was a concerted effort to obtain publicity meant to keep world sympathy stirred up on behalf of the destitute refugees. To this end, he noted, there was a series of efforts to embarrass military authorities by alleging that they were responsible for crowded and unsatisfactory conditions, for the mistreatment of individual displaced persons, and for unfavorable treatment in comparison with Germans. Early in December 1945, General Smith called Truscott from Frankfurt to inform him that a member of the UNRRA team at Landsberg, an American college professor, had resigned in a bitter letter that accused the army of poor administration and lack of care in the camp. Instead of sending the protest to UNRRA's director in the U.S. Zone whose headquarters was in Munich, or to Truscott's headquarters in Bad Tolz, the professor sent the letter to a Jewish newspaper correspondent in Frankfurt, who had called on General Smith for comments before making it public. Truscott suggested that Smith personally investigate the conditions, and that he bring news correspondents from Frankfurt. Smith and the newsmen were there the next day. After a conference in which the UNRRA team and the camp's committee voiced their complaints, the group inspected the camp and found that most of the grievances were minor matters of crowding and supply that Jewish camp officials could easily have corrected.

A little more than a month after having been thrust into the multiple roles of commander of the Third Army, military administrator of Eastern Bavaria, and overseer of DP camps, Truscott was informed that as boss of the Third Army he would be held accountable for the administration and maintenance of war crimes trials of the top leaders of the Third Reich. Although planning for the tribunals had been under way since before the end of the war, he was presented with the responsibility only a week before they were to open with great fanfare in Nuremberg on November 14, 1945.

Truscott found that friction had developed between members of the staffs of the tribunal and the Office of the Chief of Counsel over accommodations and other administrative details. The city of Nuremberg was filled with personnel of many nationalities, some assigned to duties with the trials, others on a more temporary status. Because the German civil administration was little more than embryonic, law enforcement presented a serious problem. When Truscott made a detailed inspection of the site, assisted by members of the Third Army staff, he observed that the administrative side was wholly inadequate, with authority divided among several agencies. The office of the Chief of Counsel had concerned itself with managerial details with which it was not familiar, and which interfered with its primary legal function for conducting trials. Making Nuremberg a separate area of command under Brigadier General Leroy Watson, Truscott gave him a large staff and placed all necessary army resources at his disposal.

In the bitterest passage in *Command Missions*, he recalled, "On my visits to Nuremberg, I had many discussions with officials connected with the trials. I was present on the opening day and heard the reading of the indictments. At various times, I listened to the presentation of the testimony. I saw the accused in their cells, at exercise in the prison yard, in conference with their counsel, and before the tribunal in the courtroom. It was one of imposing dignity, but it was not one to fill me with the pride I have felt in American courtrooms. I believed that these major Nazis were guilty of waging aggressive war and other crimes against humanity for which they should be brought to the bar of justice. But when I looked down upon the courtroom scene I was never able to escape the impression that I was witnessing a conquerors' triumph, for it was only the totality of the conquerors' victory that made this impressive spectacle possible."

Also in the Third Army region were trials held at Dachau. On the site of a concentration camp, the trials were of special interest to the American forces because those in the dock were accused of crimes against American personnel, or ones committed in areas allocated to American forces. Truscott felt that these trials were especially important because they involved what he called "lesser fry of the Nazi regime" and afforded an opportunity to give the Germans an object lesson in the Western method of administering justice. Present at the opening and at other times during the course of the trial, he found the setting simpler than at Nuremberg, but as dignified and effective. He recorded that because public interest was centered in the more spectacular trials at Nuremberg, the accomplishment at Dachau was not generally well understood. He believed that the first Dachau trial set the standard for those that followed. The only death warrant he ever had to sign was for the execution of several of those convicted in the first Dachau tribunal.

As he looked in on the war crimes trials in mid-December 1945, often accompanied by a visiting official from the United States, he was busy with an aspect of his duties as the military governor that would have fascinated his pals in the ranks of war correspondents. He had authority to license the German press. Although Bill Mauldin, Ernie Pyle, and Mike Chinigo would have challenged the idea of government dictating to a journalistic enterprise in the United States, they agreed with the necessity of assuring that the Germans would never again experience absolute control of the flow of information that had existed under the Nazi regime, and that no Nazis or any of their collaborators could be permitted to work as journalists.

On December 10, reporters covering the war crimes trials rushed from Nuremberg to a hospital in Heidelberg to check on a report that George Patton had been seriously injured in a car crash. On his way to hunt pheasant near Mannheim, with an aide and a hunting dog following in a jeep, his chauffeured Cadillac was struck by an army truck. He suffered a broken neck and was left paralyzed, lingering for thirteen days before he died. As Patton's body lay in repose at a nearby villa on Saturday, December 22, Truscott and almost the entire American army leadership in Germany paid their respects. On Sunday, the coffin had a cavalry escort to the Heidelberg Protestant Church and was then taken to an American cemetery at the town of Hamm in Luxembourg. With Truscott in command, contingents of British, French, and Belgian armies joined a battalion of infantry and cavalry representing the Third Army in rendering all the honors of a military funeral.

Perhaps recalling that December day when he saluted his old polo friend for the last time and remembering when they served together at Arlington, Truscott would write in his book on the cavalry experiences that he and Patton had shared, "And when the band turns away, leaves the cemetery, and strikes up a sprightly quickstep . . . it is a symbol that the living must carry on."

Two months after Patton's funeral, a task that pleased the former schoolteacher was the opening of a university for refugees. Under the auspices of the UNRRA, it was planned by the Foreign Student League, representing the students and educational leaders of thirteen nationalities, and supervised by the Third Army. It received twenty-six hundred applications, half of which were approved. At a ceremony held in the Burger Brau Keller Auditorium in Munich, where Hitler and his henchmen had conspired to turn Germany into the dictatorship that took the world to war, Truscott signed the charter on February 16, 1946.

The day before, he, three other generals (McNarney, Keyes, and Lucius Clay), several colonels, and Ambassador Robert Murphy had been forced to flee a meeting in a conference room of the former I. G. Farben munitions plant when a fire in an adjoining room burst through a wall. Although arson was suspected, an investigation found that the blaze was accidental.

A month later, Truscott again officiated at the opening of a school. In Somthofen in the southern mountains of Bavaria, it was a training facility for 120 officers and 300 enlisted men who were to become the teaching cadre for 38,000 men in a U.S. constabulary force. It was a concept inspired by the original idea of a Ranger force in 1942 that was to return to the United States to teach Commando tactics. Education of a gentler nature was offered to soldiers at Freising. In the Weihenstephan agricultural and technical school, men of the Third Army took a course in making beer. Classes were held in the oldest brewery in the world. It was chartered in 1146, but Benedictine monks were said to have made beer there as early as 850. The American students' entire production was reserved for the men of the Third Army. The school also enrolled 400 officers and enlisted men in high school and college-level courses taught by American educators in agronomy, animal husbandry, chemistry and physics, biology, and mathematics. Only Germans taught beer making.

While Truscott viewed the early months of 1946 as a repetition of his work through the autumn and winter of 1945, those who observed him found his transition from flinty combat commander to government administrator fairly smooth. At the same time, he privately bristled at what he considered the "close attention" by the press of the very difficult problem of purging ex-Nazis from the government, industry, and education. Although the principal agency for searching out and arresting ex-Nazis was the Counter Intelligence Corps, reporters seemed to him to dwell on the Patton episode and were always more than ready to pounce upon any report that a Nazi might have escaped the net. One story that rankled alleged that several wives of high-ranking Nazi officials were entertaining American officers in their homes just across Tegernsee from where Truscott was living. The story proved false.

Another favorite with correspondents was demilitarization. Truscott and others in the occupation authorities were criticized for slow progress in destroying military installations and war potential. Truscott believed that these criticisms were unjustified because the reporters failed to realize the magnitude of the problem or comprehend the inadequate means available for the dismantling of remnants of the German war machine.

To allay some of this faultfinding, Truscott noted, theater headquarters directed him to "lay on at least one good demolition" for newsmen to witness. His staff selected a huge I. G. Farben plant at the city of Kaufburen. Late in October 1945, he flew there and in the presence of most of the correspondents in the U.S. Zone pressed buttons that set off two blasts that obliterated the installation.

Twenty-eight years before Lieutenant General Lucian K. Truscott, Jr., blew up the Farben plant as a symbol of American victory in a war, Captain Truscott had seen rapid dismantling of the U.S. Army in a rush to get back to normalcy. Observing the same fervor in 1946 as the boss of the Third Army, he noted that the United States Zone of Occupation in Germany was in a continual state of reorganization. Redeployment was continuing at the maximum rate, resulting in almost endless shifts in personnel from one unit to another, requiring readjustment of areas of control as one organization after another was sent home. In this process, the only elimination of a U.S. responsibility for an occupation of territory had come when American forces withdrew from Czechoslovakia, simultaneously with the withdrawal of Russian troops, as the government of the new Czech president, Edward Benes, was restored to full sovereignty.

Prior to the pullout, Truscott had visited Czechoslovakia and Prague specifically several times and saw that the line separating Russians and Americans had become a tense scene of outposts that faced each other with no contact by the two armies. This was not because the American forces desired such restrictions, he recalled. The Russian high command had imposed the restrictions to prevent Russian soldiers from coming into contact with Americans. As Third Army commander, he observed the same Russian policy quickly applied in Germany. Like most Americans, he had been shocked to hear his friend and comrade in arms George Patton urge that the U.S. Army push on from Germany to drive the Red Army all the way back to the Soviet Union. Yet, on March 5,

1946, in a speech at Westminster College in Fulton, Missouri, Winston Churchill lent credence to Patton's assertion that the Russians were an enemy by declaring that the Soviet Union had built an iron curtain across Eastern Europe. From the Baltic Sea to the Adriatic, he said, "A shadow has fallen upon the scenes so lately lighted by the Allied victory. Nobody knows what Soviet Russia and its Communist international organization intends to do in the immediate future, or what are the limits, if any, to their expansive and proselytizing tendencies."

Of particular interest to Truscott as the military governor of Eastern Bavaria was the warning, "If now the Soviet Government tries, by separate action, to build up a pro-Communist Germany in their areas, this will cause new serious difficulties in the British and American zones, and will give the defeated Germans the power of putting themselves up to auction between the Soviets and Western democracies. Whatever conclusions may be drawn from these facts—and facts they are—this is certainly not the Liberated Europe we sought to build up. Nor is it one which contains the essentials of permanent peace."

Although in March 1946 Truscott was a lieutenant general, all of his promotions to star rank since 1942 were considered temporary. On official army roles he was carried as lieutenant colonel. This changed in April when President Harry S. Truman asked the U.S. Senate to approve elevations of sixty-three officers from temporary to permanent rank. Raised to brigadier general along with him were his friends and comrades Colonel Alexander Patch and Lieutenant Colonel Al Wedemeyer. Boosted from brigadier to major general were Mark Clark and Walter Bedell Smith. Because of formalities of administration and for the purpose of determining retirement benefits, none of the promotions affected the status of the temporary rankings. While Truscott was officially on the books as a brigadier general, he would wear three stars until he retired.

While the Senate acted to approve Truman's recommendations, Truscott and his staff were on the move in Germany. With official deactivation of the Seventh Army headquarters, based in Heidelberg, the Third Army headquarters and the office of Military Governor of Eastern Bavaria shifted to that city in order to be in a more central location and closer to theater headquarters in Frankfurt. Barely settled in the new location, Truscott received a cable from the War Department informing him that Sarah was seriously ill in Walter Reed General Hospital. Truscott rushed to Washington on a B-17 bomber lent to him by General McNarney. Satisfied after ten days that she was on the way to full recovery, he returned to Germany, expecting that once the army let dependents go overseas, she would join him there in the summer.

During the long flight to Germany, Truscott came down with a chest cold so severe that when he arrived in Heidelberg, a doctor ordered him into a hospital. After an electrocardiogram showed that he had suffered a heart attack, he was told on April 15 that he needed at least six weeks of bed rest and that his old friend General Keyes was coming from Italy to take command of the Third Army.

At the end of one small paragraph devoted to this episode in *Command Missions*, Truscott wrote, "That ended my second Army command and my last wartime mission."

He returned to the United States in July and spent six months under observation at Walter Reed, and another half year with the War Department Personnel Boards. Examined again, he was told that his cardiac condition had not improved. His only recourse was to retire. On September 30, 1947, he made it official. At age fifty-two and after thirty years and six weeks in the army, he believed that his service to the country was finished.

★ TWENTY ★

COLD WARRIOR

FOR THE FIRST TIME IN THREE DECADES, Lucian K. Truscott, Jr., found himself looking for a house he could call his own. After giving up teaching in Oklahoma for a life in the army, he'd lived in barracks and bachelor officers' quarters, then in a series of houses on or near posts with Sarah and their children. Since the spring of 1942, he'd slept in tents or rented space in England, Northern Ireland, Morocco, Algeria, Tunisia, Sicily, Italy, the south of France, Italy again, then in Germany, and in whatever accommodations his staff could find on a journey to China and back. Occasionally, he enjoyed the luxury of a trailer or commandeered villas. In Bavaria, he inherited a virtual palace that went with taking over from Patton. For meals at the front, he'd shared the rations served to his troops or the handiwork of his Chinese kitchen staff. In their twenty-eight years of marriage, he and Sarah had done their best to make a bewildering roster of temporary addresses seem permanent, knowing that one day an order would descend the chain of command telling them to pull up stakes.

For Sarah, the past five years without him had been passed in the place of her roots and the countryside she knew best, but it was new to him. Except for the handful of years of duty across the Potomac from Washington, D.C., at Fort Myer, Virginia was as foreign to him as Carrickfergus was to the fledgling Rangers and Moroccan shores, Algerian deserts, Sicilian mountains and passes, and beaches in Salerno, Anzio, Italy, and France had been to the invading dogfaces who followed him to war. In the tranquil place Sarah had chosen for them to settle down, he found golf courses and plenty of open spaces with pastures and rolling hills for getting on the back of a horse. In the heart of Loudon County at the foot of the Blue Mountains and on land rich in the history of the Civil War, they bought Bluemont Farm. Small in acreage and in need of fixing up, it was close enough to the nation's capital for him to keep in touch with friends who were still on active duty and able to use their influence to bring him out of retirement, however briefly.

After a stint of evaluating officers as a member of the War Department Screening Board, he served for a year (1948–1949) as the chairman of the Army Advisory Panel for Amphibious Operations at Fort Monroe, Virginia. Between its meetings, he began assembling material for two books The first would be the story of his war. Health and time permitting, he would then turn to a memoir of life in the old-time cavalry. Lucian III had graduated from West Point in 1945 and was serving in the infantry. A senior in high school, James had set his heart on going to the U.S. Military Academy in 1950. Mary was happily married. Once in a while, Bill Mauldin phoned and a letter arrived from Mike Chinigo in Rome, but Ernie Pyle had been killed covering the last of the war in the Pacific.

Mark Clark had come home in June 1947 to take command of the Sixth Army at the Presidio of San Francisco.

Ike had replaced Marshall as army chief of staff and Marshall became Truman's special representative to Chiang Kai-shek in China and then secretary of state.

Ike's right arm throughout the war, Walter Bedell Smith, was ambassador in Moscow.

Patton was in a grave in Luxembourg and his reputation was in the laps of historians, but his prediction that Russia was destined to be the new enemy came true.

In 1948, the Soviet Union attempted to deny the Allied powers access to divided Berlin but were eventually thwarted by an airlift of supplies and backed down. When Communist North Korea invaded the Republic of Korea in June 1950, American generals of Truscott's generation who were still in uniform or called back to service were at war again, but under the flag of the United Nations. Among the men who had been too young for World War II but were the right age for Korea was Lucian III. Now a captain, he would lead an infantry rifle company while his father watched the new war unfold from Bluemont Farm and felt what General Ted Roosevelt's father had called "the wolf rising in the heart." Despite the damage to his own, Truscott shot off a volley of letters appealing to be put back in uniform, starting on July 24 with Chairman of the Joint Chiefs of Staff Omar Bradley.

Three days later, Bradley answered, "It is good to know that we can count on you should the need arise. For the present, however, there appears to be little likelihood that retired officers will be recalled. As you know, this is a matter which will be decided by the individual services. Since their plans in this connection do not come up for consideration before the Joint Chiefs, I have little contact with matters of this kind. I am passing your letter to General [J. Lawton] Collins in order that the people in the Army will know of your willingness to come back on active duty." To Eisenhower, back from duty as the first commander of the North Atlantic Treaty Organization (NATO) and serving as the president of Columbia University, Truscott wrote in August, "I know, of course, that any general mobilization will have you back in harness. Please don't forget me." Ike replied, "It would really be like old times to be in harness with you by my side." But Eisenhower was also retired.

Truscott's letter to Clark pleaded, "Don't forget me if you have use for me."

Clark's reply was both dismissive and self-serving:

> I can well imagine your eagerness to get back in this crisis and give the assistance you were so capable of contributing in the last war. Right at the present moment with this partial mobilization only in progress, the Department of the Army has informed me that there is no intention of bringing back retired officers; however, I feel that there should be total mobilization at the present time, that the Soviets should be told that we have had enough and we are preparing for a war which we believe to be inevitable. I believe through that sort of demonstrated determination we might avoid another war. When that time comes for the greater buildup, I feel it will by then, by all means you should be brought back in to help us out. I would be the first to request it. I am delighted.
>
> We are in a pretty chaotic situation here, with crash programs descending upon us every few hours. My concern is that we not get so committed in an unimportant area of the world that we get our eye off our main goal which is in the other direction, and that we not commit all our resources which would preclude our having a halfway firm foundation upon which to rebuild. I wish I could talk with you and get your advice on some of these subjects. If it would appeal to you, I would be glad to have a plane pick you up any place you say and fly you down here for a day, just so we could check over the course of action we propose to take.
>
> Incidentally, a couple of months ago I finished my story of the Mediterranean campaign. It's to be published in the fall by Harper and Brothers. As I researched, I was more and more aware of the great contribution you made to our

victories. I always will be deeply grateful for the opportunity to have served with you for so long.

Unsure whether he was unwanted, deemed unfit because of his heart condition, or just not needed, Truscott continued the life of an ex-general and went on golfing and riding, but knowing that the Truscott name was being carried into battle by his son. He was also working on his memoir, but reliving Dieppe and the invasions of North Africa, Sicily, and Italy deepened his sense that history was passing him by. From the placid hills of northern Virginia that once felt the thundering hooves of Stonewall Jackson's cavalry and resounded with the bugle calls of the Confederacy and the Union, he followed the Korean War with the interest of a father whose namesake was in it, rather than as a former general who wished he could be there.

When Ike announced as a candidate for president in 1952 that he would go to Korea to see what could be done to end the war, if not win it, Truscott knew as well as Eisenhower that the best to be gotten was an armistice, and that the Cold War was not going to be won in Korea. That Ike was elected president in a landslide did not surprise him. That the victory would affect the future of an old soldier who'd been retired to the Virginia horse country never crossed his mind.

The chain of events that would put Truscott back in harness began with Walter Bedell Smith. As director of Central Intelligence, he decided on March 9, 1951, that as former military governor in Germany, Truscott was the right man to become the CIA station chief in Frankfurt, but with a cover story. In a secret memorandum that was declassified in 1994, Smith officially informed Truscott, "You will proceed to Germany and take station as senior Central Intelligence Agency representative in Germany." The last paragraph stated, "Your status in Germany will be that of Special Consultant to the United States High Commissioner. Where necessary, you will state but will not publicize your connection with the overt activities of the Central Intelligence

Agency. You will *disclaim* [emphasis added] connection with the covert activities of the Central Intelligence Agency, except to the following: a) Responsible United States, British, French, and German officials on a need-to-know basis; b) Central Intelligence Agency personnel on a need-to-know basis."

When Smith directed Truscott to investigate what "State Department types" had been doing on the front lines of the Cold War, Truscott replied, "I'm going to go out there and find out what those weirdos are up to."

Suddenly, the retired three-star general found himself in charge of the cloak-and-dagger operations of the CIA in the most explosive part of Europe. His duties as outlined in Smith's memo were not only those of the public representative of the CIA, but supervisor of its secret agents and coordinator between the CIA and other intelligence operations. His orders also authorized him to approve or veto secret operations, subject to review by Smith.

Just as abruptly, Bluemont Farm, which he and Sarah had thought was a permanent home, joined the long list of houses that duty required them to give up. The move was made easier because James had gone off to West Point. It was also the first time that Sarah was able to go with her husband to a posting since before the war. She also had the comfort of knowing that in his new assignment, no one would be shooting at him. Whether he told her that his title of Consultant to the High Commissioner was a charade isn't officially recorded. The only references by members of his family to his postwar government connections state that he had held various advisory posts in the Washington area. Truscott said nothing in *Command Missions* about his CIA role in Germany, or that he undertook even greater responsibility with the CIA in 1953.

The chain of events that would place him high in the echelons of the Central Intelligence Agency and in the pantheon of American espionage began when he was still adapting to the role of military governor after the war. On January 20, 1946, President Truman picked up a pen and signed an executive order setting up a Central Intelligence Group. It was a step that Truman had thought was unnecessary. Believing that an espionage system born prior to World War II had outlived its need and usefulness, he had swiftly abolished the Office of Strategic Services (OSS) in September 1945. Soon after this, he found what he later called "a stack of documents that high" on his desk that contained a report to President Roosevelt that had been written by the OSS founder, General William "Wild Bill" Donovan, on the subject of postwar intelligence gathering.

One of the most decorated men in the Allied Expeditionary Force during World War I, winning the Medal of Honor, Distinguished Service Cross, and Distinguished Service Medal, Donovan had run as a Republican for lieutenant governor in New York and had been a U.S. district attorney and assistant attorney general of the United States under President Coolidge.

For Roosevelt, these added up to a man of intelligence as well as courage. Donovan seemed to be just the man he needed for some work of a very special nature at a time when the great powers of Europe and Asia were engaged in wars that threatened to involve the United States. In 1940, Roosevelt wanted to know more about what was going on in Europe, but wanted this information to come from other sources than those that were already at his command through diplomatic channels. Roosevelt needed someone to go to Europe, to look, to observe, and to report back to him personally on what he found out. Especially, he wanted an opinion on what the prospects were for the United States keeping out of the war.

Having often expressed his private opinion that the United States not only could but ought to stay out of the war in Europe, Donovan accepted the assignment and made a number of trips that took him to Europe and the Middle East. He returned to advise FDR that the United States could not avoid the war and warned him that the United States should prepare for it. These views were largely in agreement with Roosevelt's. Deciding he needed someone to set up a government service that would collect information, digest it, and report it to him directly, he turned to Donovan. "You will have to begin with nothing," he said. "We have no intelligence service."

There had been none since 1929, when with the comment, "Gentlemen do not read each other's mail," Secretary of State Henry L. Stimson had closed down the State Department's code-breaking section, which had been known as the "black chamber." This and small intelligence units within the armed services had been the only American intelligence-gathering operation after the end of World War I. In July 1941, Roosevelt took the first step toward reestablishing a spy unit by appointing Donovan Coordinator of Information (COI). Another man with experience in intelligence operations in the First World War, Allen W. Dulles, wrote some years later of the appointment, "Donovan was eminently qualified for the job." A distinguished lawyer, Donovan had divided his busy life in peacetime between the law, government service, and politics. He knew the world and had traveled widely. He understood people. He had a flair for the unusual and for the dangerous, tempered with judgment. These were qualities desired in an intelligence officer.

Five months after Donovan accepted the job of Coordinator of Information, the Japanese attack on Pearl Harbor put the United States into the war and immediately broadened the duties that Donovan had assumed. What had been an informal group of scholars and historians working as a research and analysis organization had become more. This widened scope was recognized in June 1942, when the COI was renamed the Office of Strategic Services with the job of collecting and analyzing strategic information, and the planning and operating of special services. They included parachuting teams of agents behind enemy lines to aid underground resistance forces, including those who aided Truscott's forces in Sicily and Italy and the Maqui in France.

Countless other specialists were soon at work, all under the control and direction of the OSS. One of them was Allen W. Dulles. Based chiefly in Switzerland and masterminding a scheme that allowed American intelligence to get inside the Nazi government through an underground anti-Nazi group in the German spy apparatus (*Abwehr*), he worked closely with the British Secret Service. Toward the end of the war and after it, the OSS tracked down Germans attempting to escape, recovered art treasures that the Germans had systematically looted from captive cities and nations, and assisted Truscott's military government in rooting out ex-Nazis.

As the war neared a close, Donovan was looking ahead and remembering how the United States had virtually disbanded its intelligence services after World War I. Late in 1944, he wrote to Roosevelt, "I have given consideration to the organization of our intelligence service for the postwar period. Once our enemies are defeated the demand will be equally pressing for information that will aid in solving the problems of peace."

He recommended that intelligence control be returned to the supervision of the president and the establishment of a central authority reporting directly to the president. Roosevelt directed him to get together "the chiefs of the foreign intelligence and internal security in the various executive agencies, so that a consensus of opinion can be secured." Inheriting the presidency, Truman issued an order disbanding the OSS, many of whose agents went into army intelligence or to the State Department.

As the wartime alliance with the Soviet Union disintegrated into the Cold War, Truman realized that a president needed to know what was going on everywhere in the world. Finding the recommendations that Donovan gave to FDR and learning that FDR had referred them to the Joint Chiefs of Staff, who never followed up, Truman sent for Admiral William D. Leahy and asked him to look into it. Presented several proposals from various departments and agencies on the topic of intelligence, Truman favored one by the deputy chief of Naval Intelligence, Rear Admiral Sidney W. Souers. It recommended "a central agency to serve as an over-all intelligence organization." On January 20, 1946, Truman issued the executive order creating the Central Intelligence Group under supervision of a National Intelligence Authority, consisting of the secretaries of state, war, and the navy and a representative of the president. Truman's order designated Souers as the first director of a

Central Intelligence Agency that had been created by Congress in the National Security Act of 1947. When Souers chose to leave government, he was succeeded by Air Force Lieutenant General Hoyt A. Vandenberg. He was followed by Admiral Roscoe H. Hillenkoetter, and in October 1950 by Walter Bedell Smith.

When Smith chose to leave the CIA, Eisenhower tapped Smith's deputy to succeed him. The son of a Presbyterian minister, grandson of a secretary of state, and brother of Ike's pick for secretary of state, John Foster Dulles, Allen Dulles was born on April 7, 1893, in Watertown, New York, and grew up in a household that valued public service and where world affairs were a common topic of discussion. He graduated from Princeton with a master of arts, and in 1916 entered the diplomatic service with posts in Vienna and Berne. He also worked for the American Commission at the Paris Peace Conference (1919) and later served in embassies in Berlin and Istanbul. He returned to Washington in 1922 as the chief of the State Department's Near East Division and received his law degree in 1926. Shortly after, he served as counselor of the U.S. delegation to China.

In the 1930s, he became active in Republican politics, and in May 1941 urged the United States to enter World War II out of enlightened selfishness. Shortly after the attack on Pearl Harbor, he was recruited by Donovan to set up and run an OSS listening post in Berne. From 1942 to May 1945, he gathered intelligence information on Nazi Germany and played an instrumental role in events that led to the surrender of the German forces to Truscott's army in Italy. While Fifth and Eighth army units spread across northern Italy, secret negotiations to end the fighting that had been going on since February through Italian and Swiss middlemen had been conducted primarily by Dulles and Lieutenant General Karl Wolff. The senior SS officer in Italy, he, and later General von Vietinghoff, hoped to gain either cooperation or acquiescence of the western Allies for a continuation of Germany's war against the Soviet Union using Axis forces then engaged in Italy. Although neither Dulles nor Allied military leaders seriously considered Wolff's goals, they were interested in any possibility of ending the fighting without more bloodshed. When their exertions ultimately failed, Truscott's army had no choice but to smash German resistance.

As a government consultant in 1948, Dulles was appointed chairman of a commission to assess the intelligence system, and in 1951 he was made the deputy director of the CIA under General Smith. Having known Dulles during the war and benefited from Dulles's OSS work, Ike chose him to take over from Smith.

To serve as his deputy, Eisenhower reached out to the man he'd picked to be his field deputy in Algeria and to replace Patton in 1945, and who General Smith had tapped to become the CIA station chief in Frankfurt. All of this was formalized in a memorandum that acted on the recommendations from an intelligence advisory board. Ike's memo stated:

> I concur in the need for strong centralized direction of the intelligence effort of the United States through the National Security Council and the Director of Central Intelligence. The exercise of a more comprehensive and positive coordinating responsibility by the Director of Central Intelligence can be of the utmost value to the entire intelligence community and strengthen the national intelligence effort. I have also concurred in the recommendation of the Director of Central Intelligence that he appoint a Deputy Director for Coordination, who will review all possibilities for increasing integration, reducing duplication, and improving coordination within the intelligence community; and, after such review, will recommend, when necessary, action by the Director of Central Intelligence to coordinate all elements of the intelligence community. This work should be carried out in full consultation with appropriate representatives of all of our intelligence agencies. The Director of Central Intelligence has appointed General Lucian K. Truscott, Jr., Retired, for this duty.

The effect of this was to install Dulles as the administrative manager of the CIA and Eisenhower's chief advisor on intelligence, with Truscott running and controlling the actions of the agency's rapidly expanding network of agents, which would soon total twelve hundred. At this time, the CIA was located in a deceptive-looking building on secured land that belonged to the navy across the street from the State Department, where Allen Dulles's older brother, John Foster Dulles, was secretary of state. In vivid contrast to the dour chief diplomat, and different temperamentally and physically from Truscott, Allen Dulles was an Ivy League and Wall Street gentleman, but at the same time a jocular figure who sat at his desk smoking a pipe, his feet in velvet slippers with embroidered fox heads on the toes. Yet he was a man whose brilliance and innovation would be responsible for some of the most daring enterprises the United States pursued during the Cold War, from overthrowing unfriendly governments, sending spy planes across Russia, and planning invasions to probing the deepest, darkest secrets of the Communist world and very often America's allies.

With few exceptions, details of what Truscott did at the CIA remain wrapped in shrouds of secrecy. His papers at the George C. Marshall Library contain nothing on the CIA years. In a few instances, others related illuminating anecdotes of his role. According to one account, soon after his appointment, he discovered that the CIA was planning to assassinate the Communist Chinese leader Chou En-lai. During a banquet in Bandung, Indonesia, an agent was to slip some poison into Chou's rice bowl that would not take effect for forty-eight hours, at which time Chou would be back in China. Outraged, Truscott confronted Dulles, forcing him to end the operation.

A less dramatic revelation concerning Truscott at the CIA involved the agency's internal security chief, Sheffield Edwards, and resulted in an urgent meeting with Dulles in 1954. With extreme nervousness, Edwards told Dulles, "Mr. Director, we have a serious problem that I have already briefed General Truscott on."

Through a puff of pipe smoke, Dulles replied, "Oh?"

Anxiously, Edwards said, "Six, *six* of the men you have brought over from OSS are serious security risks."

When Dulles appeared puzzled, Truscott exclaimed, "Jesus, Allen, they are homosexuals, and I can assure you that if we know, the Soviets know!"

Presented with the possibility that the men might become prey to Soviet blackmail, Dulles agreed that the only recourse was for Truscott to arrange to transfer them to positions in the U.S. government in which they would not be security risks.

An immediate challenge to Dulles and Truscott was to persuade the army to let the CIA do the spy running, especially within Western Europe. It was a struggle that would continue until 1958, when the army grudgingly accepted Eisenhower's National Security Directive assigning primary responsibility for agent recruitment to the CIA. In the meantime, Truscott's operatives worked to engineer the overthrow of two governments that the Eisenhower government regarded as not only hostile to U.S. interests, but pro-Soviet.

The first was an Islamic fundamentalist revolutionary regime in Iran, headed by Premier Mohammad Mossadegh. With a large nose and sad-looking eyes, Mossadegh was aristocratic and a fervent nationalist. He was *Time* magazine's Man of the Year for 1951 and was presented as a sickly old man who often wore pajamas and frequently wept in public. The diplomat W. Averell Harriman observed, "He projected helplessness, and while he was obviously as much a captive as a leader of nationalistic fanatics, he relented on nothing." Prime Minister Winston Churchill saw "an elderly lunatic bent on wrecking his country and handing it over to the Communists."

Eisenhower shared this concern. When the British proposed a joint operation to remove him, Ike approved Operation Ajax. Coordinated with the shah and the Iranian military, it was run by a CIA operative and a grandson of President Theodore Roosevelt.

The namesake of both Teddy's brother and son, and the nephew of Truscott's wartime colleague, General Ted Roosevelt, Kermit Roosevelt, known as Kim, had been recruited from college for the OSS. Operation Ajax was so sensitive and dangerous a task that he was smuggled into the shah's palace in a plan that called for the chief of the royal guards to deliver a formal notice from the shah to Mossadegh dismissing him. The scheme failed when the messenger was arrested. After the shah fled the country and rioters flooded into the streets, Roosevelt was ordered by the CIA to get out of Iran. Instead, he arranged for demonstrators, most of them hired, to also swarm into the streets to protest against Mossadegh's government. Mossadegh fled and hid while the shah returned to power.

Tried for treason, Mossadegh denounced "foreign conspiracies" and after three years in prison spent the rest of his life under house arrest. He died in 1967. With the shah firmly back on the Peacock Throne, Iranian oil continued to flow into the West and Iran was counted on the side of the United States during the Cold War. In return, Iran received economic and military aid and became a bastion against Soviet designs on the Middle East.

The next problem facing Truscott as Dulles's operational coordinator was in Guatemala.

Since 1944, the small Central American country had been in turmoil. In that year, the dictatorship of General Jorge Ubico was overthrown and replaced by President Juan José Arevalo, a Socialist who turned violently anti-American. In 1950, Jacobo Arbenz, a military officer, came to power and brought with him the first Communist government ever established in the Western Hemisphere. Arbenz was not popular among his own people, many of whom found his links with the Russians as distasteful as the ties of the previous government with the United States. But if Arbenz was unpopular at home, he was even more so in Washington, D.C. One reason for this was the fact that on February 24, 1953, he announced his intention to take over 225,000 acres of unused United Fruit Company land.

Top members of the Arbenz government were known members of the

Communist Party. Others were being sent to Moscow for instruction and training. Guatemala had also withdrawn from a five-nation Organization of Central American States in order to avoid participating in a debate on an anti-Communist resolution. Arbenz had publicly parroted the Communist charge that the United States had been using biological warfare in Korea. But the most damaging of the evidence came from the new American ambassador to Guatemala, John E. Peurifoy. He reported to Eisenhower:

> In a six-hour conversation he (Arbenz) listened while I counted off the leading Communists in his regime, but he gave no ground; many notorious Reds he denied to be Communists; if they were, they were not dangerous; if dangerous, he could control them; if not controllable, he would round them up. He said, in any case, all our difficulties were due to the malpractices of American business. The trips of Communists to Russia were not to get training and instructions, he said, but merely to study Marxism, just in the same way as other Guatemalans may come to the United States to study economics.

The ambassador concluded that "the man thought like a Communist and talked like a Communist, and if not actually one, would do until one came along." Unless the Communist influences in Guatemala were counteracted, he asserted the country "would within six months fall completely under Communist control."

Eisenhower wrote, "Something had to be done quickly."

That "something" immediately became the concern of Frank Wisner. The deputy director for plans of CIA, he was a Mississippian who'd been in the OSS, working in Istanbul, Bucharest, and Germany. After the war, he returned to his civilian law practice but found that he longed to return to intelligence work. His challenge in Guatemala was to find someone to replace Arbenz who would be friendly to the United States and passionately anti-Communist. Wisner looked with favor upon Colonel Carlos Castillo Armas. Among his qualifications, not the least important was the fact that Castillo and Arbenz were old enemies. Castillo had attempted to overthrow Arbenz in 1950, failed, was imprisoned, and escaped to exile in Honduras.

Others were recruited for the developing plan to get rid of Arbenz's government, among them a handful of civilian pilots hired to fly World War II–vintage airplanes for what was to be an "invasion" of Guatemala by an army led by Castillo. These planes were to bomb Guatemala City while Castillo crossed the Nicaragua-Guatemala border. The bombs were intended to persuade Arbenz to give up. The date for the invasion was June 18, 1954. At dawn, three World War II P-47s zoomed low over San José, Guatemala's major port on the Pacific. Castillo lurched across the border in a battered station wagon. As he and his army bumped down the roads of his native country, Castillo carried with him a pledge from the president of the United States that the invasion would not fail.

"I'm prepared to take any steps that are necessary to see that it succeeds," said Eisenhower. "For if it succeeds, it's the example of Guatemala throwing off the yoke of Communism. If it fails, the flag of the United States has failed."

As the attack began, the government in Guatemala City announced it. In Washington, the State Department asserted that there was no evidence "that this is anything other than a revolt of the Guatemalans against the government."

Meantime, Truscott learned that the little air force attacked and bombed an ordnance depot in Guatemala City. Some members of the Arbenz government took the hint, packed up, and left. But the Castillo army had bogged down. Then came worse news. One of the old P-47s was shot full of holes. Another crashed. The air force had been virtually wiped out and replacements were needed immediately. At a hurriedly called meeting at the White House, Eisenhower fixed his soldier's eyes on Allen Dulles and Truscott and asked, "Allen, what do you think Castillo's chances would be without the aircraft?"

Dulles replied, "About zero."

"Suppose we supply the aircraft. What would the chances be then?"

"About twenty percent."

The president ordered the planes replaced.

As Dulles and Truscott were leaving the Oval Office with a promise of prompt delivery of new planes to bolster the sagging invasion, Eisenhower said, "Allen, the figure of twenty percent was persuasive. It showed me that you had thought this matter through realistically. If you had told me that the chances would be ninety percent, I would have had a much more difficult decision."

In Guatemala, things were going badly for Arbenz. The lone surviving P-47 had buzzed Guatemala City on June 25, causing further panic within his government. Arbenz had never had much support among the people, and the fact that they were under attack because of him made him even more unpopular. Nor had he won the confidence of Guatemala's small army, and on June 27, after a meeting with Peurifoy, he gave up and was succeeded by Colonel Carlos Enrique Diaz, chief of the Guatemalan armed forces. Peurifoy thought it was all over. But Diaz promptly went on the radio to announce that the struggle against "mercenary invaders" of Guatemala would not abate. Stating that Arbenz had done what he thought was his duty, he pledged to carry on.

When another colonel, Elfego Monzon, confronted Diaz with machine guns, Diaz stepped down and other colonels promptly took over the government.

The only war planned and carried out while Truscott was with the CIA was over. For the next four years, agents would be active in Indochina after the French colonial government in Saigon lost a war with Communists from the north. When he left the CIA in 1958, he was again the retired general from a war that after only thirteen years since the last shot was fired seemed to be as distant as the day he heard the lure of the bugle call and went off to join the army.

★ TWENTY-ONE ★

REFLECTIONS

"LUCK PLAYS A PART in the life of every man."

This opening line of *Command Missions* is not only so obvious a truth that it is a cliché, but it is a far from exciting start to a warrior's memoir. Truscott admitted that he set out with some trepidation and temerity to add himself to a long list of authors of books about personal experiences of the Second World War. Among volumes by generals that publishers had turned out since the end of the war were Eisenhower's *Crusade in Europe* (1948), Mark W. Clark's *Calculated Risk* (1950), and Omar Bradley's *A Soldier's Story* (1951). With a candor that was familiar to his family, friends, and wartime comrades, he explained in the foreword that several factors had led him to begin and continue "the onerous task" of writing without professional assistance. He wrote that unique war assignments had brought him into close relationship with those who were responsible for the concept, planning, preparation, and conduct of the war in the European theater and "afforded him some part" in them.

"If these experiences have any historical or popular interest," he said, "there is no one else to relate them for me."

Secondly, his own war experiences, he said, were "testimonials to the accomplishments of the American soldier who has no superior and few equals when adequately equipped, properly trained and afforded good leadership in the various echelons." Recalling that when the war began he had never heard a shot fired in anger and had no battle experience, but having applied himself in military and other studies during peacetime and formed opinions concerning the techniques of combat and leadership, he felt that more than most American senior commanders, he had the opportunity to apply these theories in battle in command of units varying in strength from a regimental combat team to a field army.

"In this respect," he wrote, "my war experiences may have some value as an example of development in the art of command and of battle leadership."

The final passages of *Command Missions* provided Truscott's assessments of the GI and the Allied soldiers he'd come to know in combat from North Africa to the last throes of the war in Italy. The former cavalryman wrote that even with the support made possible by mechanization both in the air and on the ground, it was the infantryman who had borne the brunt of the war.

The British soldier, he said, was the product of a far more rigorous discipline than was the American soldier. This was due to British military traditions and in part to the social structure of British life. "This stricter discipline may have made the British soldier appear more phlegmatic than his American comrade, lacking the Americans' ingenuity and resourcefulness," he wrote. "British soldiers always seemed to me more suited for defense than for attack, while with the American soldiers the reverse was true." Although the American could distinguish himself on defense when the occasion required, the British soldier could always be expected to hold to the last man whenever he was told to do so. British and American soldiers invariably got on well, and it was only among the high echelons that friction developed between the Allies.

French troops in Italy and southern France, colonials for the most part, performed well and merited the high regard in which they were held by the American troops. In both areas, the French troops were more volatile than Americans and displayed considerable dash.

"When American soldiers first came in contact with the German soldier," Truscott wrote, "the latter was already a veteran with a long military tradition, the product of long and thorough military training, led by experienced and capable officers, and equipped with the most modern weapons. The German was then better trained, especially for operations in small units, and the quality of his leadership was superior. German soldiers displayed ingenuity and resourcefulness more American than British. The American quickly adapted himself and learned much from the German. Sicily and southern Italy proved that he had mastered his lessons well. From Anzio on there was never a question of the superiority of American soldiers."

Devoting the closing paragraph of the book not to himself but to the GI, he wrote,

> The American soldier did not like war. He dreaded the uncertainty, danger, and hardship. He was rather resentful of military discipline and its interference with his individual liberties. He hated the monotony of military training and the physical effort it required. When asked why he was fighting, the answer was as often as not, "because I have to." He may not have known just why he was in Africa, or Italy, or elsewhere, but he appreciated well enough why he was fighting. War had been forced on the country at Pearl Harbor; like others, he had to do his part toward winning it. Disliking war, discipline, training, discomfort, and hardship, the American soldier accepted them philosophically as

aspects of a disagreeable task to which he applied his native ingenuity and resourcefulness. The American soldier demonstrated
that, properly equipped, trained and led, he has no superior among
all of the armies in the world.

Begun while convalescing from the heart attack and completed in
periods between 1947 and 1953 when his obligations to family and CIA
permitted, *Command Missions* was published in 1954 by E. P. Dutton
and Company to acclaim from book critics and war veterans. In a
lengthy review in the *New York Times* on February 9, 1954, titled "A
Fighting General Speaks Out," Hanson W. Baldwin cited Truscott's
chastising of other generals and Mark Clark in particular, but concluded
that the personalized judgments of men and events, although by far the
most interesting parts of *Command Missions*, did not reflect fully the
book's worth. "This narrative of a combat commander," he wrote, "is
simultaneously a study in leadership, a case book of strategy and tactics
and a solid slice of history, written from the records by a man who was
there."

Seven months after *Command Missions* was published, Congress
passed Public Law 88–508, which gave Truscott an "honorary" promotion to four-star general.

Encouraged by the praise for *Command Missions*, he started making
notes and dictating memories for a book that he intended to be a history
and a nostalgic memory of the horse army between the wars. Edited and
with a preface by Lucian III, it would be posthumously published in
1989 by the University Press of Kansas. Retired as a colonel and living in
Albuquerque, New Mexico, the proud son wrote, "As I went over these
pages again and again during the past few months, I relived much of *my*
life because I was born in chapter two, 'Hawaiian Interlude,' and I left
home in chapter seven, when the family moved to Fort Knox. There
were many times I wanted to say, 'Dad, what did you mean by this?' Or,
'Why not add a little more detail here?' Or, 'Why not tell the story

about . . . ?' But I couldn't. I had no recourse to any of his references or sources—especially the primary one: his mind. So I left things pretty much as he wrote them. Although I am listed as editor, my work has consisted primarily of correcting grammar, spelling, and punctuation (and not much of that) and eliminating occasional repetition."

Having served in Korea and Vietnam, Lucian III moved with his wife, Anne Harlow Truscott, who'd had a heart attack and bypass surgery in November 1990, into a retirement community in Redmond, Washington, close to the Seattle homes of their daughters, Susan, Mary, and Virginia. Their son, Lucian IV, graduated from West Point in 1969. Resigning his commission after thirteen months in a dispute with superiors, he became a journalist and joined the New York newspaper the *Village Voice* in time to cover a battle with police by gays at the Stonewall bar in Greenwich Village in 1969 that was credited with signaling the birth of the Gay Rights movement. In 1978, he published a first novel, *Dress Gray*, about the murder of a homosexual cadet at the U.S. Military Academy that *Time* magazine depicted "as the nastiest assault on West Point since Benedict Arnold tried to hand over its plans to the British." He later ignited a controversy among Jefferson descendants and scholars by calling for an official admission by the Monticello Association and Jefferson heirs that Jefferson had fathered children with his household slave, Sally Hemmings.

Lucian III's daughter Mary published a book that came out in the same year as her grandfather's memoirs of life in the cavalry, but with nothing close to the attention that her brother's novel had stirred up. Titled *Brats: Children of the Military Speak Out*, it was a compilation of tales of army life by others and was notable because she wrote in the introduction that her grandfather was a general, "and although the details of his career were vague to me, his booming voice and military bearing convinced me that he was no ordinary grandfather."

In 1999, Lucian III was diagnosed with a brain tumor. After two surgeries and radiation treatments, he died on March 12, 2000, and was cremated. As a descendant through his mother of Thomas Jefferson, he was entitled to have the urn buried in the Jefferson family cemetery at Monticello, Virginia.

Following graduation from West Point in 1954, James served in the air force. On August 21, 1957, he married an air force nurse, First Lieutenant Helen K. Haydock, at Hahn Air Force Base in Germany. They had four children: James, Thomas, Patrick, and Sarah. He retired in 1981, and worked in data processing for a year, then joined the Northrop Aviation Corporation until retiring in 1992. Settled in Slippery Rock, Pennsylvania, in 1999 he became president of the Monticello Association and was publicly at loggerheads with Lucian IV in the continuing squabble over the Hemming paternity issue. On January 26, 2000, James announced that the Thomas Jefferson Memorial Foundation had released results of a study of the Jefferson–Sally Hemings relationship, but that the issue remained unresolved. He stated, "I want to emphasize that the Association is determined to act prudently and responsibly regarding the granting of membership in the Association and the right to burial in the family graveyard. The criteria we are striving to develop must apply to everyone, including current members of the Association, other acknowledged descendants of Mr. Jefferson, the Hemings descendants currently seeking recognition as acknowledged descendants, and others that may come forward in the future."

The fight continued as recently as 2004 in a letter in the *New Crisis* that stated, "As a Hemmings descendant [although history books use one "m," family members contend that Hemmings is spelled with two] and a fellow participant in the ongoing fracas between the families, I wanted to point out that the Hemmingses have been invited to the annual meetings by only one Monticello Association (MA) member, Lucian K. Truscott IV, and with only one year as the exception (when Lucian's uncle, James Truscott, then president, extended the invitation at Lucian's behest). Most association members have made it abundantly clear they would rather we stayed at home. We keep showing up because

Lucian invites us, and because we wish to be treated the same as all of Jefferson's descendants and be granted the right to apply for membership to the association."

In an article in the February/March 1999 issue of *American Heritage* magazine, Lucian IV wrote of the first time he went with his family to the graveyard at Monticello. "Our parents and grandparents had taken us down to Charlottesville for a meeting of the Monticello Association," he remembered.

Our grandfather was Gen. Lucian K. Truscott, Jr., the commander of the VI Corps and the 5th and 3rd Armies during World War II. His wife was Sarah Randolph Truscott, who had been raised at Edgehill, a plantation a few miles from Monticello. The drive in those days, as much of it is today, was along two-lane blacktops that ran through hilly fields of corn and second-growth forests concealing the horrors of the Civil War battlefields beyond. I can still see the old Buick as we hung out the back windows, zooming our hands like airplanes in the super-heated dusty wind of a Virginia summer. In such conditions, back when air-conditioning wasn't even a rumor, you had to make a few stops for iced teas and Cokes, for a cold, wet hand towel for Grandma to dab on her forehead. There was a place we used to pull up to on our way to Charlottesville. It was one of those wood-frame diners with a few gas pumps out front. Inside were a lunch counter and a few booths and greasy fans desultorily stirring the fetid air. I remember one time Frank and I wanted to use the bathroom. Someone pointed out the door, around the corner of the building. We scampered outside onto the gravel parking lot and found a little outbuilding with one door marked "white" and another marked "colored." We were very young. We came from a life in the Army that even in those days—this was 1952 or 1953—was completely integrated. Yet, instinctively, we knew we were "white" and so we used the "white" bathroom, but when we got back in the car, headed south, we asked our grandparents why there were two separate bathrooms, one "white" and one "colored." There was a moment of silence before either of them spoke, and I think it was my grandmother who answered. "That's just the way things are," she said softly.

Although Lucian IV, his uncles, and his cousins were entitled to claim a plot in the Jefferson family graveyard through Sarah, her husband was not. It didn't matter. He wished to be interred at Arlington National Cemetery with all the trappings required by the army for the burial of a soldier, whether buck private or general. As a captain at Fort Myer in the 1930s, he'd been in charge of hundreds. At times there were as many as twenty a day as the families of men killed in World War I exercised an option to bring them from graves in France for final rest in Arlington.

With increasingly failing health in the brief years of the administration of President John F. Kennedy and the first two of the presidency of Lyndon B. Johnson, with Lucian III at war again in Vietnam and James serving in the air force, the ex–combat commander and former CIA man continued to work on the cavalry memoir. Recalling the Arlington rituals, he'd written: "The firing of volleys is supposedly from the ancient Roman funeral rite in which casting earth three times on the casket constituted burial. It was then customary to call the dead three times by name, which ended the ceremony, after which friends and relatives pronounced the word *vale* (farewell) three times as they left the tomb."

The black horse following the casket, caparisoned in mourning with black boots reversed in the stirrups, was a cavalry adaptation of the medieval practice in which a knight's charger in mourning followed the knight to his last resting place, with boots and saber reversed to show that his war days were ended. The use of the caisson for transporting the

soldier's remains in a flag-draped casket had originated in the horse artillery. The sounding of taps was supposed to have been adopted by the
Army of the Potomac during the Civil War's Peninsular Campaign of
1862 as a formality for all military funerals. The custom spread throughout the army and was eventually made an official part of the ceremony.

Truscott wrote, "There can be no more fitting honor to a departed
comrade or to the end of a funeral ceremony than this call which recalls
the words:

> *Fades the light,*
> *And afar*
> *Goeth light,*
> *Cometh night,*
> *And a star,*
> *Leadeth all,*
> *Speedeth all,*
> *To their rest*

In an article published after Lucian III's death, Lucian IV recalled,
"As a boy, my father learned to play the bugle from the bugler in my
grandfather's horse cavalry squadron. Today his bugle rests on its tar-
nished, dented bell atop my son's bedroom dresser. On the wall of the
room is a photograph of a mounted Cub Scout Pack at Fort Myer, Va.,
taken in 1931. My father, a tiny figure on a giant horse, holds the bugle
against his thigh. The bugle reaches up to his shoulder, almost, and
looks half as big as he is. I recall him telling me how proud he was when
my grandfather finally agreed to let him play taps as a duet with the
squadron bugler at lights out and cavalry funerals."

Lucian King Truscott, Jr., died of a heart attack on September 12,
1965, at the age of seventy. He was survived by Sarah, Lucian III, James,
Mary (Mrs. Grame Bruce of London), eight grandchildren, and sisters

Mrs. Loretta Truscott King of Amarillo, Texas; Mrs. Cecil Johnston, Ardmore, Oklahoma; and Miss Pat Truscott, Columbus, New Mexico. Attending the funeral at Arlington or sending flowers were wartime comrades, including Eisenhower.

On April 29, 1966, Sarah attended the dedication of Truscott Hall, a bachelor officers' quarters, at the Army War College in Carlisle, Pennsylvania. On August 17, 1994, she was buried next to him at Arlington.

Seven years before taps echoed down the slopes of the National Cemetery, Truscott had gone back to Italy. For yet another Memorial Day ceremony at Nettuno, not far from Anzio, he said: "It is a special privilege for me to return to this particular spot: It brings back a flood of memories. My first sight of Pontine plains and Alban Hills was on a Sunday morning more than fourteen years ago. That morning this blue Mediterranean was filled with a great invasion fleet. That fleet carried the VI Corps, which was to establish the beachhead here. In the VI Corps was the United States Third Infantry Division, the British First Division and many other elements. I waded ashore in command of the Third Infantry Division on beaches just over there. Rome, that beautiful city, and the Alban Hills did not then seem far away. But they were. More than four weary months were to pass, many thousand lives would be lost, and there was to be untold destruction of wealth and beauty before the Allied Corps would be first in Rome. It is to honor those who sleep beneath this sod, who fell here and elsewhere in this fair land, and through them all and those of our Allied Forces and of our Italian friends who have fallen in the service of their country, that we gather here today."

Recalling a return to Anzio in 1944, he said, "The battle still rumbled in the distance. The Alban Hills were shrouded still in battle smoke. Four months of siege had wrecked the towns of Anzio and Nettuno and had devastated these fair fields and farm homes. Thousands of local citizens had been torn from home and fireside and transported to a place of greater safety. Winter had passed, Spring had come. Mud had given way to dust, stirred by the trucks and tanks of moving troops. There was no green grass. The graves were mounds of raw, brown earth, row on row, marked by a temporary cross or star."

Invoking his visit on Memorial Day in 1945, he continued, "The war in Europe was ended. I thought then that I was saying farewell forever to my sleeping comrades, for I would soon be going home, to the homeland they would never see again. It was a sad occasion for me, and I told them farewell here. And now we say, again: We have not forgotten."

In the steadily enveloping mists of history as World War II became more distant in time and in the consciousness of the families of the men who had fought and won it, and were now dying, the name Lucian K. Truscott, Jr., and his deeds faded for everyone but dwindling ranks of veterans of North Africa, Sicily, Italy, and France, and a few military historians. Yet, no one in the war contributed more on the front lines to defeating Germany than the raspy-voiced ex-schoolteacher, ninety-day wonder, and tight-lipped general who liked meals with flowers on the table and did not give a damn if his name was in newspapers or written large in history books.

DECORATIONS AND CITATIONS

DISTINGUISHED SERVICE MEDAL, DECEMBER 15, 1942, CITATION:

For exceptionally meritorious service in a duty of great responsibility. General Truscott organized a wholly strange command, trained it, and planned operations in a manner that demonstrated organization and administrative ability of the highest order. His conduct of the landing operations of his command on 8 November 1942 as a part of the Western Task Force, resulted in the capture of Port Lyautey, with its harbor, against superior enemy opposition. He exhibited tireless activity and devotion to duty and complete scorn of personal danger to which he was incessantly exposed. The success of that operation was largely due to his professional ability and brilliant battle leadership.

LEGION OF MERIT, AUGUST 1943, CITATION:

For exceptionally meritorious conduct in the performance of outstanding service while in charge of the development of plans of a combined force. He constantly exhibited a keen insight into the many complexities of organizing combined operations. His untiring efforts, sound judgment, zeal, efficiency, and ability successfully to establish and maintain close cooperation with both the British High Command and the British combined operations forces were of inestimable value to the theater commander.

DISTINGUISHED SERVICE CROSS, 1944, CITATION:

For extraordinary heroism in action on 11 July 1943, near Agrigento, Sicily. Completely disregarding his own safety he personally directed the successful operation which expanded the Third Division's Licata beachhead, and by his continuous presence with the forward elements, as well as his exemplary judgment and leadership inspired his command to the early capture of Agrigento and the continuance of the attack northward. General Truscott's contact with the assault unit was maintained in the face of intense artillery, mortar and small-arms fire, and he repeatedly exposed himself to this enemy fire in order to confer with the officers leading the attack and to keep them informed of the enemy situation. When certain elements were temporarily halted by an enemy counterattack, he calmly and courageously assumed personal command and rallying his officers and men ordered a renewal of the attack, thereby regaining the initiative. By his intrepid direction, heroic leadership and superior professional ability, General Truscott set an inspirational example for his command, reflecting the highest traditions of the armed forces.

Wounded in action, January 24, 1944, and awarded the Purple Heart.

Second Distinguished Service Medal for "brilliant conduct of the final stages of the campaign in Italy in May 1945."

A third Distinguished Service Medal was awarded him in June 1946 for outstanding service while commanding the Third United States Army in American Occupied Germany.

Navy Distinguished Service Medal in April 1946, in recognition of notable contributions to the success of the combined Army-Navy amphibious operations in North Africa, Sicily, Anzio, and Southern France.

FOREIGN DECORATIONS AND AWARDS

Brazilian:	Ordem do Militar, Grand Officer War Medal
British:	Most Honourable Order of the Bath, degree of Honorary Companion
Czechoslovakian:	Order of the White Lion, First Class
French:	Croix de Guerre Legion of Honor, rank of Officer
Italian:	Grande Ufficiale of the Order of Saints Maurice and Lazarus Military Order of Italy Silver Medal for Military Valor Order of the Crown of Italy, rank of Grand Cross
Polish:	Silver Cross Virtuti Militari, Class V

BIBLIOGRAPHY

BOOKS

Altieri, James. *The Spearheaders*. New York: Popular Library, 1960.

Allen, William. *Anzio: Edge of Disaster*. New York: Dutton, 1978.

Astor, Gerald. *The Greatest War: Americans in Combat, 1941–1945*. Novato, Calif.: Presidio Press, Inc., 1999.

Atkinson, Rick. *An Army at Dawn: The War in North Africa*. New York: Henry Holt and Company, 2002.

Bahmanyar, Mir. *Darby's Rangers: 1942–1945*. Wellingborough, UK: Osprey Publishing, 2004.

———. *Shadow Warriors: A History of the U.S. Army Rangers*. Wellingborough, UK: Osprey Publishing, 2005.

Black, Robert W. *Rangers in World War II*. Novato, Calif.: Presidio Press, 1992.

Blumenson, Martin. *Anzio*. Norwalk, Conn.: Easton Press, 1963.

———. *Kasserine Pass*. New York: Jove Books, 1983.

———. *Mark Clark*. New York: Congdon & Weed, 1984.

Bowditch, John. *Anzio Beachhead*. Washington, D.C.: United States Army Center of Military History, 1990.

Bradley, Omar N. *A Soldier's Story.* New York: Henry Holt, 1953.

Brinkley, David. *Washington Goes to War.* New York: Ballantine, 1989.

Clark, Mark W. *Calculated Risk.* New York: Harper & Brothers, 1950.

Clifford, Alexander. *The Conquest of North Africa, 1940–1943.* Boston: Little, Brown, 1943.

Coggins, Jack. *The Campaign for North Africa.* New York: Doubleday, 1980.

Darby, William O., and William H. Baumer. *We Led the Way.* New York: Jove Books, 1985.

D'Este, Carlo. *The Battle for Sicily, July–August 1943.* New York: Harper-Perennial, 1991.

———. *Patton: Genius for War.* New York: HarperPerennial, 1996.

Department of the Army Historical Division. *Anzio Beachhead.* Nashville: The Battery Press, 1986.

Dulles, Allen Walsh. *The Craft of Intelligence.* New York: Harper and Row, 1963.

Dupuy, Trevor Nevitt. *Land Battle for North Africa, Sicily and Italy.* New York: Franklin Watts, 1962.

Eisenhower, Dwight D. *Crusade in Europe.* New York: Doubleday, 1948.

Farago, Ladislas. *Patton: Ordeal and Triumph.* New York: Ivan Obolensky, 1964.

Hogan, Jr., David W. *Raiders or Elite Infantry?* Westport, Conn.: Greenwood Press, 1992.

———. *U.S. Army Special Operations in World War II.* Washington, D.C.: Center of Military History, 1992.

Jeffers, H. Paul. *Onward We Charge: The Heroic Story of Darby's Rangers in World War II.* New York: NAL Caliber, 2007.

———. *Theodore Roosevelt, Jr.: The Life of a War Hero.* Novato, Calif.: Presidio Press, 2002.

King, Michael J. *Rangers: Selected Combat Operations in World War II.* Honolulu, Hawaii: University Press of the Pacific, 2004.

BIBLIOGRAPHY

―――. *William Orlando Darby: A Military Biography.* Hamden, Conn.: Archon Books, 1981.

Ladd, James. *Commandos and Rangers.* New York: St. Martin's Press, 1978.

Lock, John D. *To Fight with Intrepidity.* New York: Pocket Books, 1998.

Lyon, Peter. *Eisenhower: Portrait of the Hero.* New York: Little, Brown, 1974.

O'Donnell, Patrick K. *Beyond Valor: World War II's Ranger and Airborne Veterans Reveal the Heart of Combat.* New York: Touchstone, 2001.

Patton, Jr., George S. *War As I Knew It.* Boston: Houghton Mifflin, 1995.

Pyle, Ernie. *Here Is Your War.* New York: Henry Holt, 1943.

Rutherford, Ward. *Kasserine: Baptism of Fire.* New York: Ballantine, 1970.

Shapiro, Milton. *Ranger Battalion: American Rangers in World War II.* New York: Julian Messner, 1979.

Truscott, Jr., Lucian King. *Command Missions.* New York: E. P. Dutton and Company, Inc., 1954.

―――. *The Twilight of the U.S. Cavalry: Life in the Old Army, 1917–1942.* Lawrence, Ks.: University Press of Kansas, 1989.

Truscott, Mary. *Brats: Children of the American Military Speak Out.* New York: E. P. Dutton, 1989.

Vaughan-Thomas, Wynford. *Anzio: The Massacre at the Beachhead.* New York: Holt, Rinehart and Winston, 1961.

INDEX

Index

ABOUT THE AUTHOR

H. Paul Jeffers is the author of more than seventy books, including *Onward We Charge*, the history of Colonel William O. Darby and the Rangers in North Africa, Sicily, and Italy; biographies of Theodore Roosevelt, Grover Cleveland, Theodore Roosevelt, Jr., Diamond Jim Brady, Fiorello La Guardia, and the aviation heroes General Billy Mitchell and Captain Eddie Rickenbacker; histories of Freemasonry, the Great Depression, Jerusalem, the San Francisco Earthquake of 1906, the FBI, and Scotland Yard. A broadcast journalist for more than thirty years, he was an editor and producer at ABC, CBS, and NBC, and is the only person to have been News Director of both of New York City's all-news radio stations. He taught journalism at New York University, Syracuse University, and Boston University and has published fifteen mystery novels. He lives in New York City.